T0285117

Native Americans of the Cuyahoga Valley

SERIES ON OHIO HISTORY AND CULTURE

Series on Ohio History and Culture
Kevin Kern, Editor

Native Americans of the Cuyahoga Valley

FROM EARLY PEOPLES TO CONTEMPORARY ISSUES

Edited by

Peg Bobel and Linda G. Whitman

The University of Akron Press
Akron, Ohio

ISBN: 978-1-62922-288-2 (paper)
ISBN: 978-1-62922-289-9 (ePDF)
ISBN: 978-1-62922-290-5 (ePub)

A catalog record for this title is available from the Library of Congress.

∞ The paper used in this publication meets the minimum requirements of ANSI/NISO z39.48–1992 (Permanence of Paper).

Cover photo: Courtesy of Charlotte Gintert/Captured Glimpses Photography. Cover design by Amy Freels.

Native Americans of the Cuyahoga Valley was designed and typeset in Minion by Amy Freels.

The preparation of this book was supported in part by a grant from Eastern National, a nonprofit cooperating association supporting the interpretive, educational, and scientific programs and services of the National Park Service.

The drawing that introduces each chapter is one of twenty-two images carved in the Independence Slab Petroglyphs. Although the meaning and significance of the image is known only to the carver, a contemporary viewer likely recognizes it as a snake, which in turn suggests the sinuosity of a river like the Cuyahoga. The Independence Slab is a remnant of a larger set of petroglyphs removed from a quarry in Independence, Ohio, around 1843. The remnant slab has been mounted in a wall of the Independence Presbyterian Church since c. 1854.

Produced in conjunction with the University of Akron Affordable Learning Initiative. More information is available at www.uakron.edu/affordablelearning/

This book is dedicated in loving memory to our dear friend and colleague Lynn Rodeman Metzger.

Contents

Introduction

The Cuyahoga River is young in geologic time: its current course formed about fourteen thousand years ago, cutting through glacial deposits that remained after the retreat of the last of the ice. While it is a relatively small river, it has nourished thousands upon thousands of people during its ever-flowing, ever-changing history, the first humans arriving in the Cuyahoga River watershed in the late Ice Age, just as the glaciers were retreating. The river undoubtedly proved to be a great resource to the earliest peoples in this region: it was constant and essential as people came, moved, and changed. It likely provided nourishment and a fluid means of moving from place to place. The Indigenous peoples living along this rich and varied river valley have had a long and winding history, from the earliest people to today's urban residents who come from diverse Native backgrounds and homelands. Just as many of us are drawn to and enriched by the Cuyahoga River today, people over thousands of years have connected to this rich and varied river valley.

This book itself has also had a long journey—it has been in the works longer than we care to admit. Just as the people involved have changed over time, so have the times we all live in. When the book idea was first proposed by the late Dr. Lynn Metzger, the offensive caricature "Chief Wahoo" was still on the Cleveland Major League Baseball team's uniforms and merchandise, and the idea that a Native American would one day be

Secretary of the Interior seemed more aspirational than likely. The timing of societal changes and greater awareness of the biased or neglected parts of our nation's history have served to buoy up this project and confirm that its time has come. What has not changed over the years is the book's original intent: to compile in one volume a set of chapters by different contributors, each focusing on an aspect of the story of Native Americans in the Cuyahoga Valley and Northeast Ohio. The task would be challenging—to present a long and at times complicated history that continues to today in a volume that could still be picked up with one hand. We had to be selective and somewhat limited in what we covered. We believe, however, that our contributors have captured the essences of the various lives and experiences that Native Americans have had in this region, from the times before contact with Euro-Americans to today.

This book grew out of an awareness that although many people are interested in the history of Native Americans in this region, many myths and misunderstandings about that history still exist. Hints of the history appear in statues, place names, and sports teams' names. Stories are heard and repeated, often unexamined, and sometimes become myths only faintly based on facts. Native Americans and scholars are continuously adding to and correcting the narratives about Native American history and presence in this region. This book addresses the interest in Native American history while presenting the most current understandings of the past.

Lynn Metzger was well aware of the interest among the general public, especially visitors to Cuyahoga Valley National Park, who wanted to better understand the people who first inhabited this land. She was well aware of myths, misconceptions, neglected truths, and misunderstandings regarding Native American history and what it means to be Native American today. Though many people are curious about the people of the distant past, we wanted to go far beyond answering questions such as "Were there Moundbuilders here?" or "What tribes lived in this area?" and not leave the history in the distant past. Readers will see that the history of Native Americans in this region is neither smooth nor continuous. Most of the Native people living in Ohio today have descended from many different Indigenous groups from around the country and beyond. Therefore the writings presented in this volume address the complexity of the Native American presence in this region and attempt to clarify the Native American story as it has unfolded from long ago to today.

We approached this project more in the spirit of what Native American historian David Treuer stresses, that the true history of Native Americans is one of "complexity and depth" and likely not what most of us were taught in school. So we sought out writers who could address those questions about the first peoples—what we know, what we do not know, and the role archaeology plays in informing us of the past—as well as delve into the long periods since the first peoples, from the removal of Native groups from the region, to the ways non-Native people remembered them, to the Relocation program of the mid-twentieth century, to perspectives from Native American individuals living in Northeast Ohio today. In covering such a long period, we find that knowledge of the past informs the now, and the now enlightens our understanding of the past.

We, the editors and contributors to this book, are ourselves non-Native. We approached this work in the spirit of what the research project Reclaiming Native Truth calls "allies." We are grateful for the insights and perspectives shared with us by Native Americans we have become acquainted with, helping us to see our shared history in a brighter light. We believe that to know a place well, such as the Cuyahoga Valley and Northeast Ohio, we need, in the words of writer Barry Lopez, "to find our home." To do that, Lopez counsels us to get to know the land and the peoples who first dwelt in this physical place intimately—the richness of nature's diversity. As he poignantly notes, "This [richness of nature's diversity], along with the people we ignored, was a wealth that didn't register until much of it was gone, or until, like the people, it was a tattered, diluted remnant, sequestered on a reservation." He alludes to how the relationships between the Indigenous peoples who first dwelt in this land and those who colonized it have been fraught with conflict, often over the very precious resources non-Natives have left diminished and over the vastly different ways of viewing, valuing, and treating the land. This history has been rife with misunderstandings and bias. We have tried to be mindful of our own misconceptions and biases, yet know that in some areas we may have blurred vision and missteps. We hope, nonetheless, that this gathering of research and explanation from various perspectives brings to light some of the "rich diversity" of the many different people who were first connected to this region, those who came later, and those who today call it "home." We hope you will learn something new about a history that we only scratch the surface of, and that this small volume will entice you to learn more, to question what we think we know, and to see today's Native Americans in the bright light of inquiring minds and open hearts.

Notes on Terminology and Names

Terms evolve with new understandings and awarenesses. Today, the term *Indian* is considered by some to be controversial since it fails to acknowledge the depth and diversity of peoples descended from Indigenous groups on this continent. The term "Indian," many tribal names, and even the concept of "tribe," are European concepts imposed on the Native population by early explorers, traders, and colonizers. We prefer to use the terms "Native American" or "Indigenous" interchangeably.

In this book, readers will see the term "Indian" when it is used in an historic context or a name, such as the "Bureau of Indian Affairs." When historian George Knepper did the bulk of his research and writing, it was more common to use the term Indian or American Indian, plus he was writing about times in which all Native Americans were commonly called "Indian." Thus, he referred to "Indian agents" and the "French and Indian War." At the same time, he helps us understand the specific divisions among the Native Americans in the 1700s, how groups were organized and related to each other, and the confusion caused by Europeans assigning Anglo names to Native American groups calling themselves by their Native names. For instance, European-Americans spoke of the "Delaware," lumping several Eastern Seaboard groups together and naming them after the Delaware River, along which they lived (the name Delaware itself referring to the first European governor of the colony of Virginia, Thomas West, or Lord De La Warr), while the "Delaware" in this region knew themselves as Lenape.

In the chapter "Indians in an Urban World," Lynn Metzger also employs the term "Indian" in a historical context. Her research was based on her study of the Native American community in Cleveland in the middle of the twentieth century. At that time, the main center for Native people coming to the city was named the Cleveland American Indian Center, and the federal agency in charge of the Relocation program was the Bureau of Indian Affairs. In learning about that period, some Native Americans themselves at the time referred to themselves as "Indian," and some still do. Likewise, in Chapter 8, "White Visions of Red Men," historian Kevin Kern at times uses the term "Indian" as he explores the various ways the majority white culture saw and remembered Native Americans over time in US history.

People interested in Native American history often ask, "Who were the first tribes here?" The answer can be that there were no "tribes" as such here before historic Native groups were identified and moved to this region. White historians often gave earlier groups names based on their material culture, as understood from artifact types, or tools, left behind. In Chapter 3, "The First People," archaeologist Brian Redmond explains those names and how they help us distinguish among successive groups of Indigenous peoples who lived here over many centuries. So for instance, while we speak of a Whittlesey Tradition (named after Charles Whittlesey, early Ohio historian), there is no group called the "Whittlesey tribe."

Names can be confusing, and it can be helpful to remember that Native peoples, like any group in society, have always had their own names for their groups. Researchers believed that many of these names would translate into English as something like "the people," or "the real people," or "the allies." Native American groups can also be distinguished by the language groups to which they belonged. In the Great Lakes region, Indigenous languages can be grouped into three major linguistic divisions: Algonquian, Iroquoian, and Siouan. Many historic Native Americans probably spoke several languages, including some French and English, but not all Native people could understand each other, at times requiring interpreters. In the historic period of explorers and colonizers, most Native American groups were known by names that outsiders gave them or by where they resided. Today it is most appropriate and respectful to refer to specific groups using the tribal affiliation used by the particular group, and most Native Americans will identify themselves according to their tribal affiliation.

Acknowledgments

We, the editors of this book, are the carriers and presenters of ideas whose roots go back to the early 2000s and to friends who have passed away. We are indebted to our dear friend and colleague, the late Lynn Metzger, who first proposed the idea for such a book around 2001. Lynn, a cultural anthropologist and professor at The University of Akron, and close friend Joe Jesensky, a collector and student of Native American history, had collaborated on *Joe's Place: Conversations on the Cuyahoga Valley*, a memoir of Joe's explorations of the valley, from Cleveland to Akron. Besides his intimate knowledge of the Cuyahoga Valley and its history, Joe brought his delightful, dry sense of humor to the project. Both Lynn and Joe envisioned another book that would focus on the Native American history of the Cuyahoga Valley. These two friends, professional academic Lynn, who had an interest in the contemporary Native community in Northeast Ohio, and Joe, who focused on the ancient past, presented their bookended interests to friends and colleagues who could add their contributions. Also involved in those early discussions about a possible book were Fran McGovern, author of *Written on the Hills: The Making of the Akron Landscape*; flintknapper Carl Fry; writer Russ Musarra; illustrator Chuck Ayers; avocational archaeologist Skeeter Kish; and historian George Knepper. We are grateful to them all for the original inspiration for the book and early writings.

After Joe passed in 2008, at the age of 101, other projects absorbed Lynn's attention, including two exhibitions based on the Oak Native American Ethnographic Collection, and the project sat on the back burner for a decade. Then in 2015 Lynn brought the book project back to the forefront again. The reconstituted book committee now included Lynn, Peg, Linda, Chuck, and Skeeter, along with a new addition—Fran Ugalde, who worked with Lynn on the exhibitions and is now instructor in museology at The University of Akron.

We had barely gotten started on the revamped book project when Lynn passed away suddenly in July 2015. It did not take us long to decide that we must complete the project and dedicate it to Lynn, our inspiration and leader. She did, after all, leave us with a "projects to-do" list! In the process, many original ideas and some writings were retained, while the new committee sought out and added new contributors. The book has evolved and changed with the times. When we re-proposed the book to The University of Akron Press, we had the great good fortune of connecting with historian Kevin Kern. To his surprise, he found himself on the committee and contributing a chapter! We are grateful to Kevin for his humor, expertise, manuscript reviews, sage advice, and his contributions. We also approached Brian Redmond, now retired chair of the Archaeology Department at the Cleveland Museum of Natural History, for his contribution. His writing style makes a complex subject both enjoyable and easy to understand.

Through it all, Charles (Chuck) Ayers has been our illustrator, mapmaker, and artistic guide. We are deeply grateful to Chuck for his illustrations and design skills and for lightening up our discussions with his off-the-cuff cartoon "minutes" of our meetings. We always knew to watch out when he got quiet, and his left hand got busy sketching. (*Those* drawings did *not* make it into the book.) To further illustrate the book, under Chuck's design guidance, our friend and colleague, photographer Charlotte Gintert, headed into the field to capture images found throughout the pages. We are grateful to her for her keen eye and photographic excellence.

We also offer deep thanks to Steven (Skeeter) Kish, who has been with the project from the beginning. Skeeter and Joe were close friends and avid explorers of the valley, enthusiastically devoted to contributing to the documentation of its archaeological sites. Skeeter has served on the boards of four archaeological associations in Ohio, still serving as president of the Chippewa Valley Archaeological Society and former president of two other chapters. He also serves as archaeological chairperson of the Midwest Federation of Mineralogical and Geological Societies. Skeeter has contributed his ideas and expertise, especially regarding documenting Native American trails in the region and has advised the group as the project progressed, for which we are truly grateful.

We wish to thank Fran Ugalde for her understanding and expertise regarding museum collections, as well as for her computer savvy and organizational skills in handling the images for this book and for the preliminary research ideas for Chapter 1. We also thank her for providing meeting space for the group in the bright, spacious classroom space at the Cummings Center for the History of Psychology on The University of Akron campus.

This has certainly been a labor of love as we on the book committee have shared ideas, challenged each other, and explored new avenues of research. The joy of our fruitful and lively discussions was greatly enhanced by the warm hospitality offered to us by Jim King, dear friend and proprietor of Angel Falls Coffee Company. His generous refills on coffee, hearty lunches, occasional glasses of wine, and humorous repartee made our work sessions something we all looked forward to. Our Zoom meetings during the Covid pandemic were a pathetic but necessary substitute for our Angel Falls gatherings.

In addition, we would like to thank Mary Plazo, manager of the Special Collections Division of the Akron-Summit County Public Library, as well as her staff for their assistance and encouragement as we researched and wrote in their congenial, quiet library space, surrounded by local history resources close at hand. Thanks go out as well to Dr. Gina Martino, associate professor in the Department of History at The University of Akron, for her review and helpful advice on Kevin Kern's treatment of "White Visions of 'Red Men': Native Americans in Northeast Ohio Memory." We would like to thank Dr. Tim Matney, professor in the Department of Anthropology at The University of Akron. He shared his vast knowledge of all things archaeology, his review, and photographs. We would also like to thank Dr. Mike Shott not only for his important contribution of his research but also for his encouragement of this project.

We are forever indebted to the Native Americans and non-Natives who shared their stories and time with us. It was a privilege to include their narratives in our book. In addition to those we interviewed for the first chapter, we wish to thank Cynthia and Joe Connolly for leading us to valuable resources and helping us see things from a Native American perspective. Many of the connections we made came about through a most helpful conversation with Susan E. Bergh, curator of Pre-Columbian and Native North American Collections at the Cleveland Museum of Art. Sue served as the in-house curator of *The Art of the American Indian: The Thaw Collection*, an exhibition at the museum in 2010. Thanks to her guidance, we were able to connect to artists and leaders in the Cleveland-area Native American community.

All along, we have gratefully received encouragement and wise advice from Jennie Vasarheyli, Chief of Interpretation, Education, and Visitor Services, Cuyahoga Valley National Park. We appreciate the National Park Service's affirmation of the importance and value of this work. In addition, we are grateful to Eastern National, the nonprofit cooperating association for the Canal Exploration Center at Cuyahoga Valley National Park, for their grant that helped fund the writing and preparation of this book.

We are also deeply grateful that Rob Bobel, after his retirement from Cuyahoga Valley National Park in 2017, agreed to be our project manager, ably taking on the task of keeping us meeting and working. We would probably still be floundering without his meeting notices, minutes, to-do lists, and general meeting leadership. He undoubtedly picked up from Lynn the role we used to both appreciate and complain about, that of "prodder and poker."

And we wish to thank Jon Miller, director of The University of Akron Press, for his encouragement of the project, his wise counsel, and his immense patience as we worked through the preparation of the manuscript. Amy Freels, Sr. Editorial, Design, & Production Manager at the Press, helped relieve much of our anxiety as she quickly and expertly responded to our many questions. To you and Brittany LaPointe, Marketing and Sales Manager, we bow with great gratitude. We would like to thank the reviewers for their constructive criticism and encouragement.

Lastly, we thank Ed Metzger and the many friends and family who kept asking, "How's the book coming along?" Their kind interest and support helped keep us engaged and committed to this work, which we hope will add to a deeper understanding of Native Americans in the Cuyahoga Valley. To you all, our deepest thanks.

Native Americans of the Cuyahoga Valley

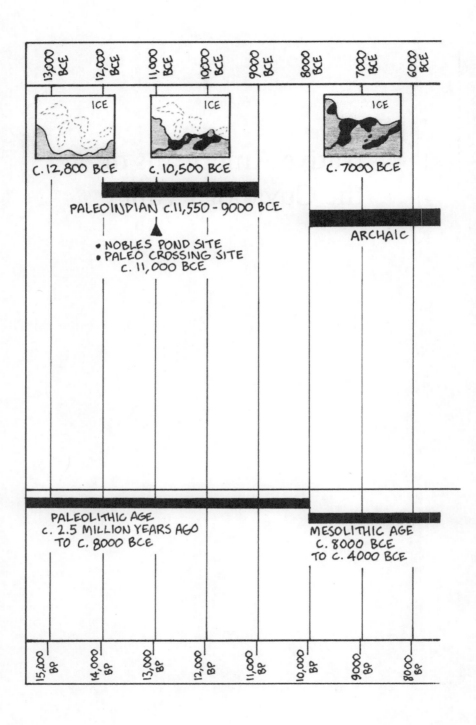

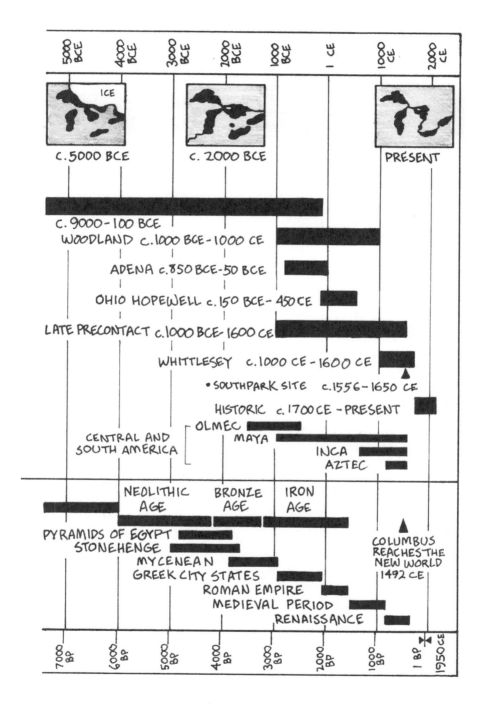

5000 BCE | 4000 BCE | 3000 BCE | 2000 BCE | 1000 BCE | 1 CE | 1000 CE | 2000 CE

ICE

C. 5000 BCE   C. 2000 BCE   PRESENT

C. 9000-100 BCE

WOODLAND c.1000 BCE-1000 CE

ADENA c.850 BCE-50 BCE

OHIO HOPEWELL c.150 BCE-450 CE

LATE PRECONTACT c.1000 BCE-1600 CE

WHITTLESEY c.1000 CE-1600 CE

• SOUTHPARK SITE c.1556-1650 CE

HISTORIC c.1700 CE-PRESENT

OLMEC
MAYA
INCA
AZTEC

CENTRAL AND
SOUTH AMERICA

NEOLITHIC AGE   BRONZE AGE   IRON AGE

PYRAMIDS OF EGYPT
STONEHENGE
MYCENEAN
GREEK CITY STATES
ROMAN EMPIRE
MEDIEVAL PERIOD
RENAISSANCE

COLUMBUS REACHES THE NEW WORLD 1492 CE

7000 BP | 6000 BP | 5000 BP | 4000 BP | 3000 BP | 2000 BP | 1000 BP | 1 BP | 1950 CE

1 "We're Still Here"
Voices and Stories from the Native American Community in Northeast Ohio Today

Peg Bobel and Linda G. Whitman

This story of Native American life in the Cuyahoga Valley and Northeast Ohio begins with a discussion of today's community and the issues that are relevant for Indigenous peoples in this urbanized region. While there are no reservations or other separate settlements of Native Americans in Ohio, more than fifty thousand Native Americans from diverse tribal backgrounds live and work in Northeast Ohio today.[1] Some are here as a result of Relocation (see Chapter 7), while others came for reasons related to career or family connections. The Native American community in Northeast Ohio represents a portion of the greater diaspora of Native peoples in the United States and Canada. For instance, the Lake Erie Native American Council (LENAC) lists over sixty tribal affiliations among its members. Although we are not ourselves Native, our intent is to tell this part of the story through contemporary Native voices from Northeast Ohio. While there are many voices we could have included in this chapter, and no one person represents an entire cultural or ethnic group, we have selected a few whose experiences shed light on what it means to be Native American today and the challenges many Native people face daily. Each person we interviewed will be introduced as his or her voice and stories contribute to the discussion. We are deeply grateful to all those who were kind enough to share their knowledge, opinions, personal experiences, and perspectives regarding relevant and pressing issues today. (For more information on the people we interviewed for this chapter, please see the short biographies at the end of the chapter text.)

We begin with the simple but central message we heard from many interviewees, best put by ceramic clay artist Peter Jones: "We're still here." Jones is Onondaga, born on the Cattaraugus Reservation. He now resides on the Allegany Territory of the Seneca Nation of Indians, in New York. Jones has a strong artistic and educational connection to Northeast Ohio through his sculptures of Native Americans on the Portage Path in Akron and his participation in Akron's North American First People's Day.[2] "We're still here" is a succinct and accurate way to express the reaction to feelings of invisibility, being "overlooked," having their needs or concerns "swept under the rug," being "erased," all feelings shared with us by those we interviewed. For Native Americans in Northeast Ohio, as is true for many across this nation, being *visible* is at the heart of what it means to feel a part of a larger community. Native American erasure has many causes and takes on many forms, as seen in the Indian boarding school education system, which began in 1860, the relocation program beginning in the 1950s, contemporary teaching of American history, and issues of racist imagery and its effects on psychological health and well-being.

The Reclaiming Native Truth initiative found that "40% of respondents did not think Native Americans still existed." According to teachers and parents in focus groups for the research, a contributing cause of this mistaken belief was that school curriculum covering Native American history is often inaccurate or under-represented. Adding to that, many respondents said they knew no Native Americans.[3] The Reclaiming Native Truth research found that the lack of representation in the media and education contributes to the problem of invisibility; the public then tends to see Native Americans not as they truly are, but through a distorted lens of myths, half-truths, and negative stereotypes. The "toxic combination of the invisibility of Native Americans in contemporary society and the pervasive negative stereotypes...leads to ongoing discrimination and lack of support for vital issues and initiatives," influencing both the general public and policymakers. As the Reclaiming project points out, "the effects are profound. The negative, persistent narrative can harm the self-esteem and aspirations of Native Americans—especially children." It can be used to "justify oppressive practices and laws, and historic and systemic racism."

The Reclaiming project lays out "pathways for change," ways to convey the "true, strength-based story" of Native Americans in this country, leading to greater support of Native Americans and Native issues.[4]

Since there is great diversity among Native Americans in the United States today, it is helpful to understand the terms used to designate Indigenous people. The US Census Bureau defines "American Indian or Alaska Native" as any person "having origins in any of the original peoples of North and South America (including Central America) and who maintains a tribal affiliation or community attachment." While some prefer one term over another, "Native American" and "Indigenous" are terms often used interchangeably with "American Indian." In the 2010 US Census, 5.2 million people self-identified as American Indian or Alaska Native (alone or in combination with one or more races). That number increased in the 2020 census to 9.7 million, a jump that surprised many and is the result of a number of factors, including an undercount in the 2010 census, successful outreach campaigns for the 2020 census, and other more complicated factors. In the 2010 census, the majority (67%) of those self-identifying as American Indian or Alaska Native (either alone or in combination with other races) lived outside Native American lands such as federal or state reservations. Many of those, however, like Native Americans in Northeast Ohio, may be enrolled members of a federally recognized tribe and maintain connections to a reservation or tribal group.[5]

Peter Jones emphasized the importance of the concept of "sovereignty," which is relevant regardless of where a Native person may be living, to understand the status of Native Americans in the United States today. According to the National Conference of State Legislatures, "tribal sovereignty refers to the right of American Indians and Alaska Natives to govern themselves. The US Constitution recognizes Indian tribes as distinct governments, and they have, with a few exceptions, the same powers as federal and state governments to regulate their internal affairs. Sovereignty for tribes includes the right to establish their own form of government, determine membership requirements, enact legislation, and establish law enforcement and court systems." In essence, tribes possess nationhood status and retain inherent powers of self-government. They are entitled to certain federal benefits, services, and protections due to their special relationship with the United States.[6] At the time of this writing, there are 574 federally recognized American Indian and Alaska Native tribes and villages in the US.

It is important to note that there is a difference between the legal/political meaning of "American Indian" and the ethnological sense of that term. As the Bureau of Indian Affairs explains it, "the rights, protections, and services provided by the United States to individual American Indians and Alaska Natives flow not from a person's identity as such in an ethnological sense, but because he or she is a member of a federally recognized tribe."[7] Eligibility for federal services differs from program to program, and eligibility criteria for enrollment or membership in a tribe can differ from tribe to tribe. Generally speaking, only a portion of individuals who self-identify as American Indian or Alaska Native are enrolled members of a tribe. All, however, are US citizens.[8]

While sovereignty gives tribes a measure of control over their lands and internal affairs, individual Native Americans, regardless of their tribal affiliation or where they are living, grapple with the effects of things they cannot control—especially the negative impact of what Reclaiming Native Truth calls "harmful and toxic narratives" and stereotypes. As the Reclaiming project explains, when a minority group lives in a dominant culture, the "dominant narrative is the lens through which history is told from the perspective of the dominant culture," a narrative that can have significantly negative effects on a person's sense of self and self-worth. The project argues that a new narrative works "best when grounded in truth." There is "power in people telling their own stories." The project aims, then, "to eradicate harmful and toxic narratives, stereotypes, structural and institutional racism, dehumanization, and the invisibility of Native Americans."[9] Each of the Native Americans who contributed to this chapter addressed not only the effects of the false narratives in their personal lives, but also shared the many ways they deal with the stereotypes and racism. Some also suggested ways non-Native allies could be effective in helping tell the true history of the Indigenous in North America and therefore increase the understanding of Native Americans in Northeast Ohio and throughout this country.

There is no better place to start than to examine how and what non-Natives have been taught about Native Americans and the experiences Native children have had through time in the educational system of the United States. Until recently, the history of Native Americans in North America as taught to non-Natives has been one that presents topics such as westward expansion and white-Indian conflicts, as all ending in the late 1800s, as if all Indians thereafter no longer existed. With several attempts to reconcile this omission, the 2019 Ohio Social Studies Model Curriculum for fourth grade covers a more comprehensive picture of who lived in Ohio throughout time, including all precontact traditions and many historic Indian tribes who lived in Ohio, along with discussions about areas of conflict and cooperation. For high school students, the curriculum stresses how the nineteenth-century western migration of white Americans was encouraged due to the increasing demands for natural resources, creating confrontation with Native Americans. In turn, this conflict helped fuel federal policy that changed the lives of the Native Americans. Although they are trying to correct the omissions, it is still apparent that what is taught is still presented with a bias towards the dominant culture's history. The Model Curriculum does not consider the Native American oral tradition of history-telling or how Native Americans see and understand their own histories on this continent.[10]

An additional hindrance to why, until relatively recently, Ohio students have not been taught much about Native American history is that there are no federally recognized Indian tribes in Ohio. It is an "out of sight, out of mind" situation. Little cultural continuity between the precontact Indigenous peoples and historic Native Americans in what is now Ohio is known and much misinformation abounds. As noted above, the Reclaiming Native Truth research found that many respondents in their surveys said they knew no Native Americans. This could be said about most people living in Northeast Ohio.

Nearly everyone we spoke with has taken steps in their lives to help correct the false narratives about Native Americans and their history. Artist Claire Heldman, who is Cheyenne River Sioux, values teaching young people the true story of the history of Native Americans in the United States. Heldman was born in Cuyahoga Falls, Ohio, but lived for a while in South Dakota, where she taught school and observed that there was no real education in the schools regarding Native American history: "People are uninformed, or ill-informed." She added, "Most white kids have never met an Indian, and the only time they [were] taught about Indians was at

Thanksgiving." She addressed that vacuum in education by visiting school classes to speak about her tribe and her family while giving the students an opportunity to interact with a person of Native heritage. Claire visited University of Akron anthropology classes to share her art and her stories of being Native American in a predominately non-Native society.[11]

Artist Marlys Rambeau is a citizen of the Cheyenne River Sioux Tribe of South Dakota. Her mother voluntarily relocated to Cleveland to look for a teaching position after graduating from college. Her mother's teaching involved traveling to different schools to teach Native American students. In all her teachings she tried to bridge the Native and white cultures, finding ways to expose non-Native children to Native children and their culturally different experiences. Marlys followed her mother's lead by becoming involved in local public education events aimed at educating non-Native society about the Indigenous community in Cleveland and beyond. She helped improve and bring authenticity to Cleveland Metroparks' First People's Day annual event by presenting on various subjects herself, sharing her art of beading, and bringing other artists, musicians, and dancers to the programs. She also worked with Lorain County Metroparks on their Pioneer Days event, explaining: "I was the one Native in the corner!"[12]

A shining example of how reciprocal education can be achieved between Native and non-Native students is the partnership between the Northern Cheyenne Reservation in Montana and The Lippman School in Akron. After a forty-five-year family connection with the tribe,[13] Sam Chestnut, Head of School, "realized kids need to experience Native Americans in their homeland, in their place." He went on to explain: "It had a big impact on me and my siblings when I was growing up ... if kids could have that appreciation, that understanding, it would have an impact on how they see the world, American History, and so about ten years ago we created a partnership with the Northern Cheyenne Tribe through Chief Dull Knife College.... They [the college] use their own people to teach their people about their traditions, and the whole idea was that Native people are more than street signs and statues; that they're alive and well and trying to hold on to their traditions, and when I learn about someone else who's different than me, it forces me to learn about where I came from, my own family's culture, religious history, whatever it may be. Find points of commonality, etc."[14]

Sam described the cultural exchange as a "partnership involving both the Lippman students going to the reservation and the students from the reservation, along with tribal educators, elders, and leaders, coming to Akron.... Many organic things grew from that naturally, the biggest being the recognition of North American First People's Day in Akron that came through a walk that we did on the Portage Path with the Cheyenne kids and elders here.... That was a profound moment for me, and I think others too, where it felt like wow, we're shining a light on something in Akron that people really only know through statues and didn't have a relationship with Native folks."[15]

Sam continued, "So people ask me, why the Northern Cheyenne? I say three things: 1) that's a relationship we have that's built on trust, and that's hard to do, hard to find; 2) they are practicing their traditions as strongly as any tribe I know in the lower forty-eight states—they have a strong tradition of trying to keep their language alive, their traditions; and 3) they held a strong connection to the Great Lakes because they're Algonquian speakers; their origins are from the Great Lakes region. I remember one elder, when we walked the Path, said, 'You know it's not impossible that some of our people walked this path,' because the Cheyenne in their history were connected to many tribes and trade."[16]

Thomas Shoulderblade, a Northern Cheyenne educator, traditional drummer, and singer, shared with us, "I have been here since the beginning of this whole coming together ... and my experience has been good, sharing our culture with the people here, helping out with the Indigenous day, because it is not celebrated nationwide." He continued by expressing sadness around the recognition of Juneteenth as a federal holiday commemorating the emancipation of enslaved African Americans, because "they can celebrate the freedom of slaves, but yet in our history they don't talk about the Dakota 38. There were thirty-eight chiefs and warriors that were hung under the order of Abraham Lincoln in front of four thousand spectators. But yet he can free slaves. You know it kind of hurt ... we are forgotten people."[17]

Recognizing "the lies, misgivings and deception in Native American history," Lippman educator Matt Russ stated that "we wanted to teach our students authentic [Native American] history ... in developmentally appropriate ways ... that still teach the truth.... But also we have this multicultural philosophy that we believe that students learn better when they are engaged with one another, engaged with people who are different from them."[18]

Our interviewees for this chapter also shared their understandings and experiences regarding how Native American children have been taught in the past and the federal policies that have influenced educational practices. Before we share their stories and perspectives, we will look more generally at the topic of education and begin this discussion with a quote from David Treuer, an Ojibwe writer who seeks to tell the story of Native Americans in this country as one not of tragedy, defeat, or even hope, but one of complexity and depth. Treuer, who grew up on the Leech Lake Reservation in Minnesota, states in an interview:

> Education was something that was done to us, not something that was provided for us. And the boarding schools are a great example of that: They were a means by which the government was trying to destroy tribes by destroying families. This is partly why education is such a tricky thing for Native people today. How are you supposed to go to school and learn about Mount Rushmore yet know that each person [represented on the monument] promoted the killing of Indian people? How are you supposed to say the Pledge of Allegiance to a country that was trying to kill and dispossess you and caused the horrible suffering of your parents and grandparents? How are you supposed to learn in an education system of which your ancestors grew deeply distrustful, and then be told we have to work hard at school to get ahead?[19]

Native American personal and cultural erasure and the attempts for eradication take on many forms. One of its more disturbing forms is the Indian boarding school education system that removed Indian children from their families, their reservations, their language, their spiritual traditions, and their culture, a program that can be singled out as the most destructive instrument in the federal policy of forced assimilation. The intent was to eliminate Native Americans and the "Indian Problem" by removing all traces of tribal cultures and replacing them with European Christian ideas of civilization, religion, and culture. The Bureau of Indian Affairs began the system in 1860 when it established the first boarding school in the state of Washington. White male reformers who espoused Protestant ideology of the late nineteenth and early twentieth centuries used education as a tool to assimilate Indigenous children into the mainstream of American society by teaching them "the importance of private property, material wealth and monogamous nuclear families." They "assumed that it was necessary to 'civilize' Indian people, make them accept white men's beliefs and value systems."[20]

Indian schools were either on-reservation day schools, on-reservation boarding schools, or off-reservation boarding schools. Most were run by the federal government or numerous Christian churches. The first schools were reservation day schools and reservation boarding schools that taught reading, writing, and the English language. The schools added other subjects such as math, science, history, and art in the hope of offering the students the possibility of becoming independent thinkers in the "American way" of individualized life. The only religious training was Christian. Schools taught classes on such topics as the principles of democracy and the political system with an eye toward citizenship training. Classes and school life were based on the belief system of the white educators: "Order, discipline and self-restraint were all prized values of white society." All these individualized trainings were directly opposite from "the basic Indian belief of communal ownership, which held that the land was for all people."[21]

However, the on-reservation assimilation into the majority culture was not sufficiently working, according to Colonel Richard Pratt who established the off-reservation Carlisle Indian School in Pennsylvania in 1879. His well-known motto was "Kill the Indian...save the man." To keep children away from their cultural heritage, the schools forcibly took children as young as four from their families and homes to live at these schools, where the schools tried to Americanize the children. The off-reservation schools began the assault on Indigenous cultural identity by obliterating any outward sign of tribal life. These schools cut students' braided hair, which ironically was a sign of mourning in Lakota culture.[22] Uniforms became standard dress. They gave the children white first and last names and banned traditional foods. These schools prohibited children from speaking their native language, even to each other. If the children did not obey these rules, the schools enforced them via harsh means, including corporal punishment.[23]

It is estimated that more than ten thousand children passed through the Carlisle School, the site of which is now the grounds of the US Army War College. Pratt had been in the military, and he ran the school along military lines. The treatment of Indian children was so cruel and tyrannical that it is estimated that over two hundred children at the Carlisle School alone are buried in the cemetery, where many children "perished due to epidemics and harsh treatment." A movement to return the children's remains to their tribes and families was initiated in 2016 at the request of a member of the Northern Arapaho because the federal agencies tasked with the repatriation of these remains were slow in responding to federal law (see Chapter 2). Efforts with officials from the US Army, the Office of Army Cemeteries, and archaeologists and anthropologists from the Army Corps of Engineers working with tribal authorities continue to return children's remains to their tribal lands. On July 16, 2021, the remains of nine children from the Rosebud Sioux Reservation in South Dakota who died at the boarding school were returned home.[24]

When many Indian families and villages resisted the schools, the authorities sometimes retaliated by withholding food rations. There were movements to "withdraw their children en masse, encourage runaways and undermining the schools' influence during summer and school breaks." Court rulings put pressure on families to keep children in boarding schools, and it was not until 1978, when the Indian Child Welfare Act was passed, that families were given the legal right to deny children placement in these schools or with white foster parents.[25]

In a June 11, 2021, editorial, Secretary of Interior Deb Haaland, a member of New Mexico's Laguna Pueblo, related how her great-grandfather was "stolen" from their family to the Carlisle School and how "these horrific assimilation policies" created generational trauma to her and her family. She writes: "Some studies suggest that by 1926, nearly 83 percent of Native American school-age children were in the system. Many children were doused with DDT upon arrival, and as their coerced re-education got underway, they endured physical abuse for speaking their tribal languages or practicing traditions that didn't fit into what the government believed was the American ideal."[26] Secretary Haaland was present at Carlisle for the repatriation of the Rosebud Sioux children's remains, and around that time she announced the Department of Interior's Federal Indian

Boarding School Initiative, the first major federal investigation into the US government's boarding school policy. The National Native American Boarding School Healing Coalition (NABS) "believes this investigation will provide critical resources to address the ongoing historical trauma of Indian boarding schools. Our organization has been pursuing truth, justice, and healing for boarding school survivors, descendants, and tribal communities."[27]

In May 2022, Secretary of the Interior Deb Haaland and Assistant Secretary for Indian Affairs Bryan Newland released Volume 1 of the Federal Boarding School Initiative Investigative Report that "lays the groundwork for the continued work of the Interior Department to address the intergenerational trauma created by historical federal Indian boarding school policies." The report is the first inventory of federally operated boarding schools and identifies 408 federal schools across thirty-seven states along with marked and unmarked burial sites at over fifty-three schools. Upon the release of the report, Assistant Secretary Newland stated, "This report presents the opportunity for us to reorient federal policies to support the revitalization of Tribal languages and cultural practices to counteract nearly two centuries of federal policies aimed at their destruction."[28]

Along with the release of the report, the Department of Interior launched a tour called "The Road to Healing" during which they met with survivors of the boarding school system to give them voice and help them connect with trauma-informed support. "The Road to Healing" also led to the start of creating a permanent oral history collection. This oral history project is being conducted through a partnership with the National Native American Boarding School Healing Coalition, which has received $3.7 million in grant funds, made possible in part through funding from the National Endowment for the Humanities. NABS has established a track record of gathering stories of survivors, making this a fitting and strong partnership which operates through a formal Memorandum of Understanding. NABS Chief Executive Officer Deborah Parker (Tulalip) stated, "This historic project is a lifeline to preserving the voices and memories of Indian boarding school survivors," while Secretary Haaland noted, "Creating a permanent oral history collection about the Federal Indian boarding school system is part of the Department's mission to honor its political, trust and legal responsibilities, and commitments to Tribes."[29]

In Volume 1 of the investigative report, Assistant Secretary Newland explains that the boarding school system was part of the federal government's larger objective to dispossess Indian Tribes, Alaska Native Villages, and Native Hawaiians. The report highlights conditions at the schools that children endured and recommends further investigation of the short-term and long-term effects of the system on Native children and their descendants. It ends with recommendations that include producing a list of marked and unmarked burial sites at federal boarding schools, approximating the amount of federal funding used to support the school system, and further investigating the legacy impacts of the system on Native children. A second report will follow Volume 1, all with the overarching goal of beginning "a healing process for Indian Country and the Native Hawaiian Community, and the United States, from the Alaskan tundra to the Florida everglades, and everywhere in between."[30]

Today most of the schools have been closed, and the number of Native American children in boarding schools has declined. The remaining ones are primarily under Native American control. Some Native Americans supported the schools because they saw assimilation as the only way for their children to survive. However, it did so by destroying family, community, and culture. Individual experiences at boarding schools varied, but separating Indian children from their families undoubtedly created generational trauma. Children did not receive the love and attention necessary for their well-being.

According to David Treuer, in spite of the harsh assimilation practices of the Indian boarding schools, many children found lasting friendships, romantic partners, and networks by bonding with other children often from different Indian traditions from around the country.[31] These relationships helped spark the Pan-Indian movement, where Native Americans from various tribes worked together to advocate for their rights and social justice for all Native Americans regardless of tribal differences.

How Native Americans were educated historically influences how they are educated today. While everyone's story is personal, they all lie somewhere on the continuum of being skeptical of contemporary education systems to maneuvering through the systems to pursue and succeed in personal desires and goals. Some of the people we interviewed told us stories of their own educational experiences and family experiences with Indian boarding schools.

Delma Ducheneaux Heldman. *Photo courtesy of Claire Heldman*

Claire Heldman's mother, Delma Ducheneaux Heldman, was Lakota Sioux from the Cheyenne River Reservation. Delma attended grade school on the reservation before she was taken from her family at the age of eleven and sent to a Catholic mission boarding school in Stephan, South Dakota, on the nearby Crow Creek Reservation, where they cut her hair. As a child, Claire remembers her mother braiding her hair with beads as a way of holding on to their culture. Delma graduated from the boarding school that is now part of the Crow Creek Tribal School System and went on to earn a bachelor's degree in elementary education at Northern State College in South Dakota. Claire's parents lived in Cuyahoga Falls, Ohio, where Claire grew up and lives today. Around 1985, her mother returned to Wakpala, South Dakota, where she passed away in 2013. Claire shared with us that throughout her life her mother kept her Native language and traditions alive, passing that culture on to Claire, who continues to share it, primarily through her art.[32]

Marlys Rambeau recalled her own experience as a minority Native young person in a dominant-culture school system. She attended what she considered a good school in her own neighborhood on the west side of Cleveland until she reached high school. Although she lived on the west side, Marlys found herself being bussed (the policy of the time with the goal of integrating the school system) to John F. Kennedy High School in the predominantly African American east side of Cleveland. Up until then she had had only limited experience with African American students; however, the main challenge for her was the not the students, but some of the teachers. One in particular would tease and taunt her in the halls. She later left Cleveland to complete her education at the Flandreau Indian School in Flandreau, South Dakota, today the oldest continually operating Federal Indian boarding school. This decision was upsetting for her grandmother, a Cheyenne River Sioux, who also had attended the boarding school as a child and was distressed by her treatment there. Marlys, however, found the conditions and atmosphere much improved.[33]

LaDonna BlueEye, a member of the Choctaw Nation in Oklahoma, tells the story of her grandmother, who was born in what was called Indian Territory (territorial holdings from 1890 onwards of the Cherokee, Choctaw, Chickasaw, Creek, and Seminole tribes in what eventually became Oklahoma). While her grandmother was able to run away from the Indian school where she had been sent, LaDonna's mother, Virginia Osborne (née Jessie) was not so lucky. Virginia spoke Choctaw exclusively until the age of five, when she was sent to the Wheelock Academy, which from 1832 to 1955 served as a mission Indian boarding school for Choctaw girls. It was located near tribal land just east of Millerton, Oklahoma. LaDonna's mother told stories of how the girls would get points for being good, which allowed them to go into town on Saturdays. Virginia went to town to try to look for her own mother. Occasionally she would see her mother and be very happy. But for LaDonna, the devastating story made her very sad, as she recognized the generational trauma the system inflicted on her family and other Native Americans. Other family stories recounted how her mother was only allowed to see her sister on Sunday when they all had to go to church, or how a parental figure was whoever was on duty that night at school.[34]

The boarding school did not allow LaDonna's mom to go home during summer breaks and instead sent her to St. Louis to work either as a nanny to a white family or to work in a laundry. All the money she made during the summer went back to the boarding school. Other stories of the poor

Virginia Osborne (née Jessie) and LaDonna BlueEye. *Photo courtesy of LaDonna BlueEye*

conditions at Wheelock are numerous. "Allegations of abuses abound at Wheelock Academy. Some members of the Choctaw Nation accuse children were regularly beaten, and stories of rape and the murder of children and babies exist at Wheelock."[35]

Peter Jones's mother was raised at the Thomas Indian School and Orphanage (formerly called The Thomas Asylum for Orphan and Destitute Indian Children) beginning at the age of five. The school was located on the Cattaraugus Reservation in Erie County, New York, and began in 1855 as a missionary school for Indigenous children from all New York tribes. Ownership was transferred to the State in 1875 where, as a state institution, "its purpose was to furnish resident Native American children with 'care, moral training and education, and instruction in husbandry and the arts of civilization.' Boys were trained for industrial work, and girls for domestic tasks."[36] Some children were sent there by their parents, while others were sent by social services. Reports indicate that some school employees harshly punished and sexually abused children, isolating others. Some say they learned valuable life lessons, while other's negative experiences caused them to become suspicious and bitter toward the white man, passing that mistrust on to others.[37] The school closed in 1957. Jones's mother went on to the State Teachers College where she met her husband, Peter's father, who was an electrician and carpenter.

Peter attended the day school at Thomas until he was mainstreamed in 1952, when he was in the fifth grade. The transition to public school was difficult for him because "the Indians were all separated when they were used to being together. We were not treated nicely." He felt they were discriminated against because they were viewed as poor and working class.[38]

The aim of the boarding school education system was to assimilate Native youth into the mainstream white culture, which involved removing the young people from their families, their reservations, their spiritual traditions, and their language. As Kenyan writer Ngũgĩ wa Thiong'o succinctly and eloquently explains: "Language is a carrier of a people's culture; culture is a carrier of people's values; values are the basis of a people's self-definition—the basis of their consciousness. And when you destroy a people's language, you are destroying that very important aspect of their heritage... you are in fact destroying that which helps them to define themselves... that which embodies their collective memory as a people."[39]

In an article in *Cultural Survival Quarterly*, Ellen Lutz describes how language loss goes to the heart of Native American identity: "Research shows that language revitalization is a key empowerment tool for Native American communities. Language learning confers cognitive advantages, enhances self-esteem and cultural well-being, and strengthens community bonds. As one Indigenous language instructor put it, 'Our language is the number-one source of our soul, our pride, our being, our strength, and our identity.'"[40]

Native Americans did not "lose" their language. It was taken from them in the unsuccessful attempt to assimilate them into white American values during the Bureau of Indian Affairs boarding school era. Many of these languages are now spoken only by a handful of elders. Many of these native language speakers have passed on, especially during the Covid-19 pandemic, which had a disproportionately negative impact on tribal communities. Revitalization programs of Native American languages have been ongoing for decades, led mostly by tribal communities themselves without substantial federal funding, training, and technical support. Today

Native Americans teach Indigenous languages in immersion language programs in their own elementary schools, high schools, and colleges.

"When people think of Native Americans, they often think of something way back in history, but my own mother did not speak a word of English until she was five years old," said LaDonna BlueEye, a member of the Choctaw Nation. She estimates that there are less than ten Choctaw speakers alive today. BlueEye learned Choctaw as a young adult at the Choctaw Center in Oklahoma; however, she described it as being a more formal version conveyed through the missionaries.

Peter Jones's mother did not approve of speaking their Native language at home when he was growing up because she was taught that the language was dead, so it would not be useful in the future. His son Michael was taught the language, but it was through commands and memorization with no understanding of how the language worked. Now Michael is a Seneca language immersion schoolteacher who uses videotaped recordings of elders to transcribe, translate, and teach the language. For Michael, conversing with the elders and teaching their language is healing some of the past trauma. "They are so relieved that someone is trying to reach them and tell their stories…there is pride and poetry in the language." The language provides "their worldview and glimpses of how they saw and see the world."[41]

One way that Native Americans keep language and culture alive today is at events where they give greetings or blessings and introduce themselves in their native language. Also, the use of land acknowledgements is a nod to Native American tribal groups who once lived and owned the land before they were forcibly pushed out by broken treaties or by federal policy. Land acknowledgments are one way for non-Indigenous people to support Indigenous sovereignty and advocate for land reparations.[42]

LaDonna BlueEye, who has a PhD in public health, remarked on how the loss of language, among other breaks in one's culture, leads to many health issues and inequities. The first year of the Covid-19 pandemic laid bare the racial inequities in the US health system and vulnerabilities of certain populations, including tribal communities. At the same time, some US representatives and senators began to recognize the intersection of the stresses of the pandemic and language issues, such as the increased risk of native-language speakers dying directly or indirectly from Covid-19 and the need for translation of the Center for Disease Control's materials into Native languages.

In 2021 the US Congress finally recognized the issue of damages associated with the loss of Native languages and its relationship to the pandemic by including a $20 million grant for "emergency Native language preservation and maintenance" in the Covid-19 relief bill. The grant was aimed at "preserving Native American languages and mitigating the effects of the Covid-19 pandemic on Native languages, which tend to be spoken more widely among older populations who are more susceptible to the virus."[43] This grant was just a part of more than $31 billion included in the Biden Administration's $1.9 trillion relief package. Overall, these funds, on top of $8 billion allocated to tribal governments in the earlier stimulus law, was a record level of federal assistance that addressed not just language retention, but health services, education, housing, and other needs. The *New York Times* characterized the money as "a potentially transformative lifeline for tribes, who were among the hardest hit by the spread of the coronavirus. It was also a high-profile step toward more equitable treatment after centuries of treaty violations and failures by the federal government to live up to its obligations."[44] Days after signing the law, the Senate confirmed Deb Haaland as interior secretary, which made her the first Native American to serve as a cabinet secretary.

LaDonna BlueEye, Marlys Rambeau, and other interviewees shared their concerns about health disparities affecting Native Americans, both on reservations and in urban settings. Research bears out what they have noted within their own families. According to the Indian Health Service (IHS), "American Indian and Alaska Native people have long experienced lower health status when compared to other Americans." A Native person born today has a life expectancy five and a half years less than the all-races US population. The IHS lists possible causes for this lower life expectancy and disproportionate disease burden as including inadequate education, disproportionate poverty, discrimination in the delivery of health services, and cultural differences, all "quality of life issues rooted in economic adversity and poor social conditions."[45]

Physician Rupa Marya and political economist Raj Patel take a deep dive into the root causes of these health disparities in the US in their 2021 book *Inflamed: Deep Medicine and the Anatomy of Injustice*. Here they analyze and show the links between our biological bodies and injustices in political and economic systems. Their analysis focuses on the many painful results of colonization and points the way to "decolonizing medicine" and "re-humanizing" health care. Along the way they note issues specific to Native Americans. For instance, they note that "Indigenous women continue to bear a disproportionate share of violence" and cite a 2016 National Institute of Justice study that showed that a staggeringly high number of Native American women—four in five—have experienced violence in their lifetimes. "Over a third have experienced sexual violence, a rate double that of white US women," violence that is most often perpetrated by someone not Native.[46]

Regarding this disproportionate share of violence, especially the crisis of missing and murdered Indigenous women, LaDonna BlueEye shared her concerns and what she has observed within her own extended family and community. She stated, "Everyone knows someone who was murdered or trafficked." Statistics show that Indigenous women and girls' murder rates are ten times higher than all other ethnicities and that murder is the third cause of death for Indigenous women. The movement Murdered and Missing Indigenous Women (MMIW) received more widespread attention after Hanna Harris was found murdered on the Northern Cheyenne Reservation in 2013. Hanna's mother, Malinda Harris Limberhand, and other advocates forcefully pushed for the passage of House Bill 21 in the Montana legislature also known as "Hanna's Act." After a tumultuous journey, "Hanna's Act" was finally signed into law by the governor of Montana in May 2019. It created a special position in Montana's Department of Justice to investigate all missing persons cases in the state and joined other state-level measures to address this serious problem.[47]

Marya and Patel also look at other issues affecting health outcomes, issues brought to our attention by those we interviewed. For instance, they describe the roles that residential boarding schools played in breaking down kinship bonds, knowledge, and ways that lead to health-damaging stresses. They examine intergenerational trauma, noting that "trauma's fingerprints last for generations." They also link language with health and cite a number of studies showing the positive health effects of maintaining and revitalizing native languages, including a protective role it might play in reducing youth suicide.[48]

In Northeast Ohio, Native Americans face health issues such as stroke and heart disease. Local leader Marlys Rambeau noted that heart disease is prevalent in her family, and she and many Native friends also have diabetes or prediabetic conditions. Rambeau advocates for strengthening the Native community and sense of Native identity as an important tool in improving health outcomes. This emphasis on restoring traditional ways and relationships is aligned with Marya and Patel's calls for a "culture of care,"—not a "caring about," but a "caring with." This includes recognizing and investing in routes to wellness rooted in deep traditional knowledge and ways.[49]

LaDonna BlueEye shared an excellent example of how to address a public health issue within Native American communities by incorporating an understanding of traditional ways, tribal history, and culture. When teaching at Indiana University, BlueEye studied and authored reports on health issues in Native American communities, particularly tobacco use and Native American imagery. She recognized that the commonly used smoking-cessation approaches, such as labeling tobacco as evil, were not working in Native communities, mainly because those methods did not take into account tribal history and culture. BlueEye believed a more effective approach involved connecting to "the real meaning of tobacco." Native Americans had been using tobacco for centuries in entirely different ways than smoking cigarettes. Her approach was to look back into Indigenous history to see and understand the traditional role tobacco played in the lives of ancestors. She reached out to elders and leaders in Native communities who could help teach younger people the traditional ways and understandings and to communicate expectations better, for instance, that smoking cigarettes was inappropriate during sacred ceremonies. Their message then was "tobacco is our medicine, and this is how we use it." She noted further: "This is a powerful message not recognized by the medical community." Tobacco was sacred, and often given as a gift; it might be burned on a fire rather than smoked. Therefore, a more effective way to address the health risks of cigarette smoking in Native populations was to help individuals reconnect with the deeply rooted traditional relationship to tobacco—one that is respectful of its sacred role. A tagline that developed for this approach is "Traditional use, not abuse."[50]

We have looked at the ways in which language loss, generational trauma, issues of identity, and disconnection from your culture can accumulate and result in biological and psychological damage. Indigenous individuals, whether living on reservations or in cities, experience some of the same stresses. The boarding school experience often had traumatic negative effects on Native American children removed from family and reservation. Having a positive and accurate sense of self can also be challenging for urban Native Americans, distanced and separated from homelands and tribal culture. While boarding schools aimed to assimilate Native Americans into the dominant white culture, the Relocation program had similar aims. In the 1950s and 1960s, the Bureau of Indian Affairs (BIA) created programs and policies aimed at assimilating Native Americans by relocating them from reservations into mainstream American society. While the stated goal was to relieve poverty through job training and jobs, Relocation also resulted in fragmenting families and tribal communities, leaving relocatees isolated and bereft of support. Recognizing that a sense of community and belonging is essential to good mental health, relocated Native peoples from various tribal backgrounds sought to build a community within their adopted locations, resulting in Pan-Indian organizations and groups, much like some Native children from various tribes met and bonded at the boarding schools.

James Workman, a non-Native who moved to Cleveland in 1995, had long been interested in the intersection of race relations and cultural issues. In the 1990s there was a rising awareness about race and identity issues, which he explored through theater. While at Cleveland State University, working on a major in history, James began working with the Native American community in Cleveland. In exploring cultural identity, he sought to understand what Native Americans did to assert their identity and focused especially on studying the effects of the BIA's Relocation Program on the local community.[51]

James believes that it is impossible to understand or discuss Relocation without first understanding "Termination," the BIA's policy from the late 1940s through the 1960s. The policy was first officially put in place in 1953 in a Congressional resolution, beginning a period of dismantling and upheaval for hundreds of tribes. The policy sought to terminate tribal status and remove Indian lands from trust status, thus ending both the reservation system and the United States government's legal obligations to Indian tribes. The resolution called for the immediate termination of some tribes by name, such the Menominee and Potawatomi, as well as all tribes in several states. In 1954, Congress sought to terminate many more tribes, including the Iroquois Confederation of Six Nations and the Seneca. During the time of Termination the federal government terminated more than one hundred tribes and bands and removed about 2.5 million acres of trust land from protection. They sold much of the land to non-Natives. Some tribes resisted the policy through civil lawsuits and some, like the Choctaw and Seneca, held off termination until the federal government ended the policy. Notably, during this period Native American rights organizations such as the American Indian Movement (AIM) gained strength, and by the early 1960s some federal leaders began opposing the policy. Both presidents Lyndon B. Johnson and Richard Nixon favored self-determination over termination, and in 1975 Congress passed the Indian Self-Determination and Education Assistance Act, which in essence ended Termination. After the policy ended, a number of tribes were successful in regaining their status of sovereignty, including the Menominee Tribe in Wisconsin.[52]

On the heels of Termination, the federal government began the Relocation program. The combination of Termination, Relocation, and the establishment of boarding schools were all part of *assimilation*, or the effort to remove Native people from their tribal affiliations and assimilate them into mainstream society and Euro-American ways and values. According to the National Council of Urban Indian Health, these policies resulted in "the creation of culturally orphaned AI/AN [American Indian/Alaska Native] people—neglected and marginalized by society."[53]

In his studies, James questioned whether the US government reached its goals with Relocation. He saw examples of how Relocation played out in real lives: how Native Americans were separated from their cultural homes but did not surrender their culture or cultural identity. While some relocated Native Americans did return to their reservations, many did not and found it hard to return. As a substitute, they gathered into community in the city, and this mixing of individuals from diverse tribal backgrounds gave rise to the Pan-Indian movement, represented in such events as regional powwows. From James's observations, the urban community was created out of loneliness and "was not what they were," but the choice, as he saw it, was to be in community in that way, or "become white people." He believes that the BIA wanted the relocated Native Americans "to be white," and some decided to make the physical move, perhaps enjoy "modernity," but still be "Indian."[54]

As with other issues discussed in this chapter, there is a range of opinions among Native Americans regarding both the goals and the results of Relocation. Those who shared their stories with us expressed various perspectives formed by their own experiences and those of their families. Claire Heldman was born in Ohio but experienced Relocation through her work at the North American Indian Cultural Center in Tallmadge, Ohio. For ten years Claire worked at the Center delivering social services to Native individuals and families, most of whom came to Northeast Ohio as part of the BIA's Relocation program. As she put it, "Relocation did not work, as far as assimilating Native people into white society. It was all about *separation*, when Natives are all about *family*." As she tried to help relocatees get training and education or find employment, she noted that they found it difficult to adjust to urban living without the support of extended family. That observation has been borne out in numerous studies and hearings held over the years that identified the major problems with Relocation, not the least of which was the culture shock—the radical difference between life on a reservation and urban living.[55]

Native Americans who have left reservations for urban life can experience complex and conflicting relationships with the reservations of their or their ancestors' birth. After losing her job with the cultural center, Claire took some time to return to her mother's ancestral reservation. Her mother, Delma Ducheneaux Heldman, was Lakota Sioux, born in 1930 at the Old Cheyenne Agency, South Dakota, today known as the Cheyenne River Reservation; she attended grade school on the reservation then graduated from the Stephan Indian School on the nearby Crow Creek Reservation. She went on to earn a bachelor's degree in elementary education at Northern State College, learned to fly, and met her future husband, Les Heldman, who was of German descent, in Florida, where he was serving in the Air Force. "My mom was short, round, and brown, and my dad was tall, with blue eyes." As an adult Claire followed her mother to South Dakota in the 1990s "to learn the background of my people." She stayed for a while on the Cheyenne River Reservation and then after leaving the reservation she studied and worked at Crazy Horse Mountain's education center, working with artifacts, as a tour guide, and in the library. "It was different there in the Black Hills—remote, with brutal winters."[56]

Claire and her mother also went on road trips to meet and learn about other tribes—their languages, their traditions. As she put it, "There are hundreds of recognized tribes. It's important to respect these different cultures." Regarding self-identity, as greater sensitivity emerged around the issue of "what to call us," Claire asked her mother, "What do *you* want to be called?" Her mother's answer came quickly: "I've been called an Indian all my life—I want to die an Indian." Claire still visits the reservation where her grandmother and aunt lived their lives and where cousins remain. The family's burial plot is there as well. But for Claire, "My career, my life, my friends are here."[57]

Marlys Rambeau is also Lakota Sioux, an enrolled member of the Cheyenne River Sioux tribe of South Dakota. She is also a Cleveland "child of Relocation." Marlys's mother came to Cleveland voluntarily through the Relocation program, having just graduated from college with a teaching degree. Marlys's father passed away when Marlys was eight years old, and her mother, a schoolteacher at a time when teachers did not get paid year-round, applied for a job at the Cleveland American Indian Center. There, around 1975, she met her future husband, Marlys's stepfather, Jerome Warcloud. The sixties and seventies were very active decades for the Indian Center. Warcloud was an educator, and at the Center he focused attention on the educational needs of the relocated Native young people.

Marlys's relationship with her tribal ancestry reflects some of the challenges of the results of Relocation. Her parents moved from Cleveland back to South Dakota to find a home for her grandmother, who wanted to return to the reservation. During that time her grandmother passed away, but her parents did buy a home in South Dakota, and for a while her stepfather Jerome Warcloud traveled back and forth between Ohio and South Dakota to operate the Cleveland American Indian Center. As of this writing, Marlys has not been back to South Dakota since her grandmother died. Her parents still live there, but she finds the systemic racism in the communities outside the reservation to be very troubling. "People there just take it—I myself do not understand how people treat each other that way."[58]

How does a Native in a predominantly non-Native community maintain their own culture and cultural identity? Marlys's response: "I get it—it's really hard in Ohio because there are no Indigenous people originally from here—we're all imports." She noted that is where local groups such as the Lake Erie Native American Council steps in. "Our main goal is to keep our culture alive, and because we all come from different tribes we try to keep programs generic." She gave the example of teaching how to make moccasins—different tribes have different style traditions, and she encourages young people to research what pattern their specific tribe used. Their creative work would then be showcased in an event called "Rock Your Mox." Classes would run through the winter culminating with a mini powwow in the spring, honoring attendees and high school graduates. Likewise, the regalia and dancing differ according to the particular tribe. She finds that today it is difficult to find skilled teachers of the traditional crafts, and the Covid-19 pandemic hampered many of the classes and events. She concluded: "It saddens me that so many people have no interest in their cultural traditions—they have left their people behind. We have such a beautiful rich culture—how can you ignore that?...This isn't what your ancestors survived for, for you to go to Starbucks and yoga classes, forgetting who you are at the core. I find it really sad."[59]

Rambeau has also taught traditional dances and continues to help organize events and dance performances, such as the performance by Native American youth at the Xtinguish Torch Fest celebration of the Cuyahoga River in 2019. She sees a dual value in such performances, as they help young members of the Native American community retain their cultural identity while reminding "the rest of Northeast Ohio that Native Americans are still here." Her art, performances, and participation in community events are ways she finds "to give our people a voice, so we can be noticed more, and invited to the table, and have our voices heard."[60]

Marlys's programs teaching Native arts leads us now to focus on how art and creative expression play a part in your sense of individual identity and well-being and connection to your cultural heritage and retention of that culture—traditions, beliefs, and values. First, it is important to understand the concept of cultural appropriation. To *appropriate* is to take something for your own or exclusive use, often without permission. *Cultural appropriation*, therefore, refers to the taking of something from another's culture that does not belong to you, especially if a dominant group takes from a minority group that has been historically exploited. This is especially problematic if, for example, something that is considered sacred to a culture is used in a nonsacred way by someone of the dominant culture.

Creating your own art, then, can be a way of "taking back," reclaiming and reconnecting to the richness and specificity of your culture. Put simply, in the words of the late George Horse Capture, formerly Assistant Director for Cultural Resources at the National Museum of the American Indian, "art is a testimony to existence."[61] Or as scholar David W. Penney puts it, "Art is, and has been, one of the principal strategies of Native American 'survivance,' to use writer Gerald Vizenor's term." Penney goes on to explain the difference between "survival" and Vizenor's term "survivance": "While the word 'survival' summons up images of last-gasp tenacity, the term 'survivance' refers more to the wisdom of memory and adaptability, and the strategies of resistance, accommodation, and transformation." Penney notes that while some Native Americans criticize museums and collections because they place the culture in the historical past, as if no Native American culture exists today, he believes this is unfortunate when considering Native American arts, since Indigenous artists have always been, and still are now, among those who most actively "reconcile the traditions of the past with the circumstances of the present."[62]

Ceramic artist Peter Jones is doing just that. Jones told us he feels he has always been an artist, noting that when he was growing up, neighbors who were teachers in his neighborhood brought him clay and other art materials to experiment with and fired clay pieces for him. Jones attended school in New York through the tenth grade then moved to Santa Fe where he could attend the highly regarded Institute of American Indian Arts (IAIA), at that time a high school. At IAIA Jones studied under Hopi artists Charles and Otellie Loloma. As he described it, the school instructors were successful Native artists and "more like family." Instruction included how to sell their work and manage financially. The school has changed and grown since he attended and today is fully accredited and one of thirty-seven tribal colleges in the United States. It houses the acclaimed Museum of Contemporary Native Arts' permanent collection, which includes many of Jones's works.[63]

Jones points out that Native people are storytellers, dealing with the past more than the present, keeping stories alive, and with his art, "I try to do both—when language died out arts picked it up." Art, in effect, "documents," or as Jones put it, "art is everything you know about forever." Jones has studied and worked to understand ancient Indigenous pottery for more than thirty years, researching how it was made and what it was used for. He feels he has come to understand the methods used by his ancestors and has created a style he calls "neo-traditional," adding that his pottery is "mostly trial and error." He explains that his pottery is a "combination of old and new... I'm not trying to replicate but to move the tradition a notch."[64]

Today Jones also teaches ceramics, having nurtured Native American ceramic artists on Six Nations reservations in New York, Wisconsin, and Canada. He shared with us that there are now one or two Native American potters on nearly every reservation, and a group of at least sixty ceramic artists are now doing a type of pottery reminiscent of early Iroquois (Haudenosaunee) pottery created in the region where he lives. The method involves pit firing, and some mistake the pottery for raku, a type of low-fired Japanese pottery, but it is not the same. Jones is encouraged by the "good people coming up" in the ceramic arts field. His biographer and retired Colgate University museum curator, Carol Ann Lorenz, said, "I believe it is safe to say that Peter nearly single-handedly revived the making of clay pots in Iroquois country. Largely through his efforts, there are dozens of Haudenosaunee artists working in clay today." In 2018, through a nomination put forth by Lorenz, Jones was awarded the Community Spirit Award by the First Peoples Fund, a nonprofit that honors and supports First Peoples artists and culture bearers. In her remarks regarding Jones, she stated, "Peter epitomizes the ideals of community connectedness and the giving spirit that the Community Spirit Award is designed to recognize and honor."[65]

As far as Jones's views of "White art," he explained: "I don't understand White art. White people don't have anything to base it on; it is so amalgamated. They have wonderful stories from their past ethnic groups, but it is all mashed together." To Jones, he finds the basis for much of white art to be "to justify 'me,' not from the heart—very seldom does it depict what you've gone through.... We've been experiencing things since 1492—you all started a whole new history here. It's important for you to know who you are and where you came from." Jones finds that non-Native people "don't know what to make of *our* art." He reflected that in the 1940s some art historians tried to categorize Native American art, calling it "modern art." He added that a lot of art has become a commodity and that the Native artists have bought into that idea to some degree, but "we and our art are much more complex" which makes selling the art complex as well.[66]

He believes that many people "don't understand us, don't want to be reminded of all that stuff, how we were treated. They feel guilty and are like walking on eggshells." But he added that all the social justice movements going on will change things: "It's important to take responsibility for what has happened."[67]

Jones's largest works to date are the identical bronze statues marking the north and south ends of the Portage Path in Akron, depicting a typical Native American male portaging a canoe. While earlier Indian statues in Akron and other Northeast Ohio cities were all created by non-Native sculptors, often depicting a standardized figure in the image of a Euro-American, those involved in the project to re-mark the Portage Path in 2002 wanted to select a Native artist to create a sculpture specific and authentic to this place and the time period in which the Path was used. Even with these careful intentions, the final work still came close to being "European-ized": The foundry in Pennsylvania did a mock-up based on Jones's maquette, but when he went to check it out he found that the artist who made the mock-up used his imagination and made changes to the figure. To Jones's eye, the figure now looked how Europeans saw Native Americans, with round faces—and a larger rear-end! As Jones put it, "I had to carve twenty pounds off his buns!" He noted that though this may not be obvious or important to a white viewer of the pieces, it is important to a Native person—and is an example in public art of "taking back" control over images of Native people.[68]

Jones's most recent public art project in this region is located in Cuyahoga Falls, Ohio. Funded by The National Endowment for the Arts and the City of Cuyahoga Falls, the bronze sculpture of a Native American paddling a canoe, titled "River Trade," celebrates the history of the Cuyahoga River.[69]

Another artist whose work illuminates his cultural heritage is Cherokee painter Edwin George who passed away in June 2022 as this book was being completed. George was an Eastern Band Cherokee who grew up in the Smoky Mountains of North Carolina. Though he was raised in a log house in the forested mountains, in a household that spoke only Cherokee, George later spent decades of his adult life in Kent, Ohio, where he worked as a resident hall custodian at Kent State University. While in Ohio, George began experimenting with art, all self-taught and inspired by stories he was told by his mother, father, and aunt. Around 1991, at the age of forty-seven, George began painting, sharing his personal history and culture through his vibrantly colorful works. George used to explain when discussing his art, "My primary purpose for painting is to help people understand my Cherokee culture."[70]

Although George had returned to live on the Eastern Cherokee Reservation in North Carolina before his death, his art lives on in Kent and in local collections. His 2005 public outdoor mural on North Water Street in Kent, entitled "Love," exemplifies the style and intent of his work. Through the use of vibrant colors and designs, George in essence paints a story, incorporating images from Cherokee myths—turtles, the shape-shifter raven "who travels between this world and the spirit world," and bear. Turtles, the raven, a deer, a bear, humans, and other creatures populate the mural, all around a central image of turtles, water, hills, and the sun.[71]

The bear often appears in George's paintings, such as in "Bear Washes His Face." As George explained in a 2004 artist statement, "Observations of the habits of the bear are very important to my people. The bear in the painting is seen at dawn, washing his face.... This ritual was practiced by my father. When I was a boy I had to rise early in the morning with him to go to the creek and give thanks to the spirit of the water."[72]

George also often included the Cherokee syllabary (language symbols) in his paintings, because, as he put it, "it identifies my people." George hoped that doing so also helped keep the Cherokee language alive. He was raised speaking only Cherokee and also found that his art served as a "visual language," as he was taught the stories in Cherokee and found it difficult to translate those stories into English. Instead, they come through powerfully in visual form.[73]

In the late 1990s and early 2000s, George's work reached a larger audience through a number of ways. In 1994 he was a featured craftsperson at the Cuyahoga Valley Heritage Festival in Cuyahoga Valley National Park, where he shared his paintings, carvings, and storytelling with thousands of visitors. In 2011, George was awarded an Ohio Heritage Fellowship in folk and traditional arts from the Ohio Arts Council. He also participated in the Akron Art Museum's Native American Festival in the 1990s, and was in numerous other festivals and art shows. His works have also been shown in the Ohio Arts Council's Riffe Gallery in Columbus, Ohio. His work continues to inspire others and his granddaughter, Janis Wunderlich, an artist herself and assistant professor of art at Monmouth College in Illinois, credits George as being "one of the huge influences in my life and my art."[74]

While Edwin George worked primarily with acrylics on canvas, artist Marlys Rambeau's materials are beads, sinew, bones, and feathers. Rambeau, an enrolled member of the Cheyenne River Sioux Tribe of South Dakota and director of the Lake Erie Native American Council (LENAC), has been beading since high school, having first learned the traditional art of beading from Sioux beadworker Faye Brings Them, at the Cleveland American Indian Center (CAIC), where Marlys's stepfather, Jerome Warcloud, was executive director. Faye Brings Them was the daughter of Irmlee (Irma Lee) Yellow Eagle, a respected elder in the Cleveland Native American community in the 1970s, and director of the CAIC just prior to Warcloud becoming director. Beadworking also runs in the family. Rambeau's mother was a self-taught beadworker, creating since she was eleven years old. Rambeau highly praised her mother's beadwork as "gorgeous," modestly saying "mine not so much—some I bead well, others I have to work on." Her mother had come to Cleveland during Relocation to take a teaching position after college, and all paths crossed through the Cleveland American Indian Center. One of the missions of the center was to provide social and educational programs for the relocated Native Americans and their children, including opportunities for the elder generation to teach the younger generation skills and knowledge, beliefs, and practices of the Native cultures. This included beading and sewing skills, making regalia, and learning Native dances. Rambeau in turn has worked to continue that transmission of culture and cultural arts by teaching beading, the making of dream catchers, and preparing regalia and traditional dress, noting that every tribe has its own traditional dress and that there are seven different types of dances.[75]

Rambeau's designs and techniques are traditional—she uses high-quality beads and other materials and backs her pieces with buckskin and leather, not synthetics—but with a contemporary twist. Her works include intricately beaded flip-flop sandals and beaded phone grips, as well as earrings, chokers, and bracelets. She has been practicing her art since she was a teenager, and as an adult was a featured artist at a Cleveland Museum of Art's Native American exhibition. She has taught classes for various organizations in Northeast Ohio and has participated in festivals and powwows. Rambeau played a major role in Cleveland Metroparks' First Peoples Day events, finding and organizing other Native artists to participate and demonstrate their particular skills, such as carving pipestone, flute-making, or working with quills.[76]

Artist Claire Heldman creates contemporary Native American art in her drawings, paintings, and wall hangings. She uses traditional culturally significant media like rawhide, sinew, horsehair, and cattle skulls as well as found objects such as slate and driftwood to create art that teaches others about her culture and Indian ways of life. She believes it can create a bridge between cultures with the hope of creating a better understanding between them.[77]

Heldman has been sketching since she was a little girl. When her high school art teacher saw how accomplished she was in art, she was moved into advanced classes. Today much of her work is visualized through prayer and meditation. "I pray for a vision and it comes." It reflects her proud heritage, and she is inspired by other Native American artists. Her mother, Delma Ducheneaux Heldman, was a very accomplished traditional bead artist who created beautiful beaded moccasins, earrings, and necklaces. Heldman believes that traditional Native American arts and crafts such as beadwork need to be taught, preserved, honored, and treasured every day.[78]

Heldman has participated in many local arts events at venues such as Summit County Historical Society, Summit Art Space, The University of Akron, and powwows in Cuyahoga Valley National Park. In 2004 she was recruited to restore a fifteen-foot-high Tlingit totem pole named "The Raven's Vision" which was probably created in the mid-1800s. She stripped the paint that covered the carved symbolic images of an eagle, frog, raven, child, and warrior, which have spiritual significance and who watch over families, clans, or tribes of the Northwest Coast. Taking the paint down to the bare yellow cedar revealing its original colors, Heldman then repaired cracks and repainted it as to how it may have originally looked in its Alaskan fishing village.[79] She saved the thick, colorful paint chips she removed to live on in her own paintings of the sun, moon, and stars. Heldman has exhibited extensively in Northeast Ohio, New Mexico, South Dakota, Colorado, Florida, and Louisiana, and her work hangs in the Ohio Governor's Multicultural Gallery in Columbus. She was named Artist of the Year by the Ohio Arts Council in 2004.[80]

Artist Valerie Evans is an enrolled member of the Delaware Tribe from Six Nations Reserve, Ohsweken, Ontario, Canada. She moved to the Cleveland area over twenty years ago and worked until 2013 as community liaison at the American Indian Education Center in Cleveland. There she organized focus groups between local health services providers and the Native American community regarding health disparities and the need for more holistic traditional healing methods to be included in the current health care system. She continues to be a community liaison today in various capacities.[81]

Evans is a nontraditional, contemporary Native American portrait artist. Her medium is colored pencil. Using historical photographs, she recreates Native American portraits of family members and friends, often clad in ceremonial regalia or placing them in different settings, illustrating her interest in Indigenous self-identity. The Cleveland Museum of Art asked her to be a community liaison and gallery guide when the Thaw Collection of American Indian Art was exhibited in Cleveland in 2010. The museum placed a very high importance on seeking out local Native American community members for collaboration, input, and involvement, contributing to the success of the exhibit.[82]

In 2016 Evans was involved in an extraordinary Sister City cultural and arts exchange experience between the City of Rouen, France, and the City of Cleveland. Several Cleveland-area Native Americans had the unique opportunity to examine Indigenous ceremonial artifacts that were collected by a French explorer in the 1830s and had previously been housed in the basement of the Muséum d'Histoire Naturelle de Rouen (Natural History Museum of Rouen) for many years. Blessings were offered to these sacred objects before possibly being repatriated back to their respective tribes in America.[83]

The cultural exchange group was treated royally on their visit to Rouen, attending many events, meetings, and banquets given by the mayor. They took private guided tours of the city, attended concerts, and art museums, as well as providing several Native American presentations to local university students. On a visit to the beaches of Normandy and the nearby American cemetery, the Cleveland contingent blessed the Native American soldiers' graves with tobacco.

Shawnee artist Julia Edwards grew up immersed in her culture at the local Native American Indian Cultural Center. There she participated in local powwows as a traditional singer and dancer, especially as a Fancy Shawl Dancer. As a teen at the center, she felt very connected with friends from many different Native American nations who lived in the Akron area at that time. She laments not having that fellowship anymore as people moved on and cultural centers closed.[84]

Edwards's parents encouraged her and her brother in the arts and to be intimately connected to their Native identity and heritage. Her father is Shawnee, and to the best of his knowledge, his ancestors have always lived in Ohio. He is an artist too, a heavy metal rock musician. He recently gave her a rare book of Shawnee vocabulary. Edwards's mother, of Hungarian descent, is a farm-to-school teacher in Akron Public Schools who teaches children about nature and sustainability through community gardening. She actively encouraged her children to know their roots. Edwards's brother pursues art through acting.

Through the time she spent at the Indian Center, Edwards became aware that the American history she was taught in school was inaccurate and one-sided. She found it exhausting to try to teach the real Native American history and to answer questions, like how much Native American blood she had, to those who perceive all Native Americans through the stereotype of Hollywood western movies. She states that other stereotypes—such as Disney's Pocahontas, the former Cleveland Indians' Chief Wahoo logo, or the idea that all Native Americans are peace-loving—hurt because they do not allow for Native Americans to be seen as real people who still exist and still suffer. "I can't just be me!" she exclaims. The older she becomes, the more she wants to learn about her Native culture which is invisible to others, as are current Native American issues of sovereignty and land reparation. She comments on how many non-Natives think Indians get everything free, when many live in poor conditions.[85]

Edwards attended Miller South Middle School for the Visual and Performing Arts and Firestone High School in Akron, where she learned oil painting. Now she expresses herself through the lens of a camera. She captures the ordinary elements of nature such as birds, animals, and plants with creativity and imagination. "Art keeps me grounded...being outdoors connects me to nature...all my artwork is nature based, it goes with my culture," she states. She attended the Myers School of Art at The University of Akron before she began studying law enforcement. Edwards is currently a Park Ranger with Stark Parks where she is surrounded by her artistic subject matter. She feels it is important for non-Native people to know that Native Americans are regular people doing regular jobs like law enforcement and do not live in wigwams.[86]

These few artists that we have become acquainted with and who have connections to Northeast Ohio represent a wide variety of styles, media, and diversity of background, expressing a range of age, experiences, and viewpoints on what it means to be Native American in the dominant non-Native culture. Their work often bridges both cultures and time, and in many ways addresses all the issues that have been discussed in this chapter. They offer us glimpses and insights into the role that art plays in their particular lives: connecting them to ancestors and to ancestral knowledge, cultural understandings, and ways of life. Their experiences and expressions through art sometimes reveal how those cultural inheritances have been assaulted, neglected, or torn apart through separations, losses, and assimilation, and how art might be one avenue of healing and connection.[87]

The history of Native Americans in this region is a still unfolding story. It takes hard work to keep the stories alive and to tell and retell them. Although this task is painful, it is crucial that this work continues. The individuals with whom we have connected and who have enriched our lives remind us that the Native American presence is alive and well in Northeast Ohio. The community has evolved since the Relocation program brought more Native peoples to this region—while some retain connections to the leaders and matriarchs of the mid- to late-1900s, a younger generation of leaders is helping shape the next chapter of local history. Every individual we interviewed has been partly shaped by their ancestors' experiences and by some of the challenges discussed in this chapter. Some have focused their attention on addressing the negative effects of stereotyped images in sports team names and logos, while others have devoted energies to keeping true to deeply valued cultural ways and traditions. Each, in their own way, is an affirmation of how their Native roots enrich their everyday lives and how these roots flower into gifts and talents expressed in our contemporary society.

Edwin George, *Love*. Outdoor mural in Kent, Ohio, latex on tile. *Photo courtesy of Peg Bobel*

Claire Heldman, *Yellow Tipi*. Acrylic on slate. *Photo courtesy of Francisca Ugalde*

Valerie J. Evans, *Tree of Peace*. Colored pencil on paper. *Photo courtesy of Valerie J. Evans*

Julia Edwards with her photographs. *Photo courtesy of Julia Edwards*

The following are brief biographies of the people interviewed for this chapter presented alphabetically.

LaDonna BlueEye, an enrolled member of the Choctaw Nation in Oklahoma, is the Indigenous consultant for Summit Metro Parks in Akron, Ohio. She is a relative newcomer to Northeast Ohio. Prior to coming to Akron, LaDonna taught in the Health Science Department of Indiana University in Bloomington, Indiana, the first and only Native American PhD in public health at the university. While there she focused her research and published reports on health issues in Native American communities. Her work on tobacco use among Native Americans received national recognition and support and led to her formulating a culturally relevant approach to smoking cessation for that population. (See for instance the "Native American Action Plan, Addressing Tobacco Abuse Among Pregnant and Postpartum Women," funded by the National Partnership to Help Pregnant Smokers Quit, a national program funded by The Robert Wood Johnson Foundation.) BlueEye's ancestors came to Oklahoma as a result of the forced removal of Choctaw and other Southeast tribes from their traditional homelands via what is now called the Trail of Tears.

Sam Chestnut is the head of The Lippman School, an independent school in Akron, Ohio, that offers K-8 education based on Jewish values and cross-cultural learning. He graduated from Kenyon College in Ohio and earned a Master of Arts in Educational Administration from The University of Akron. Sam was born in Seattle, Washington, the son of Steve Chestnut, a partner in the Seattle legal firm Ziontz Chestnut. This western firm has a national practice representing Indian tribes in such areas as tribal water rights, mineral rights, the protection of culturally and economically important natural resources, and reservation boundary disputes. While a young student in middle school, Sam became acquainted with the Northern Cheyenne in Montana through his father's work on behalf of the tribe. Stemming from these early experiences with the Northern Cheyenne, Sam has created an experiential learning partnership between The Lippman School and the Northern Cheyenne.

Julia Edwards is an artist/photographer and a law enforcement ranger for Stark Parks. Her father is Shawnee, tracing his roots far back in Ohio history, and her mother is non-Native. Cherishing her Native ancestry,

Julia, as a young girl, immersed herself in Native traditions by participating in programs at the Native American Indian Cultural Center. There she learned traditional songs and dances, attended powwows, and became an accomplished Fancy Shawl Dancer. She studied art in middle-school and high-school, and enrolled in The University of Akron, intending to become an art teacher, but chose a different career path, becoming a park ranger. She continues her art, primarily through photography, finding her favorite subject matter in local parks and natural areas.

Val Evans is a portrait artist and community liaison, currently working at Career Development and Placement Strategies in Cuyahoga County. A member of the Delaware Tribe from Six Nations Reserve in Ontario, Canada, Val now lives in Cleveland, Ohio. She notes that she has ancestral tribal ties to Ohio: The Delaware (an Anglo name given to Unami and Munsee of the Delaware and Hudson River valleys) were displaced, forced westward to what is now Ohio and then later removed to Oklahoma Indian Territory. A small band of Evans's ancestors were forced to the Munsee Delaware Reserve near London, Ontario, Canada. The journey on foot was long and arduous, and the small band sought winter refuge along the Grand River near Six Nations Reserve, eventually being adopted into the Lower Cayuga Tribe, becoming officially a part of the League of Six Nations, a recognized First Nation of Canada. Val considers her art nontraditional Native American art but explains that she sometimes puts a Native spin on some of her Native American subjects by placing them in traditional regalia or having them posed in different settings. She is interested in issues of Native American health care, sports team logos, and self-identity. Her art can be found at https://3-valerie-evans.pixels.com/.

Edwin George, an Eastern Band Cherokee Indian, was a folk artist who painted the stories and myths of his people. He wanted to teach these stories using symbolic images because he learned them in his native language, and it was easier to paint them than to find the English words. Edwin worked at Kent State University before returning to North Carolina. His work can be seen in a public art mural in Kent, Ohio. He passed away in June 2022.

Claire Heldman Oyate Wankan Wia is a Cheyenne River Reservation Lakota Sioux (South Dakota) artist. Claire grew up in Cuyahoga Falls, Ohio, with her feet in two worlds—Native and non-Native—as her mother was Lakota Sioux and her father was of German descent. In the past Claire worked at the North American Indian Cultural Center in

Tallmadge, providing social services to Native Americans in the region, many who arrived in Northeast Ohio via the Relocation program. She also lived on the reservation for a while, lived and worked in the Black Hills, then moved back to Cuyahoga Falls. She has participated in programs through the Summit County Historical Society, demonstrating Native American foods, clothing, and drumming. In 2021–22 her art was featured in a one-woman show, "Lakota Wia," in the Lynn Rodeman Metzger Galleries at the Cummings Center for the History of Psychology and Institute for Human Science and Culture Galleries, The University of Akron.

Michael Jones is of Onondaga/Seneca descent, born in Oklahoma and now living on the Cattaraugus Reservation in New York State. He is a ceramic artist who apprenticed with his father, ceramic artist Peter Jones. Michael's work has been exhibited widely, and he has recently begun showing pen and ink drawings, which are drawn from personal experiences, imagination, and dreams. His passion and pride in his ancestral Seneca language has influenced him to become a Seneca language immersion schoolteacher.

Peter Jones is an acclaimed Onondaga clay artist who lives and teaches on the Allegany Territory of the Seneca Nation of Indians in New York State. He studied at the Institute of American Indian Arts in Santa Fe, New Mexico, where he learned about traditional Southwest pottery. He returned to New York to research Iroquois pottery, working for several decades to understand how ancient Iroquois pottery was made and for what uses. He calls his art neo-traditional, utilizing some traditional methods but not duplicating traditional pottery. New York's Metropolitan Museum of Art has acquired one of Peter's works, and the National Museum of the American Indian in Washington, DC. has commissioned Peter to assemble an exhibit on Haudenosaunee pottery. Peter has a strong artistic connection with Ohio, as seen by his sculptures of Native Americans portaging canoes at the ends of the Portage Path in Akron. He returns to Akron each year for the North American First People's Day commemoration and has contributed to a public art project in Cuyahoga Falls, Ohio.

Marlys Rambeau, born in Cleveland, is a citizen of the Cheyenne River Sioux tribe of South Dakota. Her mother voluntarily relocated to Cleveland to look for a teaching position after graduating from college. Marlys is a beadwork artist who has taught various Native American arts and crafts classes as well as traditional dancing, along with doing presentations about Native American culture to many different groups throughout Northeast Ohio. As chair of the Lake Erie Native American Council (LENAC), Marlys has been active advocating for Native Americans in the region and was especially instrumental in Cleveland's Major League Baseball team name change from the "Indians" to the "Guardians."

Matt Russ is the principal at The Lippman School. He has a Bachelor of Science degree in Journalism from the Appalachian State University in Boone, North Carolina, and a Master of Arts in Philosophy and Religious Studies from John Carroll University in Cleveland, Ohio. Matt has worked closely with the head of Lippman, Sam Chestnut, on the experiential learning partnership the school has with the Northern Cheyenne tribe in Montana. A significant outgrowth of that partnership was a student project to write and propose to the Akron City Council a resolution to establish the first Monday of October as "North American First Peoples' Day." Matt guided Lippman middle-schoolers in gathering ideas for the resolution, writing it, and presenting it to council, learning about the process of law along the way. Students submitted the resolution to Akron City Council in January 2018, and it was unanimously approved into law a week later.

Thomas Shoulderblade, a Northern Cheyenne leader, has been partnering with Sam Chestnut and Matt Russ of The Lippman School on their educational/cultural exchange program for middle-schoolers. Thomas is committed to helping others learn the real history of Native American people, from a Native person's perspective, and beyond what might be routinely taught in public schools. He lives on the Northern Cheyenne Reservation in Montana and comes to Akron annually to participate in North American First Peoples' Day events. In turn, he hosts students and teachers from The Lippman School on their visit and learning experiences on the reservation. Thomas has also been a leader and educator at The Lippman School's summer camp held at Crown Point Ecology Center.

James Workman, a community educator, received a Master of Arts in History from Cleveland State University, with a special interest in the American Indian Relocation program. As a non-Native, he for many years presented to groups of all ages the facts about Relocation and its effects on Native American individuals, families, and communities. James now lives in Asheville, North Carolina, serving the community as operations director for a juvenile assessment center.

2 Archaeology
A Way to Understand the Past and Present

Linda G. Whitman

No academic endeavor is created in a vacuum. It reflects the worldview of the dominant culture of a particular time and place and reflects the biases of that culture. As a discipline beginning in the late-nineteenth- to early twentieth centuries, anthropology and its subdivision archaeology began primarily as a way to describe non-European cultures before they disappeared. The reality is that anthropology and archaeology come from a colonial framework where cultures with their individual practices, histories, languages, voices, material remains, and biological remains were viewed as objects or sources of information, not as a part of dynamic people and cultures who may still exist today.[1]

Over the past few decades, archaeology has been in the process of acknowledging and changing many of these practices, starting with apologizing for the damage it has done.[2] For archaeology, indigenous archaeology began to take its form in the 1990s with a call for including Native American values and worldviews within archaeological practices including how sites are discovered, interpreted, and who benefited from these practices along with a full partnership in decisions of their heritage management. Indigenous archaeology is a method, an intellectual framework, and a political agenda to change and improve the field of archaeology as well as further the goals of Indigenous people to control their heritage.[3] Responses to current social justice calls for reforms may be seen in the creation/implementation of heritage protection laws (see below), the creation of the Smithsonian Institution's *National Museum of the American Indian*, and the ongoing movement in museums—especially natural history museums with Native American dioramas—to rethink their exhibitions and move away from the traditional Eurocentric perspective from which they were created. However, the field of archaeology is slowly responding to these concerns.[4]

What is archaeology?

It is obvious from movies, television shows, web pages, magazines, YouTube videos, and travel tours that people love archaeology, but they are not really sure what it is. And what it isn't. Unfortunately, these misunderstandings are fed by stereotypes in popular culture like Indiana Jones, so the general public is unable to distinguish between what is and what is not archaeology. Additionally, the fact that archaeology/anthropology is not typically part of our school curriculum only feeds this misconception. This chapter is intended to provide some understanding of what archaeology is and what archaeologists do.

For a more textbook definition, archaeology is the study of people and their cultures that lived in the past through *artifacts*, portable material remains of actual things people made, used, modified and then left behind. Other remains are non-portable, and they are called features representing activities that leave behind evidence such as a hearth or fireplace, the remnants of a building or a soil stain in the location of a rotted house post.

Archaeology in the United States is a subdiscipline of *anthropology*, which can be simply defined as "the study of what makes us human." Anthropologists take a holistic or "broad approach to understanding the many different aspects of the human experience" through understanding the relationship between human biology, language, and culture, both past and present.[5] Anthropology at its core maintains the importance of cross-cultural comparison and a central methodology of ethnography. *Ethnography* is the scientific description of the shared customs of individual peoples and cultures to gain a deep understanding of a group's culture and social dynamics. These concepts distinguish cultural anthropology from the discipline of sociology.

While it may be true that archaeology is fun, it cannot be reduced to a cinematic adventure. So much more than just "playing in the dirt," archaeology is a scientific discipline. It uses a set of scientific methods and techniques to recover and analyze material remains and rigorous theories to interpret the findings. These theories change and evolve when different questions are asked of the archaeological record. The material remains may be garbage, debris that has been accidentally abandoned, as in a broken ceramic pot, or intentionally abandoned, as in a settlement. Archaeology is unique in its ability to study changes in human societies over long periods of time.

We study the past mostly because it enlarges and enriches our human experience by recognizing our common humanity and our cultural differences. It promotes respect for other people and helps preserve our shared cultural heritage. We want to know how people lived in the past. By knowing and understanding the course of events that shaped individual cultures, we can better understand who we are and what we can become.[6]

On a broader level, archaeology is culturally relevant, helping us address current issues such as environmental change and social inequities. Studying how past societies responded to climate shifts over decades, centuries or even millennia can help put today's climate issues into perceptive and offer ideas affecting modern environmental policy.[7] Social inequities described in terms such as race, gender, ethnicity, class, and caste can be seen in the interpretation of the archaeological record throughout time. Studying these variations of power and privilege in the past can shine light on what is seen as social inequality in the present.[8]

The goals of archaeology as a discipline include 1) to find and record the past, preserving a record of it for the future; 2) to reconstruct cultural histories or timelines; 3) to reconstruct and interpret past lifeways; 4) to explain the processes of cultural change; 5) to preserve, protect and manage archaeological sites for the present and future generations; and 6) to educate people about the very distant as well as the relatively recent past. Keep in mind that the goals of any discipline are refined as new interpretations of data are recognized.

While the goals and interests of the archaeologist are primarily humanistic in nature, after all it is a social science, much of the methodology employed in archaeology is borrowed from the hard sciences, which are based on concrete laws and rules. Doing archaeology is complex and interdisciplinary; scientific and not romantic. Archaeologists work with scientists in many disciplines such as astronomers, epigraphers, geographers, geologists, geochemists, soil scientists, paleobotanists, paleontologists, biological anthropologists, microbiologists, physicists, and zoologists, to name a few. They specialize in areas such as human remains, ancient plants and animals, ancient pollens, stone tools, ancient ceramics, ancient glass, mapping with noninvasive geophysical techniques, mapping with drones, classical archaeology, historical archaeology, underwater archaeology, Biblical archaeology, settlement systems, ritual, and religion. In contrast to other scientists, archaeologists are in a unique position because they actually "destroy" sites, their subject of study, as they collect data. Precise and accurate data collection is necessary to recreate a site and interpret it in written words, graphs, statistics, photographs, and maps.

It is a common misconception that archaeology only occurs in faraway places and only involves the investigation of people who lived a very long time ago. This is not an accurate picture of what archeology is or what archeologists do. Some archaeologists do study the remains of ancient cultures located far from Northeast Ohio and through the course of over five million years of human evolution. Others study the material remains of people who lived just one hundred years ago in the old farmstead just down the road, or the first mill in Akron to produce oatmeal, or the Indigenous peoples who lived here before European contact and colonialism.

The archaeological record is made up of data on many scales, those as small as what can be seen under a microscope such as ancient pollen (which enable environmental reconstruction) taken from a broken pot, to those as large as ancient cities. An archaeological site is the basic unit of investigation. It is more than a collection of things waiting to be dug up. It represents complex relationships within a once-living group of people, between them and other people, and between them and the environment. Artifacts or features by themselves have little scientific value without knowing the *context* of where and how they were found. *Context* is a term archaeologists use in a very specific way: it refers to the spatial association and distribution of artifacts, features, natural remains like animal bones or minerals (called *ecofacts*), and even sites themselves that are necessary for the reconstruction and interpretation of past human behavior. These relationships can provide information such as what people ate and how they cooked food; what plants and animals were available for consumption, clothing or building materials; how raw material was acquired, manufactured and used for tools; how they buried their dead and what they may have died from; what types of climate they lived in and how it is different from today's climate; and where they lived at a given time of year.

Archaeologists also look at how these materials were left behind. Are there *patterns* informed by this process, which takes material artifacts from an active role in human behavior and deposits them into the archaeological record? Has the original location of abandonment of materials changed through time by temperature, humidity, human activity, natural disasters like earthquakes or volcanic activity, or climate change? We also look at whether a site is similar in size, content, date, location, etc. to other settlements nearby, such as a line of encampments along the length of the Cuyahoga River or on its terraces.

Finding Sites

So, what do archaeologists do? Archaeologists do not just start digging anywhere to look for sites, nor do they excavate every known site. All archaeological investigations begin with a research design to plan how evidence of the human past will be collected and evaluated. This process of building a research design provides a place to discuss the historical and environmental setting of a site, a practical plan of action for fieldwork, and a theoretical framework for interpretation and analysis. It sets the research questions that guide the excavation to meet both the specific objectives of the research and the broader goals of archaeology.

Archaeological sites are found by conducting an archaeological survey, which is used to find data from sites or regions. Archaeologists who are looking for sites use three main methods: surface survey, aerial survey, and subsurface survey. Each method uses specific techniques, some simple and some complex, to detect and record archaeological evidence.

A surface survey (also called a pedestrian or walkover survey) is conducted by systematically walking over terrain on a grid, visually looking for evidence on the surface of the earth. In Ohio, as with most Midwestern states, agricultural fields have been plowed for over 250 years,

University of Akron student digging a shovel test survey unit. *Photo courtesy of Tim Matney*

disturbing the soil and mixing possible archaeological sites with the soils around them. Since plows can move artifacts several hundred feet from their original deposit, finding something on the surface might not indicate the exact location of a site. Or a site may be found buried under the plowzone of an agricultural field. Surveys may not find sites because the sites are small, or too disturbed and scattered by plows, or buried deeper than a farmer plowed.

An aerial survey may be conducted using aerial photography via airplanes, balloons, or drones equipped with remote control cameras. Nonphotographic aerial images like radar, thermography, or satellite scanners can also be used. Using remote sensing techniques, archaeologists look for differences in soil or vegetation color, patterns of crop markings only visible from overhead, buried ditches that hold more water (thus making the vegetation grow differently), or other differences that suggest the presence of potential archaeological sites.

Subsurface survey is used to locate sites beneath the surface of the earth when the ground surface covering is too dense to allow good visibility, such as in a woodlot or field of soybeans. It can make use of auguring (a drill-like tool used to take small samples of subsurface deposits), coring (a hollow tube driven into the ground to sample the subsoil for stratigraphic change or layers of soil deposited over time), and shovel testing (digging test holes with a shovel to determine whether the soil contains any cultural materials that are not visible on the surface) to look for subsurface sites. These methods are conducted systematically on a grid. The soil or "matrix" is sifted through a screen, and the archaeologist records information, including the total depth of the unit dug, soil type(s) and color changes, and at what depth the soil comes from, and the presence of any artifacts.

Other subsurface methods used to locate sites are geophysical surveys such as magnetic field gradiometry, electrical resistivity, and ground-penetrating radar. These methods are considered nondestructive because they do not alter the ground surface. Each of these methods use sophisticated instruments that can detect anomalies or inconsistencies that may indicate buried archaeological features or even some artifacts when their physical properties contrast measurably with their surroundings. Readings from the equipment taken in a systematic pattern create datasets, which are translated into an image map of an area indicating areas of potential interest. Because these methods are nondestructive, they can also guide excavations, informing archaeologists exactly where to excavate and preserve sites when avoiding disturbance of a culturally sensitive area such as a cemetery.

In addition to these archaeological methods, archaeologists rely on other sources of information, especially in the study of precontact sites. Farmers are a great source of information. They know the details about their land, noticing if there are any mounds, unusual depressions, rock shelters, or interesting things pulled up by their plow. Farmers and people who collect artifacts as a hobby or avocation can thus become local informants who aid archaeologists. They are frequently consulted and work together for the benefit of documenting archaeological sites (see Shott Chapter 4).

When searching for historic archaeological sites, historic and archival documents such as historic maps, deeds and wills, photographs, written and oral histories, etc. are used. Finding lilac trees, English ivy, or daffodils in the woods while conducting a pedestrian survey might suggest

University of Akron students conducting a magnetic field gradiometry survey. *Photo by Linda Whitman*

the location of a former house. Archaeological sites can also be found by accident! Any human activity that changes the surface of the earth such as grading for a road or ballfield, or digging to construct a building or pipeline, or digging in a garden can expose artifacts from a buried site. Natural processes such as drought, wind, or water erosion can also expose buried sites.

Excavation

Once a site is located, excavation is the procedure archaeologists use to recover, identify, and record cultural remains dug from the ground. It is the only way to verify the presence and characteristics of site survey evidence. However, most archaeologists excavate as little as possible of a site because of the destructive nature to this nonrenewable resource. Once it is dug, it's gone forever. We have the artifacts and the information in the form of notes, photographs, and maps, but the actual site is gone. The entire excavation process and what happens after the dig is expensive and very time-consuming. After excavating, cleaning, identifying,

Photograph of an excavation taken by a drone. *Photo courtesy of Jerrad Lancaster*

reconstructing, and describing our finds, the process of analysis and interpretation is undertaken on artifacts and the other information recovered. A report is written describing and interpreting all data collected, and all types of data and artifact curation needs to be conducted in perpetuity. Archaeologists generally only excavate when the site is threatened for destruction or if it can provide new, significant cultural information.[9]

Many methods are used for excavating an archaeological site, and the choice of how to dig is usually dependent on the research questions being asked. The excavation uncovers the past both in its horizontal and vertical dimensions. The horizontal dimension gives us a picture of the site at one particular fixed point in time, a detailed snapshot. The vertical dimension provides the timeline, giving us the sequence of change within a site over time. The best preserved and least disturbed remains found underground provide a *primary context* or the condition where things have not been disturbed since they were originally discarded.

Archaeologists need a really good reason to excavate an archaeological site. That is where a research design comes in. This document "outlines the 'who, what, where, when, how, and why' of the fieldwork."[10] Doing archaeology entails a detailed research design, which is necessary to obtain permission to excavate a site from the landowners of a site and to find funding for the research.

How Old is It?

A common question asked of archaeologists is "How old is an artifact or a site?" There is evidence that the Cuyahoga River Valley has been inhabited by people from at least 13,500 BP. How do we know this? Two main types of dating methods are used in archaeology: relative dating and absolute (or chronometric) dating. Relative dating methods tell us if an artifact, site, or culture is older or earlier than another and does not give us an actual calendrical date. For example, we know that a Paleoindian spearhead is older than a Middle Woodland spearhead based on how it looks and how it was manufactured. In this case, the style of the artifact tells us the age of one sample relative to another. In contrast, absolute dating methods provide an actual estimated age of an object or occupations as a range of actual dates. These two types of dating—relative and absolute—are discussed below.

Some of the most common methods archaeologists use to determine relative dates are stratigraphy, seriation, and environmental sequencing. Stratigraphy is based on the idea that archaeological deposits are layered with the youngest material on top and the oldest material on the bottom. While excavating from the ground surface down, we dig through a series of layers (called *strata*), which provide a relative order (or chronology) for artifacts found within the strata.

Seriation is based on the concept that styles of material culture such as the design of cars, clothing, hairstyles, stone tools, and pottery jars change through time. Because of this, it is possible to assign relative dates to them based on the style. Think of the different styles of blue jeans you have worn throughout your life. These change a lot quicker than the architectural style of the buildings downtown. By studying the characteristics of change through time, archaeologists can construct the order that reflects the passage of time.[11]

In a similar way, but on a different scale than style, geologists have developed many methods to determine the age of geological formations and to examine environmental or climate change through time, both natural and through the actions of human groups. Long-term geological and environmental processes consist of glacial advance and retreat, fluctuations in climate, fluctuations in land and sea levels, and annual soil deposits in glacial lakes. If the chronology of the geological event is known, archaeological materials associated with those changes can be fit into the known chronology.

In contrast to relative dating, absolute dating methods provide an estimated calendric age of an object. This is typically thought of as a calendrical date with a range of years and a statement of the statistical probability that the "true" age falls within that range. The true age of most artifacts is never known. Some absolute methods of dating include: radiocarbon dating, dendrochronology, obsidian hydration, potassium-argon dating, thermoluminescence dating, and archaeomagnetic dating. Each method is used on a different type of material, such as organic material (charcoal, shell, wood, bone, and hair), wood, obsidian (volcanic glass used for making tools), rocks, ceramics, or a variation in the Earth's magnetic field over time for a specific range of dates. Dating historic sites can be accomplished through historic records and by knowing the history of the manufacture and production of artifacts such as ceramics, nails, kaolin pipe stems, window glass, and glass bottles.[12] Historic sites are also dated via archival or historic documents whose dates are already known. In general, historic materials provide more precise dates and, in several cases, we can date archaeological materials to small date ranges, or even a single year.

Our Shared Heritage

Archaeological sites are protected in a variety of ways. However, as the Society for American Archaeology notes, "the past belongs to everyone, and it is everyone's responsibility to help preserve and protect it."[13] While many federal laws protect archaeological sites, only a few will be discussed in this chapter.[14] The National Historic Preservation Act (NHPA) of 1966 and its many amendments was passed to protect our nation's cultural heritage from federal development. NHPA sets historic preservation policy and creates partnerships between the federal government and states, and between the federal government and Native American tribes. This law requires that federal agencies take into account the effects that any of its actions may have on historic properties (meaning precontact and historic archaeological sites as well as historic sites) by identifying these sites, assessing the negative effects, and resolving those negative effects.[15]

A new kind of archaeology came about with the passage of this federal law. The broad term we use for the archaeology that developed out of this concern for our shared cultural resources is Cultural Resource Management (CRM). When any new development uses federal or tribal funds or needs licensing, such as a new highway, sewage treatment plant, cutting a forest, or improvements to a dock, an archaeological survey is legally required to see if any archaeological sites are present and if sites with important information will be destroyed by the project. CRM, also called compliance archaeology, is the industry that evolved to assist agencies in meeting these federal and tribal requirements. This law does not apply to projects on private property. Ohio does not have state laws that protect sites on state property; however, there are local preservation ordinances.

The Archaeological Resources Protection Act (ARPA) of 1979 builds on the Antiquities Act [of 1906] by defining and regulating legitimate archaeological investigation on federal and tribal lands and outlining the enforcement of penalties against those who loot, vandalize, or destroy archaeological resources. The act requires a consultation process with the affected Native American peoples by anyone who wants to conduct an archaeological investigation before a permit is issued and allows the tribe to attach its own terms and conditions to the permit.[16]

The Native American Graves Protection and Repatriation Act (NAGPRA) of 1990 went into effect in January 1996. "It addresses the repatriation of American Indian, Native Alaskan, and Native Hawaiian human remains, funerary objects, sacred objects, and items of cultural patrimony currently held by federal agencies and institutions that receive federal funds and defines 'ownership' of human remains and items of cultural importance when excavated or otherwise found on lands under federal or tribal control by setting up a ranking of control of remains of cultural importance from individual family, related kin, and tribal group."[17]

NAGPRA states that it is illegal to traffic in human remains and cultural items, and people who violate this law can *and will* be prosecuted.

The law requires that all federal agencies, museums, or other institutions, such as universities that receive federal funds, to inventory their holdings of Native American human remains and funerary objects and provide written summaries of other cultural items. These organizations are required to consult with Indian Tribes and Native Hawaiian organizations "to attempt to reach agreements on the repatriation or other disposition of these remains and objects. Affiliated Indian Tribes or affiliated Native Hawaiian organizations then determine the disposition of cultural items."[18]

How Can You Help?

If you are interested in archeology there are a number of ways in which you can help or participate. If you find a possible artifact or an archaeological site, it is important to report it so it can be properly recorded and documented, especially if the area may be destroyed. If you are in the Cuyahoga Valley National Park or any of the county or state parks here in Ohio, contact a person of authority, such as a park ranger or naturalist. If you are out of state and find an artifact on tribal property, contact the relevant tribal police. *Do not remove an artifact.* Depending on where you found it, removing an artifact may be against the law and punishable by fines and even jail time.

Another reason to not remove an artifact is because much of its scientific value is in recording its context. Record as much information as possible about where you are when you find an artifact. Use your cell phone to photograph it and its GPS to document its location. You might even draw the artifact and record its location on a paper map. If found on public land, contact those who are in charge of the property. If found on private property, share the information with a professional archaeologist in local colleges or university departments of anthropology or with a city or state natural history museum. Each state has a Historic Preservation Office that records the exact information of archaeological sites. Within Ohio, the historic preservation Office is in Columbus. It is a division of the Ohio History Connection, previously called Ohio Historical Society.

Additional ways you can get involved in archaeology are by visiting archaeological sites around the state, volunteering at local museums, and taking courses at local university anthropology departments and museums. County parks systems and museums have Citizen Scientist programs where you may be able to volunteer to participate in archaeological field and lab investigations. Ohio Archaeology Month is an annual event which takes place all over the state in parks, museums, and universities during the month of October with events, lectures, atlatl demonstrations, flint knapping, artifact exhibits, and more.[19] An excellent resource for information about Ohio archaeology is Bradley Lepper's book *Ohio Archaeology*.[20]

Many people who are interested in archaeology become avocational archaeologists or collectors. Avocational archaeologists are people who have passion for the past through archaeology but have not chosen to follow it as a professional career. They volunteer in their spare time without receiving personal income or profit.[21] Private collectors have been collecting archaeological artifacts mostly in the form of stone tools found on private property for a very long time. Many collectors work with archaeologists to help document and preserve the archaeological record (see Shott Chapter 4).

This chapter has been a quick introduction to what archaeology is and what archaeologists do. It is much more that digging up artifacts or popular images like Indiana Jones. Archaeology is scientific and multi-disciplinary. It's a systematic way to find and use data from the past to inform our present understanding of issues like social inequity, resource management, and climate change. It is fieldwork, and it is also work in the laboratory, the classroom, the museum, and its results are published in scientific and popular literature. It is archaeologists as well as personnel in government agencies, museums, universities, farmers, and collectors. And, if you want to be, archaeology is you.

Like all scientific disciplines, new data and new methods of collecting and interpreting that data are constantly evolving. It is a discipline with a problematic past that has evolved into a more inclusive and wide-ranging field of study. Each generation of archaeologists has a slightly different perspective on the ancient world, and, because of this, we constantly re-examine and debate older interpretations, sometimes confirming, sometimes modifying or even abandoning previous interpretations.

3 The First People
Ancient History of the Cuyahoga Valley
and Northeast Ohio

Brian G. Redmond

Who were the first people to enter the Cuyahoga River Valley? Where
did they come from, and what were their lives like once they arrived?
All good questions—and many more are possible. The truth is that not
much can be said in detail about many aspects of their lives, for two
main reasons. First, the native peoples of this region kept no written
records of their lives and histories. For this reason, the cultures of this
early time are often referred to as *prehistoric*, meaning before the time of
written records. However, many people take offense to this label, since
they feel that this word implies that Native Americans had no history.
This is a valid concern, and out of respect for this sentiment, I use the
term "pre-European contact" or "precontact" for short. So, the absence
of any written histories for this precontact era requires us to use another
approach that involves the science of archaeology.

To put it simply, archaeology is the study of past human cultures and
societies using the material remains they left behind. Archaeologists often
utilize historical records, when available, but for regions like our own,
careful study of the artifacts and sites remaining from early cultures has
proven to be a viable means to examine this ancient human past. In most
of eastern North America, this extended past is traditionally divided into a
timeline consisting of long *stages* of cultural development (i.e., Paleoindian,

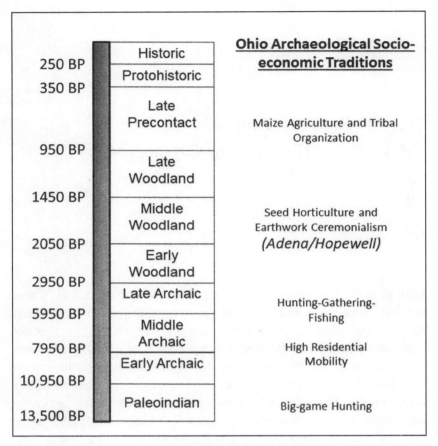

Timeline of Northeast Ohio Precontact History. *Courtesy of Brian Redmond*

Archaic, Woodland, and Late Precontact) and *periods* within each stage (usually divided into "Early," "Middle," and "Late" segments). We will follow this basic scheme as my narrative moves forward through time.

What follows then is an account of these early human histories based on material evidence interpreted through the lens of archaeology. As such, this "view" may appear somewhat blurry at times, particularly when the archaeological record is poorly known, and clearer when more detailed evidence is available, such as for the last few centuries prior to the arrival of Europeans. Regardless of such changes in clarity, archaeological work in this region has provided enough information to construct an account that extends back to the end of the Ice Age, which is at least 13,000 years BP (Before Present).[1] This account will begin with this earliest cultural stage and extend up to just before European contact (300 BP) when the Cuyahoga Valley, and indeed much of northern Ohio, was apparently vacated by its Indigenous inhabitants.[2] So, let us begin.

Coming of the First People

The earliest archaeological evidence for the presence of humans in northern Ohio are collections of stone tools dating to at least 13,000 BP.[3] Archaeologists refer to these people as "Clovis" or "Paleoindian," with "Paleo" meaning ancient. Many of the earliest sites on record produce small numbers of chert (flint) hunting and butchering tools, the most prominent of which is the Clovis fluted point. These tools are easily distinguished from later artifacts by their long, "lanceolate" shape and distinctive flute or groove-like flake scar on one or both sides of the point. The purpose of this flute is still up for debate but has most often been explained as a modification to aid in the attachment of the point to the split or beveled end of a wooden spear shaft. Other ideas include the possibility that indigenous hunters devised the modifications to create channels to increase bleeding of speared prey, or a way to thin the base of the point for hafting (tying onto a wooden shaft or handle), or most recently, to serve as a shock-absorber to prevent the point from breaking when penetrating the body of an animal. Other artifacts in the Paleoindian toolkit included hide-scrapers, large flake knives, "spoke- shaves" and small spurred gravers (engraving tools). Undoubtedly, this was a toolkit designed for hunting large game animals, possibly mammoths or mastodons, but more likely caribou, in the open spruce-fir forests that covered most of northern Ohio at the time. Due to the loss of most organic remains, we are surely missing much of the other hardware made and used by Paleoindian families that roamed across the region. Occasionally we get lucky, such as at a site called Sheriden Cave (33WY252)[4] in Wyandot County, Ohio, where two well-preserved bone spear points and a miniature Clovis point were found in the small cave. But Sheriden Cave also contained thousands of animal bones, including those of several extinct species such as Giant Beaver, a rodent the size of a black bear; Great Short-faced Bear, a huge carnivore larger than a modern grizzly bear; and Stag-moose, a moose-sized deer/

Fluted points and tools from the Paleo Crossing site (33ME274). *Photo courtesy of Brian Redmond (This and following images taken by Redmond illustrate artifacts curated at the Cleveland Museum of Natural History.)*

elk with a huge rack of antlers. The most common fossil bones found in Sheriden Cave belonged to the Flat-headed Peccary, a pig-like animal about the size of a white-tailed deer.

Of the over twenty thousand animal bones recovered from Sheriden Cave, only *one* bone—a snapping turtle neck vertebra—showed any sign of butchering by people. A few other bones were exposed to fire, but this could have occurred when local grass fires spread into the mouth of the cave. It now seems likely that most of the bones found in Sheriden Cave accumulated when animals fell into the open sinkhole that exposed the cave entrance. Other remains may be from kills that carnivores brought

14 FEET
12
10
4
2

• CARIBOU   •STAG MOOSE • GIANT BEAVER   • MAMMOTH
  •SHORT-FACED • FLAT-HEADED   • HUMAN
   BEAR   PECCARY   • MASTODON

Artist interpretation of megafauna. *Illustration courtesy of Charles Ayers*

into the shelter of the cave. How did the bone points and mini Clovis points end up in the cave? I have two possible explanations in mind. One is that a small group of Paleoindian hunters stopped off in the cave to camp and left some of their weaponry behind for use at a later time. Such "insurance caching" was a common thing to do among traditional hunting and gathering societies around the world. The second possibility is that people deliberately left bone and stone artifacts in the cave as an offering to ancestors or other spiritual entities. Historic accounts reveal that Native Americans in the eastern US made offerings of food, arrows, and other implements in caves and rockshelters, which they often viewed as entrances to the underworld realm.[5] So, this may be our first sign of ritual behavior by Paleoindian people in the region.

Unlike Sheriden cave, evidence for people who used Clovis technologies living in the Cuyahoga Valley during the late Ice Age is meager. Private collectors have found a small number of Clovis points along Tinkers Creek and a few other locations. This suggests that the Paleoindian presence was light, which may have to do with the rather inhospitable conditions that likely existed.

The current Cuyahoga River formed during the late Pleistocene, probably about 14,000 years ago, as the series of glacial lakes that filled the valley began to empty toward Lake Erie. Such young drainages are marked by steep valley walls and fast-moving streams, with few of the wide floodplains and terraces that are desirable for human settlement. The lack of such accessible landforms would have made movement through the Valley difficult and likely hazardous. One interesting exception may be a fragment of an early stage Clovis point or "preform" found at a site called "Norman P." (33SU15) located on the floodplain of Tinkers Creek in Summit County.[6] This find suggests that some Paleoindian groups were able to make their way through the valley at this early time. More sites may exist but were well buried beneath accumulating river sediments, and are now difficult to detect. Also found at Norman P. is a complete Dalton point that dates to the very end of the Paleoindian stage, about 12,500 BP, when fluted points were no longer in fashion.

Fortunately, we have much better evidence for Paleoindian people living in the uplands and away from the major streams. One of the most heavily occupied Clovis locations is the Paleo Crossing site (33ME274), situated just west of the main valley in southeast Medina County. Paleo Crossing was discovered in the late 1980s by an artisan named Jim Remington while collecting artifacts from the surface of a plowed field in Sharon Township.[7] Among his finds were several Clovis points that he eventually showed to Dr. David Brose, then Curator of Archaeology at the Cleveland Museum of Natural History (CMNH). Museum crews conducted more surface collections and excavations at the site from 1991 to 1993. Several additional Clovis points and hundreds of other tools were found along with a few small pit features marked by soil stains and at least one post mold (i.e., a small soil stain remaining from where a wooden post was set into the ground). Small bits of charcoal collected from this post mold were radiocarbon dated to between 13,021 and 12,718 years BP. This research revealed that Paleo Crossing covered an area of about three acres and was most likely a seasonal campground for several Paleoindian families, who may have planned communal hunts, traded artifacts and raw materials, got married, or even performed hunting rituals. But due to the lack of preservation of any non-stone artifacts, we can only speculate on the details of such activities. We don't even have bones to indicate what kinds of animals were hunted. My guess is caribou, since some burned bones of this animal have been found at sites in Michigan, Massachusetts, and New Hampshire.

One insight is that much of the chert used to make the Clovis points and other tools came not from Ohio, but some five hundred miles away

Dalton point and base of Clovis preform from the Norman P. site (33SU15). *Photo courtesy of Brian Redmond*

in the lower Ohio River Valley in what is today Harrison County, Indiana. The large quantity of tools made from this "Wyandotte chert," along with the relatively small amounts of Ohio cherts, seems to be telling us that the people living at Paleo Crossing migrated into Northeast Ohio from very far away and brought their Hoosier chert with them.[8] These may be some of the first people to enter northern Ohio at the end of the Ice Age.

We cannot say why these early folks came to northern Ohio, but we do know that even larger settlements followed at places such as Nobles Pond (33ST357) in Stark County. At this site, professional and avocational archaeologists worked over many decades to identify several concentrations of Clovis artifacts. These concentrations are thought to represent communal gatherings of Paleoindian families, possibly covering many acres.[9] Research by similar groups of scholars in southern Michigan and southern Ontario tell us that this Clovis migration spread farther northward, perhaps to keep up with the movements of great herds of caribou.

Many people assume that mastodon or mammoth were on the menu, since these large animals still survived when the earliest people came to

Northeast Ohio. Unfortunately, direct evidence for humans hunting these great creatures in Ohio is sketchy, even though the discovery of mammoth and mastodon bones in our state is not uncommon. The many peat bogs (old Ice Age ponds) that cover much of the glaciated regions of Ohio nicely preserve the bones of these animals. One fine example is a nearly complete mastodon skeleton found in 1953 just east of Mogadore in Portage County during the draining of a peat bog. The remains are now stored at the Cleveland Museum of Natural History. In only a few intriguing cases, stone tools have been found in association with the skeletons or possible butchering (cut) marks observed on the bones. One of these is the Martins Creek Mastodon from Holmes County which was found with a few chert cutting tools.[10] Blood residues identified on one of the flake knives reacted positively to elephant blood, suggesting that hunters may have butchered this creature. A few other finds provide more circumstantial evidence, such as the absence of limb bones and unusual cuts and scrapes on the bones. So, it may be that dinners of mastodon or mammoth steaks did occur at Clovis campsites, but probably not all that often.

Settling In During the Archaic

In contrast to the meager evidence for Paleoindian people in the Cuyahoga Valley is a relative wealth of Archaic stone tools found at many sites in the drainage. The Archaic is the longest single cultural interval in the ancient history of the Cuyahoga Valley, extending from 12,500 to 3000 BP. It was a time after the Ice Age, known as the Holocene, when the climate was warming and the environment slowly transformed to the landscape we see today. Gone were the mammoths and mastodons, and caribou had migrated farther north to today's subarctic region. Replacing them were elk (wapiti), white-tailed deer, raccoon, wild turkey, and the other denizens of the modern deciduous forest. The spruce-fir woodland also receded northward and was replaced by oak-hickory and beech-maple forests on the uplands and elm-ash woodlands in wet areas.

The toolkit of the earliest Archaic peoples looks quite different from that of their predecessors. Early Archaic spear points and knives are generally large, deeply notched, and sometimes serrated with wide, triangular blades and grinding on the basal edges. Over several millennia, projectile points manufactured by Archaic peoples became gradually

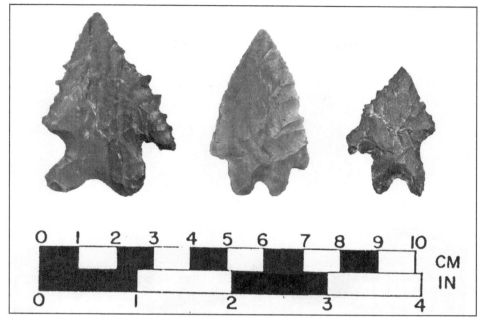

Selected Early Archaic points from the Norman P. site (33SU15). *Photo courtesy of Brian Redmond*

smaller on average and methods of modifying the bases (i.e., notching versus forming a stem) shifted back and forth in popularity. Narrow chert drills or perforators began to appear along with ovoid hide-scrapers, not unlike those used by Paleoindian hunters. One of their newest innovations was the stone axe marked by a conspicuous groove pecked around one end to aid in hafting to a wooden handle. By about 5000 BP, the style of axes shifted to ones without grooves called *celts*. These slightly smaller and more streamlined tools came in several sizes. These tools were most likely used for a range of cutting, chopping, shaving, and skinning activities. The appearance of stone axes in all these forms points to the increasing importance of woodworking, the products of which (e.g., wooden house posts, household implements, dugout boats, etc.) no longer survive to this day. Other ground stone artifacts that people used during the Archaic were food grinding and processing tools such as the slab mortar or metate, bell-shaped pestle, mano, and other hand-held grinding implements. The increased numbers and diversity of such tools

Selected Cuyahoga Valley Late Archaic points and drill. *Photo courtesy of Brian Redmond*

Full grooved axe fragment from site 33SU31. *Photo courtesy of Brian Redmond*

Celt from site 33CU18. *Photo courtesy of Brian Redmond*

Groundstone mano and mortar from the South Park site (33CU08). *Photo courtesy of Brian Redmond*

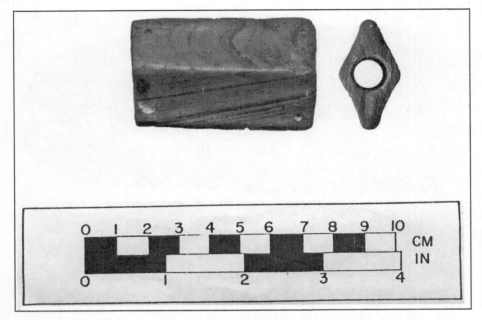

Slate bannerstone from the Norman P. site (33SU15). *Photo courtesy of Brian Redmond*

reflect that Archaic folks relied more on the growing importance of plant foods, including seeds, nuts, tubers, and root crops, in their diets. The small number of later Archaic sites where animal bones survive reveal a diversification of game to include smaller animals such as raccoons, muskrats, rabbits, squirrels, birds, and fish, all in addition to white-tailed deer, which was the main meat staple.

Perhaps the most inscrutable artifact form to appear in the Archaic is the bannerstone. Bannerstones first developed in Ohio around 7000 BP and take the form of a carefully ground and polished section of banded slate or limestone with a hole bored longitudinally through the center. The archaeological record shows that over time Archaic peoples changed bannerstones from simple implements with round to squared cross-sections to more elaborate forms including a winged variety. Archaeologists are divided on the functions of these artifacts. One popular explanation is that they were counterweights attached to the "atlatl" spear-throwing stick. The atlatl was likely the primary hunting weapon during the Archaic, used to propel a long, thin spear or "dart" tipped with a stone point. The

THE THROWING STICK, OR ATLATL, INCREASED THE VELOCITY AND RANGE OF THE THROWN SPEAR. IT WAS USED BY NATIVE AMERICANS FOR MORE THAN 10,000 YEARS.

BANNERSTONE

Artist interpretation of atlatl use. *Illustration courtesy of Charles Ayers*

bannerstone may have provided added weight at the back end of the atlatl to counter the weight of the long dart with stone point that extended forward. Such a balancing act would have allowed hunters to steady their weapons while stalking game and perhaps provided for a nice smooth throw when the time came. This explanation makes sense to anyone (including myself) who has tried using an atlatl to launch a dart. It does seem to improve the accuracy of the throw—and your arm doesn't get so tired.

For many archaeologists, this explanation seems incomplete. If the function was simply to serve as a counterbalance, then why did later bannerstone-makers take the extra time and effort to fashion these "weights" into elaborate forms, such as the winged variety, and search out attractive varieties of stone? More than one person has commented on the resemblance of this form to a bird and suggested that a symbolic, and perhaps spiritually powerful, significance was also attached to these artifacts. Possibly an association with birds and flight may have increased the hunter's fortunes during the hunt and maybe helped propel the dart farther, faster, and with more accuracy given this inherent power. Some have proposed that bannerstones possessed religious properties that were not necessarily associated with hunting and atlatls, given that they also turn up in other special contexts such as human burials and what appear to be ritual deposits or caches. In addition, many of these bannerstones were deliberately broken prior to burial, perhaps to release the spirit of the artifact.

As for where in the Valley people lived during the Archaic, we have little detailed information about the sites where artifacts are found. The vast majority have been subjected to only one or a few surface collections by amateurs and a small number of others to limited test excavations by professionals. Even so, the large number of Early Archaic projectile points observed in private collections alone makes it clear that shortly after the Paleoindian stage (ca. 12,000 BP) human habitation of the Cuyahoga Valley increased significantly. Given the drastic stylistic differences between Early Archaic points and lanceolate Paleoindian points, some archaeologists have proposed that these new populations came from areas to the south of the Ohio River Valley, where similar forms of points occur even earlier. In other words, these Archaic populations of the Valley may not be the direct descendants of the Paleoindian. This is an interesting issue for further investigation, but it cannot be answered with the current data in hand.

At present, sites with large surface exposures of Archaic projectile points, chert flaking debris or "debitage," and a few groundstone tools are thought to represent seasonal basecamps where two or more families of hunters and gatherers congregated for a few days or weeks to procure seasonally available plants and animals. Smaller versions of such surface sites are most likely the temporary camps of small groups of hunters or collectors. But in many cases, we can't really be sure of the true nature of these sites, given the lack of intensive professional investigations. In addition, many of these sites are *multicomponent*, meaning that they were occupied during more than one time period. On such sites, the accumulation of many artifacts over time can make it difficult to judge the duration, size, or purpose of any single occupation. Yet, given the evidence we have, it does appear that over the eleven millennia of the Archaic, the sheer number of sites increased over time. This steady increase most likely represents more people and heavier utilization of the natural resources of the Valley with the largest and densest occupations taking place during the Late Archaic period (ca. 5000 to 3000 BP).

Near the end of the Late Archaic, we see a shift in how people treated their dead, from individual burial in or near living areas to the establishment of formal cemeteries. The latter burial places were often founded on natural elevations like the sand and gravel knolls or "kames" scattered throughout northeast Ohio. We have few detailed accounts of what was found, as sand and gravel mining destroyed the sites decades ago. We do have a bit more information about two of these former kame cemeteries in the Valley from accounts made at the times of their destruction. At the Terra Vista 2 site (33CU18), situated on the high bluff overlooking Tinkers Creek, quarrying of a gravel knoll in the 1950s uncovered at least six human skeletons that were covered with red ochre paint.[11] Among the burial artifacts were several marine (ocean) shell pendants. The use of red ochre pigment and marine shell artifacts in burials occurred over an extended period in the Ohio region; however, the placement of these remains in a gravel kame suggests that they date to the very end of the Late Archaic after about 4000 BP or so.

A second possible location of a kame cemetery is the Jaite Papermill site (33SU13).[12] Local informants report the former existence on the property of a large gravel kame measuring some fifteen feet in height. Quarrying operations removed much of this feature in the 1960s, and numerous artifacts, including some human remains, were destroyed in the process. Among the reported finds was an ovoid artifact of ground slate with three drill holes. Known as a "gorget," such drilled slate pieces are commonly found in burial and other ritual contexts dating to the succeeding Woodland stage. The particular placement of the drill holes on the Jaite site gorget (i.e., two toward one end and one near the opposite end of the gorget) is similar to the pattern seen on large marine shell (sandal-sole) gorgets typically found in so-called "Glacial Kame" cemeteries in western Ohio.

Just about four miles west of the Cuyahoga Valley in Bath Township several other Late Archaic human burials were discovered in a small rockshelter called Krill Cave.[13] Excavations by archaeologists from Kent State University in the mid-1970s revealed cultural deposits about five feet deep across the floor of the shelter. Stone tools and pottery from these soils testified to a series of precontact occupations dating from the Early Archaic period to the Late Precontact stage. Among the Late Archaic remains were four human burials covered with red ochre. Two of these consisted solely of the lower leg bones of two adults laid side by side. No parts of the upper skeletons were found. A third grave was the burial of a five-year-old child laid out in a flexed (fetal) position, a common posture for Late Archaic burials. The fourth burial was a "bundle" burial

Two-hole slate gorget and pendant from Summit County, Ohio. *Photo courtesy of Brian Redmond*

that consisted of the disarticulated (disconnected) bones of an eighteen- to twenty-year-old person placed between two pieces of roof-fall (rock) from the shelter ceiling.

Interments of this last kind are thought to represent a type of secondary phase of burial in which people removed selected bones from the original grave, then cleaned and "bundled" together for burial in another location. Two radiocarbon dates place the timing of these interments between about 4500 and 3500 BP. Although no artifacts were directly associated with any of these burials, small notched projectile points of the Late Archaic "Brewerton" series were found in the surrounding deposits. Also found were three freshwater snail shell beads of the genus *Leptoxis*, one *Marginella* marine shell bead, and several fragments of bone tools. *Leptoxis* snails may have been traded into northern Ohio from as close as the Ohio River Valley, but *Marginella* shells could only have come from the Gulf of Mexico or southern Atlantic coasts.

The use of red ochre paint and marine shell artifacts in mortuary contexts at Krill Cave provides yet another example of Late Archaic ceremonialism in the region of the Cuyahoga Valley. But the human remains found at Krill Cave may also tell a richer story, particularly in regard to the apparent burial of just the lower legs of two people. This unusual custom was apparently repeated at a few other Late Archaic cave and rockshelter sites in Ohio and involved the depositing of only partial skeletons. The true meaning of this practice may never be known, but it undoubtedly involved a complex, multistage process of burial ceremonialism followed by interment in places (caves and rockshelters) that were most likely viewed as portals to the underworld. In fact, the discovery of the scattered remains of up to fifteen other people in the deposits of Krill Cave may also point to this place as an important interface between the worlds of the living and the dead. As we will see, this evidence for complex ritualism involving the use of human remains becomes even more common in the subsequent Woodland stage.

Gardeners and Earthwork Builders of the Woodland Stage

Most archaeologists today identify a set of distinct cultural changes or innovations that began by about 3000 BP in the Ohio region and introduced the widespread use of pottery, the growing of squash and native seed plants, and the construction of earthen enclosures and mounds. Many people claimed this was the time of the "Moundbuilders," a term that conjured up racist images of a lost (typically "white"), civilization that was ultimately destroyed by "savage" Indians but left behind the wondrous earthworks best known for the central Ohio Valley. Today, this term is understood by most people to refer to the Native American ancestors themselves, who created impressive earthen monuments and complex religious systems now most commonly known as "Adena" and "Hopewell." Modern archaeological research has shown that these "cultures" actually consisted of diverse groups of native societies who shared a distinctive set of ritual and ceremonial practices and utilized certain kinds of iconic artifacts in common.[14] This social and religious florescence involved not just Ohio, but much of the Eastern Woodlands between about 3000 and 1500 BP, that is, within the Early and Middle Woodland periods of our chronology.

The archaeological record indicates that the people of northern Ohio in general, and the Cuyahoga Valley in particular, shared these new cultural innovations, but perhaps not at quite the same scale as southern Ohio, at least when it comes to the building of mounds and earthworks. So, during the Early Woodland period (ca. 3000 to 2100 BP), we see that the Indigenous peoples introduced domesticates such as the common squash and bottle gourd and several kinds of native seed plants such as Maygrass, knotweed, goosefoot, and sumpweed. These seed plants are probably unfamiliar to most readers, given that they are today looked upon as common weeds. However, carbonized seeds from these plants become increasingly more common in botanical samples from Early to Middle Woodland sites. This, in turn, indicates that these plants became important food crops and were likely cultivated by Woodland peoples in small gardens located in and around most settlements.

Few traces of squash, gourd, or any of the previously listed seed plants by Woodland peoples in the Cuyahoga Valley have yet been found. This may be due to archaeological sampling problems rather than a deliberate choice by local groups. This explanation seems likely given that just to the west of the Valley, direct evidence for the cultivation of these plants has readily come from the Early to Middle Woodland occupations at the Leimbach site (33LN09) in Lorain County (squash) and the Heckelman site (33ER14) in Erie County (squash, bottle gourd, chenopod, Maygrass, knotweed, and sumpweed).[15] Nonetheless, it is not likely that these plants were staple foods (gourds were most likely used as containers), but more like supplements to a regular diet of deer, fish, and other game, as well as various wild plant foods, especially nuts.

Boiling is the best method to efficiently process lots of seeds or nuts. It is highly likely that people processed much of their food by boiling, even though we have no direct evidence for this. We can say with assurance that Archaic peoples boiled much of the nut surpluses we detect, in the form of carbonized nutshells, on large habitation sites such as the Burrell Orchard site (33LN15) along the Black River in Lorain County.[16] This is because experimental research shows that processing of large quantities of nuts, particularly hickory nuts, is most efficient when the crushed shells and meats (the kernel or edible part) are added to a container of boiling water.

After a few minutes, the shells sink and the meats float to the surface to produce a calorie-rich oil. But how did Archaic folks boil anything without fired-clay pottery? This can be efficiently done by placing hot rocks in hide-lined pits, bark containers, or water-tight baskets over and over again until the water temperature reaches the boiling point. So, it now appears that the advent of pottery-making may have just improved the efficiency of an already useful technology. Ceramic pots can also serve as rodent-proof containers for dry storage.

It now appears that the earliest pottery found in northern Ohio was made, not for cooking directly over a fire, but for hot-rock boiling. Support for this notion comes from the form of these early pots. Most are rather rugged containers, much like modern crock pots, with walls up to 0.7 inch thick and flat bottoms. Such thick walls are not efficient for transferring heat from a fire to the liquid contents but perfect for retaining the heat from hot rocks placed inside the pot. In addition, the sturdy sides and base would help prevent the vessel from cracking as the heavy rocks were placed inside. It now appears that the earliest pottery in northeast Ohio was adopted near the end of the Late Archaic period, based on the discovery of a vessel of this kind at the Kendera site (33ER53) in Erie County. The Kendera pot was recovered from a cooking pit dated to about 3600 BP, making it one of the oldest vessels ever found in northern Ohio.[17]

After about 3000 BP, the remains of Early Woodland pottery vessels are rather commonly found; however, few have been dated. One exception is the Early Woodland occupation documented at the Stanford Knoll site (33SU138) in the Cuyahoga Valley of Summit County.[18] In the 1980s, several fragments of thick pottery, tempered with pieces of crushed stone grit to prevent cracking, were found in a small shallow pit by CMNH archaeologists. Also recovered were two fragments of an apparent sandstone bowl and what might be an unfinished tubular-shaped pipe of limestone. One of the vessel sherds was dated using a process called thermoluminescence (TL) dating that permits an age to be calculated directly on the vessel itself, rather than the more common method of indirectly dating of charcoal or other organic material found near the artifact.

The resulting TL date was 2900 BP, which is just at the interface between the Late Archaic and Early Woodland periods, sometimes called the "Transitional" Archaic period. The great antiquity of this pot is also supported by the inclusion of the sandstone bowl fragments in the same

Early Woodland vessel fragment (left), sandstone bowl fragment (right), and limestone pipe preform from the Stanford Knoll site (33SU138). *Photo courtesy of Brian Redmond*

pit. On a few sites in northeast Ohio, stone bowl fragments have been found in Archaic contexts, suggesting that these containers preceded the ceramic form. The possible tubular pipe "preform" from Stanford Knoll is another artifact type that is likely to turn up in Terminal Archaic contexts.

In 2015, archaeologists from Cleveland State University documented another Early Woodland occupation at the Stanford Field site (33SU608), located just north of Stanford Knoll. Excavators uncovered a deep cooking or fire pit that contained thick, cordmarked pottery including a decorated rim sherd. Dating of organic material found with this sherd revealed an age of about 2700 BP, which is nearly contemporary with the TL date from Stanford Knoll.

In 2000, CMNH excavations at the OEC 1 site (33CU462) on the Cuyahoga River near Independence, uncovered the remains of what appears to be another Early Woodland vessel.[19] Although this specimen could not be directly or indirectly dated due to the lack of associated organic material, its shape is much like that of the early vessels already described. The pot was in poor condition when found, but about half of what was originally a complete vessel was carefully reconstructed. It has

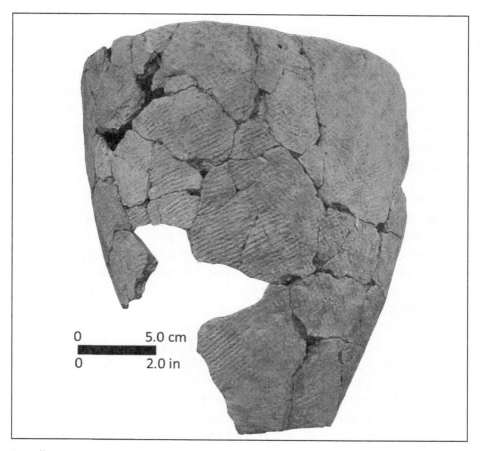

Partially reconstructed Early Woodland vessel from the OEC 1 site (33CU462). *Photo courtesy of Brian Redmond*

a flat bottom and out-sloping walls with a height of about twelve inches. Unlike the vessels mentioned above, the OEC 1 pot has slightly thinner walls and the exterior surface is covered with fine cord impressions, possibly from a woven fabric that was impressed into the wet clay before firing. The remains of the pot were found in a small pit without evidence of fire. Such a context suggests that this was a vessel used for dry storage and kept in a cache pit, possibly within a dwelling.

The construction of mounds and earthworks, the hallmark of the Woodland stage, is well represented in northern Ohio, including the Cuyahoga Valley. Unfortunately, this fact is not well known among the general public. This is partly to do with the lack of professional research as well as past efforts by landowners and property managers to play down their existence to prevent potential looting and vandalism. In addition, the mounds and earthworks of northern Ohio are generally much smaller in scale than the magnificent Adena conical mounds (up to sixty feet high) and the Hopewell geometric earthworks of southern Ohio (enclosing up to hundreds of acres). In fact the average height of a Woodland mound in our region is just one or two feet and perhaps no more than eight to ten feet across. Thus, most of the mounds go unnoticed by casual hikers, hunters, and fishermen of the area.

Even though most mounds are rather inconspicuous, a few relatively large mounds have been recorded in the Cuyahoga Valley. One of these is the Gleason Mound (33CU19) situated on a river terrace near the village of Valley View.[20] This mound is rather well preserved, despite some past looting, with a height of about twenty-six feet and diameter of up to 130 feet. This mound has never been professionally investigated; however, local collectors report the discovery of projectile points and small amounts of pottery that appear to date to the Middle Woodland, ca. 2000 to 1500 BP. Another earthwork of comparable size is the Botzum Mound (33SU21), in Summit County.[21] Unlike the Gleason Mound, Botzum has been subjected to several investigations, beginning with a tunnel by a local farmer and ending with test excavations by archaeologists from CMNH and the National Park Service. Each of these projects turned up few artifacts and no human burials. Close inspection of the mound stratigraphy by the latter investigations indicates that this edifice may in fact be a natural feature, like the glacial kames discussed above. Such may also be the case for apparent large "burial mounds" reported in the past. If so, mounds such as these may have contained intrusive burials similar to those found in the Late Archaic kame cemeteries. Nevertheless, true burial or mortuary mounds did exist in the Valley according to early testimony from local antiquarians and others who discovered small numbers of human remains during their explorations. These finds generally included few artifacts and more often occurred in the smaller, more common versions of mounds mentioned above. Unfortunately, few of these discoveries were adequately recorded and many of the mounds are long gone.

Drawing of Gleason Mound by Joe Jesensky, 1928. *Illustration courtesy of Charles Ayers*

Fortunately, there is another type of earthwork that is better documented, and many examples survive to this day. These are small, hilltop
enclosures that were constructed on high shale bluff-tops throughout the
Cuyahoga Valley and across much of northern Ohio from Toledo to the
Pennsylvania line. In most cases, these enclosures were formed by the excavation of one to three parallel ditches across the narrow entrances to these
hilltops. Many were first recorded in the nineteenth century by scholars
such as Colonel Charles Whittlesey of Cleveland. As a trained geologist,
Whittlesey surveyed many of the natural rock outcrops and valleys of
Ohio. In the process, he also mapped and recorded earthen mounds and
earthworks, including the hilltop enclosures in northeast Ohio. One of
his best-known works is *Ancient Earth Forts of the Cuyahoga Valley, Ohio*
(1871), in which he documented eleven hilltop enclosures and associated
mounds. Whittlesey referred to these sites as "forts," since, like many of

his contemporaries, these enclosures were thought to be of a military nature and relics of ancient combat between the so-called "Moundbuilder Race" and Native Americans. Although no modern archaeologist holds to this romantic explanation, some still see these enclosures as defensive works utilized during warfare between precontact tribal groups. Indeed, most of these locations feature potential natural defenses, such as steep bedrock cliffs bordering the hilltops and narrow, "hogback," entryways. In general, though, direct evidence of warfare, such as the remains of wooden post stockades, is lacking. In fact some of the hilltop enclosures contain few artifacts and provide little evidence of occupation. Others, such as the Leimbach site (33LN09) on the Vermilion River,[22] Burrell Fort (33LN14) on the Black River, Seaman's Fort (33ER85) on the Huron River, and Greenwood Village (33SU92)[23] in the Cuyahoga Valley contain domestic features such as hearths, cooking pits, and post mold outlines of small dwellings, which point to at least seasonal settlements of a few families.

Some hilltop enclosures, such as the Heckelman site in the Huron Valley, were definitely occupied but for ceremonial purposes rather than group settlement. Ten seasons of excavation by archaeologists from the University of Toledo, CMNH, and Firelands Archaeology, a local avocational-professional volunteer group, identified clusters of post molds from the erection of ceremonial poles within an oval ditched earthwork measuring up to 150 feet in length.[24] Little evidence for everyday, domestic activities, or house construction was found. The use of this location as a ceremonial center began during the Early Woodland period, ca. 2300 BP, and extended into the following Middle Woodland period, around 1800 BP. Most notably, this Middle Woodland occupation shared many material similarities with Hopewell culture populations residing in southern Ohio.[25] What appear to be Late Woodland and Late Precontact period village occupations followed with direct evidence of wooden post house structures and an extensive stockade defense built during the Late Precontact period.

Artifacts and features perhaps indicating similar kinds of Woodland ceremonialism have been found at the Soldat site (33CU20),[26] another hilltop enclosure situated on a bluff overlooking the mouth of Tinkers Creek in the Cuyahoga Valley. The site is now identified with Charles Whittlesey's "Fort No. 4," and his original survey located a single earthen embankment closing off the narrow entrance to the promontory and a small mound near the tip of the hilltop.[27]

Early Woodland stemmed point and expanded center slate gorget from the Soldat site (33CU20). *Photo courtesy of Brian Redmond*

Subsequent professional excavations in the 1970s and 1990s identified an Early Woodland occupation marked by characteristic contracting stemmed points and a rare expanded-center slate gorget. Unfortunately, these testing projects were unable to determine whether or not the site functioned as a domestic settlement or ceremonial enclosure. As with Heckelman, the Soldat site also saw a later, possibly village, occupation by Late Precontact period people of the Whittlesey Tradition (named after Charles Whittlesey).[28]

The subsequent Middle Woodland presence in the Cuyahoga Valley is clearly marked by a few sites where classic Hopewell culture artifacts have been found. Most prominent of these locations is the area around the small village of Everett. The mid-nineteenth-century construction of a school in Everett disturbed a mound containing artifacts of copper, chert, mica, and slate, which are likely affiliated with the Hopewell culture. The mound itself was reported to contain a possible mortuary structure made of limestone slabs which is typical of other Woodland mounds in northeast Ohio. In the early 1970s, CMNH archaeologists surveyed the Everett area and found Hopewell-style artifacts during test excavations around the former canal and the floodplain of Furnace Run south of the village.[29] This general area was designated the Everett Knoll site (33SU14). Additional testing recovered typical Hopewell corner-notched points, a bladelet core, stone and bone ornaments, galena crystals, and thin-walled, plain and decorated pottery, all resembling Hopewell types from southern Ohio. Later investigation in the 1980s and 1990s discovered additional concentrations of Hopewell artifacts in several house lots in the village.

Salvage excavations in one property exposed twenty-two features that included post molds and roasting pits containing Hopewell bladelets, notched points, and thin, cordmarked pottery. Seven radiocarbon dates revealed an occupation dating to between 1880 and 1610 BP.

The cooking pits and diagnostic artifacts found at the Hopewell sites point to a more than temporary occupation; however, the lack of recognizable post patterns of dwellings makes it difficult to characterize just what people were doing at this location. It seems likely that at least some activities would have been focused on mortuary rituals related to the nearby mound. For example, the remains of cooking pits may point to the preparation of food for feasts related to such ceremonies. The archaeological evidence at hand indicates that the Everett area was a congregation point for local groups practicing mortuary ceremonies in the Hopewell style. This in turn reveals important social ties between the Middle Woodland occupants of the Cuyahoga Valley and populations to the south, possibly in either the Muskingum or Scioto River Valleys.

Woodland people conducted another form of ceremonialism, represented by groups of finely made chert bifaces (i.e., artifacts flaked on both faces) that were found deposited in pits. Such biface caches are most often interpreted as ritual deposits and tend to occur in upland locations away from river valleys. In the early 1930s, a farmer began plowing a formerly swampy area of his property and discovered a cache of 150 well-made,

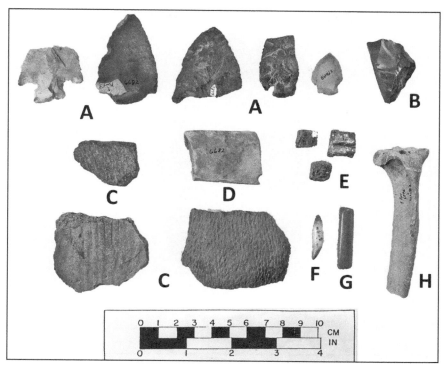

Selected Hopewellian artifacts from the Everett Knoll site (33SU14): A. projectile points; B. bladelet core; C. pottery sherds; D. gorget fragment; E. galena crystals; F. partially drilled raccoon canine tooth; G. bird bone bead; H. cut dog tibia (leg bone). *Photo courtesy of Brian Redmond*

ovate-shaped bifaces or "blades." Known as the Koth's Cache (33CU58), the site was located south of Tinkers Creek and east of the Cuyahoga River on a flat bluff top.[30] Most of the artifacts were given away with only one biface ending up in the collections of the CMNH Archaeology Department. The CMNH specimen measures 4.5 inches long, 2.5 inches wide and is very thin at 3/8 inch. This well-made artifact is made from a light gray variety of Flint Ridge chert and may have been burned. Local accounts of the discovery relate that the remaining artifacts were equally well-crafted with a few examples measuring up to 7 inches in length.

In 1982, a similar cache of finely made bifaces was discovered in a peat bog on the Lukens farm located about 2.5 miles northwest of Kent, Ohio

Chert biface from the Koth's Cache site (33CU58). *Photo courtesy of Brian Redmond*

in Portage County. A total of 356 bifaces were recovered after plowing a section of the recently drained bog near a small tributary of the upper Cuyahoga River.[31] Archaeologists from Kent State University recorded the find and determined that the bifaces most likely dated to the Early Woodland period based on their overall form; however, the feature has never been directly dated. A few of the cache blades were coated with red ochre pigment. Fragments of oak wood, some of which appeared to have been worked, were also found with the stone artifacts. So, it seems that Native Americans originally placed the bifaces in a wooden container of some kind and then buried it in this rather remote spot.

The Koth's and Lukens caches are examples of a cultural phenomenon that is somewhat widespread across Ohio after about 4900 BP. There are several similar caches in other parts of northeast Ohio, such as the Valentine Cache (33LA25) in Lake County, which consisted of more than

144 Flint Ridge chert bifaces found during excavation of a drainage ditch near the Chagrin River in 1977.[32] As a group, these kinds of caches feature burial of a tight cluster of finely made, ovate bifaces in swampy conditions such as ponds or peat bogs.

Most archaeologists interpret these caches as ritual deposits rather than storage of stone tools for later use. However, the depositing of well-made stone tools in watery locations is known in many parts of the world. For example, caches of stone axes, flint tools, and other implements have been found in ponds, lakes, and river deposits dating to the Neolithic and Bronze ages of Western Europe, Great Britain, and Ireland. In any case, the caching of these materials in rather remote, wet, and boggy places suggests that the intention was never to retrieve them. Thus, the place-ment of what were likely seen as valuable and possibly ritually charged items in bodies of water may reflect the carrying out of sacrifices to perhaps incur the favor of some kinds of supernatural entities. And, like the caves and rockshelter sites discussed above, such wet places may have been seen as convenient entrances to the underworld realm, which facilitated more direct contact with spirits or ancestors.

After 1500 BP, Native American societies in northeast Ohio appear to have given up some of the elaborate ceremonialism and earthwork construction that marked the Early and Middle Woodland periods. During the following five centuries of the Late Woodland period, popu-lations appear to have increased and larger congregations of people made greater use of both upland and lowland/riverine resources. Also during this time hunting technology shifted significantly from the atlatl spear-thrower to the bow and arrow. This change is only detected through the changing form of projectile points, from relatively large and thick to smaller and thinner, and anything amounting to an atlatl weight (banner-stone) disappeared. Small mounds were still constructed, but most appear to be incorporated into settlements. The hilltop enclosure sites first built during the Early Woodland period also continue to be used, since Late Woodland points and pottery are present. One of the best studied exam-ples of the Late Woodland use of these places is the Greenwood Village site (33SU92) located in Northfield Township, Summit County.

The Greenwood Village site has been identified as Whittlesey's "Fort No. 5," and is perched atop a mesa-like bluff that overlooks the Cuyahoga

River floodplain. The landform is almost island-like, as it is attached to uplands by only a narrow hog-back ridge. Information from Whittlesey's maps revealed that this enclosure was somewhat different than the others. Only about half of the bluff top's surface was enclosed, and this was done using four earthen walls with adjoining ditches that formed a somewhat rectangular enclosure. Two or three small mounds were located on Whittlesey's maps, and these were situated near the bluff edges.

CMNH archaeologists carried out excavations on the plateau in the early 1980s and found evidence of occupation dating primarily to the Late Woodland period. The artifact assemblage consists of crude-looking stemmed and notched projectile points and a few ground stone tools. The remains of moderately thick, cordmarked pottery were found in several of the pit features, including a good portion of an elongated jar with a round base and slightly out-turned lip. This vessel somewhat resembles early Late Woodland (ca. 1400 to 1200 BP) pots found in the central Ohio River Valley. Although excavations were limited in scope, several small and a few large earthovens containing abundant charcoal and burned rock were recorded. Notably, only a few post molds and almost no animal bones or burned plant remains were recovered. These results suggest that the Greenwood Village site was occupied only periodically for purposes other than everyday living. In short, it is not what we would consider a "village." One surprising discovery was an extensive stone pavement lying beneath an apparent gateway in one of the earthworks. Such prepared entrances are known for some of the large Hopewell enclosures in southern Ohio, which suggests that this complex may have been constructed prior to the Late Woodland. This feature also indicates that activities at this site were of a ritual and ceremonial nature. In fact, the many earthovens were likely used for preparing food for large groups of people attending these festivities.

Although Late Woodland sites generally increase in number and are found in a wide range of environmental zones, in earlier times, many families spent much of their time at warm season campsites or small villages situated on the low terraces bordering the Cuyahoga River. For example, a 2009 testing project by Cleveland State University archaeologists at the Clark site (33SU106) in Boston township revealed a deeply buried (thirty inch), one-foot-thick midden layer containing burned earth

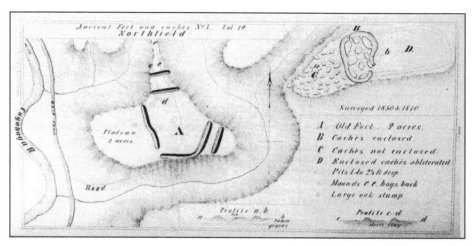

Whittlesey's 1871 map of Fort No. 5 or the Greenwood Village site (33SU92). Reprinted from Colonel Charles Whittlesey, *Ancient Earth Forts of the Cuyahoga Valley, Ohio*, Western Reserve and Northern Ohio Historical Society Tracts, Number 5, Fairbanks, Benedict and Company (Cleveland, 1871)

and rock, ash, nutshell, burned and unburned deer and small mammal bone, and charcoal deposits. A charcoal sample collected from this feature dated the occupation to ca. 1100 BP. Also found were earthovens and other cooking pits, as well as small storage pits and a sufficient number of post molds to suggest that the people living there constructed nuclear family-sized (three to six people) houses. By this time, most of the stone tool technology had evolved into small, thin, and notched arrow points along with flake hide-scraping tools and bone and antler implements. Pottery vessels become somewhat larger with the addition of collars around the rim and heavily cordmarked bodies.

Village Farmers of the Late Precontact Period

Beginning around 1000 BP distinct cultural changes took place among the Native American societies living in northern Ohio and particularly in the Cuyahoga Valley. I have already noted the technological shift from the atlatl spear-thrower to the bow and arrow, as seen from the reduced sizes of Late Woodland projectile points. Many scholars believe this switch resulted in an advantage for stalking deer and other game animals. For instance, it seems much easier and more efficient to shoot deer from the cover of vegetation or perhaps a tree stand using a bow and arrow rather than to stand up and heave a spear among overhanging tree branches. But Archaic and Woodland hunters must have done so for millennia.

Another explanation for this technological shift is that the bow and arrow is a more efficient weapon for warfare. Again, because the warrior can conceal him/herself in the brush but also because arrows can be shot in more rapid succession and in greater numbers than possible with an atlatl and darts. Unfortunately, archaeology cannot give us a definitive explanation; we just know that this technological change took place. This is particularly evident in the large number of triangular-shaped arrowheads that are found everywhere on Late Precontact settlements. We also have independent evidence that points to a likely increase in hostilities during the Late Precontact period. But first, let me mention some of the other significant changes that occurred during this time.

Perhaps one of the most important developments by Native peoples was their adoption of corn, or more appropriately, "maize," as a staple food. Archaeologists have found early forms of maize in sites in southern Ohio as early as the Middle Woodland period, but only in small quantities in what were likely ritual contexts at a few large mound and earthwork enclosures.[33] Native peoples purposefully selected this tropical grain after about 1200 BP, resulting in larger quantities of charred maize kernels in Late Woodland pit features. By about 800 BP, maize is found on most excavated village sites across the region. Native Americans continued to grow squash and gourds and introduced the common bean at just about this time. By the historic period (after ca. 400 BP) most Native American societies in the Midwest heavily depended on maize, beans, and squash for much of their diet and supplemented these crops by seasonally available harvests of fish, nuts, deer, turkey, and small game animals.

This dramatic dietary shift is also reflected in changes in pottery forms developed from Late Woodland peoples forward. For example, most Late Precontact period vessels are on average thinner than in the past with more rounded bases. These changes would have increased the efficiency of boiling, which, based on historic period accounts, was the primary way to prepare maize-based soups and stews. But ceramic modifications also featured elaborate decoration on vessels. Cordmarking was still popular on pot bodies, but now the necks and rims often featured

Late Precontact triangular arrow points from the OEC 1 site (33CU462). *Photo courtesy of Brian Redmond*

complex geometric patterns that were stamped or incised on the moist clay surface prior to firing. In some cases, people added small loop or strap handles and substituted crushed mussel shell temper for the long-term use of crushed stone grit. Fortunately for archaeologists, these designs are not random but involve a limited range of motifs for each social group. Because of this, pottery made by Native Americans from northeast Ohio sites can be distinguished from assemblages found in northwest Ohio and beyond. In addition, the basic forms of decoration changed over time and these shifts help us identify the approximate period when any particular decorated pot was made and used. Furthermore, these characteristics have allowed archaeologists to identify ceramic "style zones" that are geographically distinctive regions across the Eastern Woodlands. In the recent past, clusters of sites in any particular area that shared ceramic styles of decoration—as well as other cultural attributes such as house forms or burial practices—were grouped into "phases" with distinct, radiocarbon-dated "life spans" of several centuries.[34] The phases in one area over time were then grouped into "traditions." In northeast Ohio, the Late Precontact archaeological record is known as the "Whittlesey Tradition," after Charles Whittlesey, since he was first to record some of the key sites. To the west of the Cuyahoga River Valley is the "Sandusky Tradition," which shares many cultural similarities with the Whittlesey Tradition but distinct pottery styles.[35]

One of the most significant cultural developments in northern Ohio was that people were choosing to live in seasonal village settlements after about 800 BP. Archaeologists find that on the ground, these take the form of dense artifact scatters and plowed-up, dark midden soil covering two acres or more. Excavations at a number of these sites have exposed post mold patterns from circular and rectangular houses and encircling stockade defenses, some with adjoining ditches. These stockade and ditch constructions are solid evidence for the drastic increase in interpersonal violence and outright warfare between Native peoples during this period. Equally convincing is a related increase in the discovery of triangular arrow points in skeletal remains from these sites. The remains of pit features of many forms are also found, sometimes numbering in the hundreds. Over the years, these locations have been the focus of many excavations, often by artifact collectors but also by trained archaeologists. Consequently, we have more information about the lives of these Native American residents of the area than for any earlier time period.

One of the earliest professional investigations of a Whittlesey Tradition village was by Dr. Emerson Greenman at the Tuttle Hill site (33CU07) in Independence, Ohio.[36] Today the site no longer exists due to modern development; however, it used to sit on one of the high shale promontories on the west side of the Cuyahoga Valley, just south of where Interstate 480 crosses the river. In the 1930s, Dr. Greenman worked for the Ohio State Archaeological and Historical Society (now known as the Ohio History Connection) in Columbus and spent several years in northern Ohio investigating its precontact archaeological sites. He determined that the Tuttle Hill site was the same as Charles Whittlesey's "Fort No. 3," and in 1930 conducted excavations of a portion of the hilltop. He uncovered eighteen pit features and the same number of human burials, along with a large collection of pottery, stone tools, and bone and antler implements. A number of the features were described as "refuse" pits, since they contained layered deposits of charcoal, ash, animal bone, pottery and other artifacts. Some of these pits were very large, with straight sides and flat bottoms and measuring up to six feet in diameter and five and one-half feet deep. Today, we believe such pits were initially used by Native peoples as storage features, somewhat like underground silos for preserving the maize harvest. Once the pits were emptied of the stored

Tuttle Hill Notched vessel section from the OEC 1 site (33CU462). *Photo courtesy of Brian Redmond*

food, the hole was filled with village debris. A few smaller versions of these pits appeared to have served as cooking facilities as well.

Greenman's work at Tuttle Hill aided in his formulation of the "Whittlesey Focus" to describe the similarities in artifact assemblages and village settlements he went on to document in Northeast Ohio. Since radiocarbon dating had not yet been invented in 1930, Greenman was unable to calculate a precise date for the Tuttle Hill site's occupation, but he believed it was at least a few centuries prior to the arrival of Europeans in the area, since no historic metal or other trade goods were found. But his close examination of the decorated pottery, with its distinctively notched collars, convinced him that the Whittlesey Focus (now "Tradition") was ancestral to an Iroquoian tribal group. Today, most archaeologists are looking elsewhere for the historical descendants of the Whittlesey folk.

During the 1930 field season, Greenman had time to examine another village site in the Cuyahoga Valley known as South Park (33CU08). The site is located about 2.5 miles upriver from Tuttle Hill, but unlike the former, South Park site was apparently never visited by Charles Whittlesey. Today it represents the most extensively excavated archaeological site in the Cuyahoga Valley. Like Tuttle Hill, South Park sits atop a high shale bluff along the west side of the river and produced a very similar set of artifacts and features. By the 1960s, shale bedrock mining threatened the destruction of the site. In an effort to protect this important historical resource, extensive salvage excavations were undertaken by archaeologists from CMNH and Case Western Reserve University, primarily under the direction of Dr. David Brose.[37] The results produced a wealth of information that revealed that the site had been occupied several times during the Late Precontact period, between about 805 BP and 425 BP.

Intermittently over this time, South Park people lived in a variety of houses made from wooden posts and likely covered with bark or cattail mats, as used in historic dwellings of the Great Lakes. Initially, houses at South Park consisted of a few small circular or rectangular, single-family dwellings scattered across the flat bluff top. In contrast, the latest inhabitants occupied a rather crowded living area filled with larger, possibly multifamily, longhouse-like structures. No direct evidence of an enclosing stockade was found during excavations; however, a few post molds discovered across the narrow entrance to the bluff-top may represent the remains of such a defensive barrier.

In 2000 and 2001, CMNH archaeologists discovered a previously unknown village component at the OEC 1 site located just upriver from South Park.[38] This work uncovered artifact forms resembling those from the South Park village along with plant and animal remains testifying to a mixed hunter-gatherer/horticultural life way. Radiocarbon dates placed this occupation at about 500 BP.

During the Late Precontact period there were also distinct changes in pottery decorations, from incised and stamped geometric motifs to

Rendering of South Park village (ca. 400 BP) showing multifamily dwellings during the winter (Artwork by Kathy S. Kraus). *Drawing courtesy of the Archaeology Department, Cleveland Museum of Natural History*

notched collars similar to those found at the Tuttle Hill site. Found among the remains of the Whittlesey ceramics were a few pots with decorations more typical of those made by Native people of the Sandusky Tradition in northwest Ohio and the Fort Ancient Tradition in southwestern Ohio. In 1930, Emerson Greenman recovered an unusually shaped vessel from South Park that is identical to Late Precontact period pottery from Wisconsin called "Oneota." Such finds point to the high level of social interaction and trade that was going on across the Great Lakes and Midwest regions during this period.

Carbonized maize fragments were found in many of the pit features at South Park, along with smaller quantities of bean and squash. The few fragments of stone and ceramic smoking pipes recovered point to the use—and likely cultivation—of tobacco in the village. Native peoples may have grown some maize and the other crops on the bluff-top, but the lower terraces and floodplains of the Cuyahoga River would have been much more productive. At a few of the latter locations, archaeologists have uncovered the remains of what might be small farmsteads where fields of these crops may have been grown. One likely example is the Sweet Corn site (33CU46), located on the floodplain directly across the river from South Park. Limited excavations here in 1995 by Dr. Fred Finney revealed ten small cooking and storage pits containing charred maize remains and Whittlesey Tradition pottery and stone tools. Also uncovered was a six-foot-long row of post molds that may represent the wall of a dwelling. One radiocarbon date placed this occupation at about 600 BP.

Despite their growing dependence on maize, the Whittlesey villagers were only part-time farmers, as seen in the abundant samples of animal bone, nutshells, seeds, and freshwater mussel shells that show a continuing dependence on seasonally available wild foods. Deer bone is found everywhere, and other popular species include black bear, raccoon, fox, woodchuck, beaver, muskrat, rabbit, and even elk. Native peoples fished for catfish, perch, freshwater drum, and caught redhorse sucker in the rivers and probably during fishing expeditions on Lake Erie. Some birds were also popular foods including ducks, geese, and wild turkey; several species of turtle were on the regular menu as well. Dog bones may represent both faithful pets and an occasional meal.

Most of these foods would have been available from spring through fall, but winter occupations are not out of the question. If we follow the seasonal pattern practiced by many tribes living in the Great Lakes at contact, families would congregate in groups of a hundred or more at warm-season villages then disperse to small family campsites in the interior forests during the late fall through early spring. The archaeological evidence for such cold-season campsites is meager in northeastern Ohio, but may be represented by some of the many sites where only a few triangular points, several handfuls of pot sherds, and a hearth pit or two are found. Most of these assemblages are reported from the uplands and rockshelters such as Krill Cave, Boston Ledges (33SU19),[39] and Stow Rockshelter.[40]

The religious life of the Whittlesey Tradition people is mostly unknown. The presence of a few small mounds near river bluff village

Engraved slate fragments depicting a hand and a bird from the South Park (33CU08).
Courtesy of Brian Redmond

sites such as Staas (33CU224) and possibly the Soldat site may represent
ritual burial of the deceased members of the community, or may instead
represent Woodland monuments. At villages like South Park and Tuttle
Hill, small clusters of human burials have been identified; however, most
are too few in number to be the remains of everyone who died during
the occupation of that settlement. The rare occurrence of engraved pieces
of ground slate found in middens or refuse pits might represent artifacts
made and used by shaman or tribal religious leaders. Most seem to have
been deliberately broken and deposited in pits after use. It may be that
during the Late Precontact period, religion was a more personal affair
with a general lack of the large communal gatherings envisioned for the
Woodland earthwork enclosures.

One of the greatest questions derived from our archaeological research
is: What happened to the Whittlesey, Sandusky, and other precontact
tradition peoples in northern Ohio? We see that the material record of
pottery, stone tools, and village sites ends abruptly at 350 BP. The earliest
historical references to this area describe a land essentially abandoned of
permanent Native American occupation for almost a century, at which
point tribal groups such as the Wyandot, Ottawa, Miami, Delaware,

Seneca, and others begin to filter into northern Ohio.[41] But since we know that these groups originated from outside our region, they are unlikely to be the direct descendants of the Whittlesey and other precontact groups.

At this point in time our archaeological trail runs out, since by 250 BP or so, the clay pots, stone tools, and other materials that we have used to trace native groups over centuries of time and vast geographic regions are quickly replaced with European trade goods such as brass kettles, glass beads, copper arrow points, and iron axes and knives. By 150 BP, much of the utilitarian Native American material culture in the Great Lakes looks very similar. So, for now our discussion of the precontact Indigenous inhabitants of northern Ohio must come to a close. But we hope that the trail can be picked up again with the use of new techniques of analysis and the coordinated study of the many artifact collections curated from Ohio, the greater Midwest, and beyond.

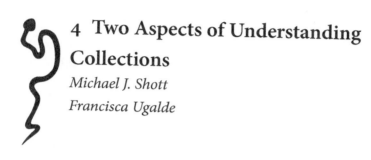

4 Two Aspects of Understanding Collections

Michael J. Shott

Francisca Ugalde

The following two contributors discuss different aspects regarding collecting and collections. Michael J. Shott discusses the role that collectors can have in contributing to our understanding of the archaeological record and how they can collaborate with professional archaeologists. Francisca Ugalde discusses the stewardship of Indigenous property. —Editors

Collecting the Material Record
Archaeologists and Others
Michael J. Shott

Written documents are the raw material of history. Whether rare originals like the United States Constitution or widely disseminated texts like newspapers and books, the written record is reproducible. Ownership of historical documents is not a zero-sum proposition; my possession of a copy of the Constitution does not prevent others from owning it as well. But imagine if, as before Gutenberg, all written documents were irreproducible originals. Then my possession of documents prevents you from owning them; now distribution of the historical record is a zero-sum game, its collective value diminished by every act of unwitting exclusion. Imagine further that thousands of people, often with benign motives, seek scraps and snippets of rare documents. The result is a fatal scattering of a vital, irreproducible record that, no matter how much it gratifies each individual to own a small piece, impoverishes us all. If I am exclusive owner of the first line of the Preamble to the Constitution, you of the second, and thousands of others of entire words to isolated characters, then there no longer is a Constitution but only scattered, irretrievable scraps dispersed beyond hope of compilation.

Ohioans legitimately are proud of the state's recent history and the role that some of their Euro-American ancestors played in its early years. When we look back to the late eighteenth and early nineteenth centuries, we routinely describe Euro-American predecessors as pioneers. These people, their times and their deeds, unquestionably deserve study and respect. However, Ohio's true, original pioneers came here at least thirteen thousand years ago, and not from Europe.

This book is about the Native American in what today we call Northeast Ohio. As the book shows, Native American history deserves just as much respect and study as does the much shorter history of Euro-Americans here. Across Ohio and eastern North America broadly lies a rich, diverse record of these peoples' times and their deeds. We are accustomed to thinking of and describing Ohio's landscape before the arrival of Euro-Americans as "pre-settlement," yet the countryside whose abundance excited the wonder, even awe, of early European observers itself was the product of deliberate, thoughtful landscape management by settled natives who not only sowed and harvested, first, domestic crops like *Chenopodium* and, later, maize and others imported from Mexico. They also planted or cultivated vast tracts of nut-bearing walnut and hickory trees and created complex patchworks of fallow fields in various stages of ecological succession around their villages that promoted the growth of dense populations of everything from saplings for fuel and timber to strawberries and deer as food sources.

For at least two millennia before European invasion of North America, then, Ohio was a settled landscape. Early in that period, it was dotted with scattered farmsteads and small towns of wooden houses, whose people occasionally congregated to construct and use the geometric earthworks that are well-known in south-central Ohio but also occurred in numbers in Northeast Ohio before mostly being destroyed in the nineteenth century. Later, parts of the state featured large towns and, elsewhere in the Midwest, cities were built around earthen skyscrapers. Even earlier, Ohio's true pioneers encountered near-Arctic habitats that contained megafauna like mammoths and mastodonts; whether these people drove such animals to extinction is unclear, but there is no doubt that these earliest Ohioans possessed the skill, cunning, and intelligence to hunt them and other game as well.

Yet precontact Ohioans, like prehistoric Europeans until about three thousand years ago, had no use for writing, even though their distant relatives in central America invented several written languages. As a result, we have no written history of early Ohio any more than we have a written history of Europeans before the Classical Greeks or, for western Europe, much later still. Instead, the archaeological record is our only source of information on the thirteen thousand years of Ohio's human occupation that preceded Euro-Americans.

Speaking of "the archaeological record" evokes images of King Tut's tomb or Indiana Jones's (highly) fictional escapades. Yet the vast majority of the archaeological record worldwide reflects what ordinary people did during their ordinary lives. Of course, ancient Ohioans ate food, wore clothes, and lived in wooden houses, but our climate and soil conditions do not conduce to the preservation of perishables like these. Instead, besides the monuments like the Hopewell Culture National Historical Park in Chillicothe and the log tombs and copper ornaments that some contained, Ohio's precontact archaeological record consists mostly of the bones of animals that people hunted, the stone tools they used to hunt them along with the industrial by-products of the tools' manufacture, and fragments of the pottery vessels in which they cooked and stored their food. What is more, and what surprises many today to learn, that record accumulated on or just under the ground surface on which ancient Ohioans lived, a surface that, over much of Ohio, remains unchanged. Accordingly, much of what ancient people lost or discarded lies near the modern surface, although some is deeply buried depending upon local sedimentary regimes. Where that modern surface is in cultivation—and anyone who drives Ohio's back roads during the summer knows that there are a few cornfields here and there across the state—things that people made and used 1,000, 5,000, or 10,000 years ago may lie on the surface.

Many in Ohio, not least farmers, have known that much for over two centuries. In that time, some among them found and kept precontact tools, usually spear or arrow points (what archaeologists turgidly call "projectile points"). These people are collectors, selectively and sometimes casually but often quite seriously, of the archaeological record. There is over a century of professional, or nearly professional, archaeological research in Ohio, yet archaeologists always have been many fewer in number and much more limited in distribution than are collectors. As a result, widespread collectors probably have found many more spear and arrow points than have archaeologists; a rare comparative study from just across the state line from Toledo suggested that archaeologists have found about 3–5% of points, collectors the remaining 95%+.[1] Archaeology is the rare science to which those not professionally trained can make important contributions, depending on the documentary quality of the evidence they collected.

A document can be reprinted, but the archaeological record is irreproducible. To know prehistory requires access to the entire record. Midwestern prehistory is written predominantly in points. We must know the distribution and abundance of as much as possible of its thousands of precontact sites and millions of points. Some scholarly value of artifact collections resides in the artifacts themselves, but artifacts without context are useless curiosities, just as all the scissors-snipped, isolated letters in all of the Constitution's words are useless piles of characters. Therefore, the value of private collections in contributing to the serious study of Ohio's past depends upon their documentary quality. We thus confront a real equivalent to the imagined constitutional diaspora: an irreproducible record, rich in context and detail, but dispersed among thousands of private collectors unknown to one another and to the professional community. Ohio precontact history may be written in points but, without well-documented private collections, reading it is like trying to read a text riddled with letters and words snipped out by scissors.

Since archaeology arose as a scholarly discipline in North America, archaeologists and collectors have maintained a sometimes collaborative, but usually fraught, relationship. There is blame all around for this state of affairs, but both in the past and today there are good reasons to work together on the serious, responsible study of Ohio's past. Like all professions, archaeology is governed by ethical precepts. Consistent with those values, archaeologists practice and promote preservation of the record, excavate most sites only when necessary—i.e., when the sites are threatened with destruction—permanently curate the collections they amass for study into the indefinite future, and refrain from commercial traffic in antiquities, which only promotes the wrong sort of interest in collecting artifacts.

Not all archaeologists are ethical saints, but neither are all collectors sinners by comparison. Many collectors, arguably most of them, feel and act the same way as do archaeologists, or similarly. Those among them who: 1) document their collections (i.e., keep records of which artifacts were found where, and identify and group those artifacts by their discovery sites); 2) make artifacts and associated documentation available to other interested scholars, professional and nonprofessional; 3) do not buy or sell artifacts as commodities; and, ideally, 4) make arrangements for their collections' permanent disposition after their own deaths, are *responsible collectors*. Opposed to them are the fewer who selfishly destroy the archaeological record for the sake of personal possession or gain.

Ironically, many archaeologists slight responsible collectors and the significant contributions they can offer to the systematic study of Ohio's past. Yet if already-collected artifacts are an informative part of the record, and if archaeologists are enjoined to promote the record's preservation, the very ethical standards–established by regional and national organizations–by which some archaeologists justify their views require collaboration with responsible collectors.[2]

Whatever the limitations of the archaeological record, whatever the damage and degradation that more than a century of undocumented collection has wrought upon it, many of the scattered scraps of Ohio's prehistory are not yet irretrievable. If archaeologists and responsible collectors collaborate in the documentation of collections, if the artifacts and documentation are digitized and archived in well-organized initiatives, we can preserve vital context before the shreds and tatters are irreparably scattered. In the process, we overcome archaeology's dilemma.

My colleague Kevin Nolan of Ball State University and I, inspired by the redoubtable Jonathan Bowen, have sought to do precisely that, admittedly for a study area in southern, not Northeast, Ohio.[3] With a gratifying number of responsible collectors, we are engaged in a research project that leverages the great information residing in their collections to learn much more than we once knew about ancient Ohioans' use of the landscape, their population trends, and the historical and adaptive processes that jointly governed the progressive, usually minute, changes that they made over time to their stone-tool technology. If and when archaeologists and responsible collectors in Northeast Ohio undertake similar collaborations, then books like this one can be revised and updated to reveal even more than we knew before about the region's precontact history. Some of Northeast Ohio's archaeological record remains to be documented, in part hopefully by the responsible collectors who can at once esteem their own ancestors' recent history and Natives' much longer precontact history. Together, we owe no less to those true pioneers of Ohio.

Material and Archival Collections
Stewardship of Indigenous Cultural Property
Francisca Ugalde

It is human nature to collect things, partially due to a deep-seated need to learn about cultures of the past through the objects that represent them. Unfortunately, the act of collecting is inextricably linked to colonialism and is rooted in outdated attitudes and behaviors that commonly placed white Eurocentric cultures above Indigenous ones. In many instances, non-Indigenous collectors removed Indigenous materials from their people/culture/context with the supremacist excuse that they could provide better stewardship and would preserve cultural materials from a "vanishing race" unable to provide proper care for their own materials. Fortunately, there is a current trend within collecting institutions to become more culturally sensitive through efforts to decolonize their collections and collecting practices by bringing Indigenous voices into leadership, curatorial, interpretive, and collections care roles.

Collections can be big or small, of narrow or broad scope, privately or publicly kept, and stewarded by either organizations or individuals. Collections are comprised of *musealized* objects—those that have undergone the collecting process and transformed from being a commonplace thing into material culture (the physical representation of a group of people's culture through the objects they created and used). Material culture can be described as cultural objects (anything created by humans that provides information about the culture of its creator and users) and are carriers of cultural heritage (the legacy of physical objects and intangible attributes of a group or society that are inherited from past generations, maintained in the present and bestowed for the benefit of future generations). Cultural heritage can be *tangible* (buildings, historic places, monuments, artifacts), *intangible* (folklore, traditions, language, knowledge), or *natural* (culturally significant landscapes, and biodiversity). Indigenous material culture can be contemporary goods or art, ethnographic (objects from the past, other than archaeological artifacts, originating with and/or used by a group of people and representative of their culture), or archaeological (material remains or information that tells about human activity in the ancient and recent past).

Institutions responsible for the care of cultural property are bound by legal, social, and ethical obligations, guidelines, and standards to provide proper physical storage, management (including exhibition), and care of collections and associated documentation. Additionally, effective collection stewardship ensures that the objects the institution owns, borrows, or holds in its custody are available and accessible to present and future generations. The standard care of collections includes, *at a minimum*, the practice and implementation of safe handling methods and procedures, the use of safe storage materials, the maintenance of proper and secure storage facilities, and the recording and safekeeping of accurate information and documentation. All these requirements address the physical conservation/preservation needs of an object. Yet, these basic standard measures do not address the cultural and spiritual needs of Indigenous cultural property, which require additional procedures that respect traditional Indigenous values, through culturally responsive care.

Materials that require specific culturally sensitive procedures include those associated with sacred ceremonial practices and rituals, objects with symbolic use (may not possess sacred attributes but are culturally significant to a tribal community based on its age, association with a ceremony, a historic tribal leader, or craftsmanship), and those implemented in end-of-life practices (when religious or cultural practitioners ritually end the life of an object to cease its sacred attributes). Culturally responsive procedures will vary by object type and by Indigenous group, meaning that there are no hard and fast rules that can be applied across the board. Some examples of these procedures include object handler gender restrictions (some objects should never be touched by women), the placement and position of an object in storage or display (and whether the object is meant to be on display at all), the materials used to protect objects, the methods of transportation, as well as the execution of religious rituals. Regarding the latter, it is of *utmost* importance that non-Indigenous individuals *do not* attempt to practice any type of Indigenous religious practice or ritual to satisfy this requirement.

Indigenous archival materials that may be culturally sensitive from an Indigenous perspective must also be treated with an additional level of care that goes beyond the standards of the archives field that address access and privacy of archival materials. Culturally sensitive archival materials, both physical and digital, include still or moving images of human remains, religious or sacred objects, ceremonies of any kind, burials or funerals, archaeological objects, or sacred places; recordings or transcripts of songs, chants, music, religious practices, healing or medical practices, myths, or folklore; and cartographic materials of sacred or religious sites or areas. Non-tribal stewards of Indigenous archival materials must consider Indigenous values and perspectives when managing these types of materials and must aim to provide proper, updated, and accurate context of Indigenous esoteric, ceremonial, or religious knowledge and information sources, and work directly with tribes to learn and apply the proper levels of access to their archival materials.

Each tribe, band, and Indigenous community is unique and will interpret the term *culturally sensitive* differently. It is crucial that these materials are viewed through their own cultural context, and for that, the most important step to take is to actively reach out to, develop a relationship with, and request assistance from tribal representatives to guide you in the specific culturally sensitive needs or limitations of their cultural materials.

An additional level of care and procedures must be applied when dealing with Indigenous ancestral remains (human skeletal remains that have an ancestral connection to Indigenous peoples today) and associated burial objects (objects that by their attributes or location can be demonstrated to have been placed in direct association with the burial of a human being as part of the burial rite). These materials, as well as sacred objects, and objects of cultural patrimony are protected under the 1990 Native American Graves Protection and Repatriation Act (NAGPRA), which requires federal agencies and institutions that receive federal funds (including museums, universities, state agencies, and local governments) to actively assess their collections for the purpose of repatriation (the process of restoring or returning something to its place of origin).

The guidelines and standards above are but a few that collecting institutions are ethically and legally expected to follow. Organizations such as the International Council of Museums (ICOM), the United Nations Educational, Scientific, and Cultural Organization (UNESCO), and the American Association of Museums (AAM), have well-established, regularly reviewed and updated publicly available ethical standards that address, among many other topics, collecting practices and care of and access to collections.

Unfortunately, private collectors are not bound by the ethics and laws that are expected from collecting institutions, but it is strongly recommended that they strive to follow them as well.

For some helpful resources for further information on topics discussed, see the following:

Dillon, A. "Collecting as Routine Human Behavior: Motivations for Identity and Control in the Material and Digital World." *Information and Culture* 54, no. 3 (2019): 255–280. https://www.researchgate.net/publication/336587786_ Collecting_as_routine_human_behavior_motivations_for_identity_and_ control_in_the_material_and_digital_world.

Goskar, Tehmina. "Top 10 Tips to Start Decolonising Your Practice," October 30, 2020. Curatorial Research Centre. https://curatorialresearch.com/top-tips-in-curating/top-10-tips-to-start-decolonising-your-practice/.

Ogden, Sherelyn, ed. *Caring for American Indian Objects: A Practical and Cultural Guide*. Minnesota Historical Society Press (2004).

Shoenberger, Elisa. "What Does It Mean to Decolonize a Museum?" *Museum Next* (February 23, 2022). https://www.museumnext.com/article/what-does-it-mean-to-decolonize-a-museum.

Ugalde, Francisca. "A Case for Collections Management Policy for Passively Collecting Institutions." Masters thesis. The University of Akron, December 2012.

American Association of Museums Standards. "Collections Stewardship." https://www.aam-us.org/programs/ethics-standards-and-professional-practices/collections-stewardship-standards/.

International Council on Archives, Committee on Best Practices and Standards Working Group on Access (August 24, 2012). "Principles of Access to Archives." https://www.ica.org/resource/principles-of-access-to-archives/.

American Philosophical Society. "Protocols for the Treatment of Indigenous Materials." *Proceedings of the American Philosophical Society* 158, no. 4 (December 2014).

International Council of Museums. "Code of Ethics." https://icom.museum/en/resources/standards-guidelines/code-of-ethics/.

United Nations Educational, Scientific, and Cultural Organization. "Ethics and Intangible Cultural Heritage." https://ich.unesco.org/en/ethics-and-ich-00866.

American Alliance of Museums. "Code of Ethics and Professional Practices for Collections Professionals." https://www.aam-us.org/wp-content/uploads/2021/03/Code_Ethics_Collections_Professionals_2021_02_24.pdf.

5 Along the Lower Cuyahoga
1740–1805

George W. Knepper, revised and updated by Kevin F. Kern

The story of historic Native American activity in the Cuyahoga Valley is elusive. This region was off the main track of Indigenous-white relationships. With few exceptions, Natives of the Cuyahoga played a less visible role in the struggle for control of the Ohio country than did larger and more permanent Indigenous communities located in the Sandusky, Tuscarawas-Muskingum, Scioto, Great and Little Miami, and Maumee River regions. Natives of those watersheds regularly encountered British and American traders, Indian agents, land scouts, soldiers, and even missionaries. In diaries, letters, journals, and reports, these white sojourners left accounts of Indigenous lifestyles, leaders, and tribal activities. Captivity narratives written by whites once held prisoner tell us much about the Native peoples of Ohio, but aside from James Smith's limited observations (he mentioned no Cuyahoga towns or resident tribes) while hunting with Wyandots along the Cuyahoga in the mid-1750s, we have no captivity narrative describing Native American life along the river and its valley. [1]

The general outline of Indigenous affairs in the Cuyahoga Valley has long been described by local enthusiasts, but primary sources are far too scarce to provide the detailed documentation that would allow us to address with confidence subjects such as the number of inhabitants at a particular time, tribal relationships, village sites and dates of occupancy, semi-permanent versus transient settlements, tribal leadership, participation of Cuyahoga warriors in eighteenth century warfare, exact trail locations, and the like. Indigenous life along the Cuyahoga can be seen only through an informational mist that obscures the fine points.

By the time the first white settlers recorded their memories, Native American life in the Valley was so unstructured as to make statements about who was where at what time a risky proposition. The oral tradition of a frontier people was often distorted by long repetition before it found its way into a written account, resulting in conflicting stories for every notable frontier event. For example, more often than not, early sources refer to the Cuyahoga River simply as "Cuyahoga," with no indication as to whether that means the river, the river and its valley, the important village location called Cuyahoga Town, or the larger region centering on the river.

And then, of course, the physical landscape has been drastically changed. Nature changed the course of the river from time to time, but that is nothing compared to what humans have done. Excavations, land-fills, roads, canals, railroads, utility and power lines, dams, trunk-line sewers, golf courses, real estate developments, and parks limit our ability to see how things used to be. It is little wonder that we puzzle over village sites and course of trails. Only a powerful imagination, and an informed one, can convert today's adulterated landscape into what it might have been more than two centuries ago.

Along the Cuyahoga

The Lower Cuyahoga River, flowing from the big falls[2] to Lake Erie, is one of the great historic highways of America. Precontact Ohio Natives coveted its valley and adjacent escarpments for village sites, "forts," and caches. They traveled the Portage Path between the Cuyahoga and the Tuscarawas River to its south, engaged in trade with distant people, and left ceremonial and burial mounds as witnesses to their presence. They inhabited the Valley in reasonable numbers, at least seasonally (see Chapter 3).

In the mid-seventeenth century, Iroquois (also known as Haude-nosaunee) warriors from what is now New York State drove the last of the precontact Natives from the Valley and all of Ohio after a series of conflicts prompted by French and British colonial rivalry known as the Beaver Wars. For many decades thereafter, the Cuyahoga was a no-man's land, avoided by the Iroquois themselves and by other peoples intimidated by Iroquois claims of suzerainty. But early in the eighteenth century, the rivalry between France and Great Britain for control of the Trans-Appalachian west and its lucrative fur trade heated up, and the Cuyahoga was too important a strategic location to remain unclaimed.

In the 1660s France and Great Britain started a power struggle that set them against one another in periodic wars that finally ended with Waterloo in 1815. They fought in Europe, on the high seas, and in their colonies. One chapter in this continuing saga was played out in Europe in the War of the Austrian Succession (1744–48). British colonials called its counterpart in North America, "King George's War."

In the struggle to control the interior parts of North America, both France and Great Britain recognized the advantage of controlling access to the western Indigenous groups and their fur trade. At the same time, the Indigenous people of the Trans-Appalachian region recognized that the Anglo-French rivalry provided leverage for them to achieve their own goals by selective and judicious use of their support or neutrality. The interests of all these groups intersected shortly after 1740 when hundreds of Iroquois, primarily Senecas and Cayugas, began moving westward to relocate along the Cuyahoga River, separating themselves from control by the Six Nations Council.[3] They established temporary villages near the river's mouth and upstream to the vicinity of modern Akron. These settlements, located between the French stronghold at Detroit and the British post of Oswego on Lake Ontario, were of obvious strategic importance.

It appears that a shortage of game brought on a famine that persuaded these migrants to tap into the rich hunting grounds along the pristine Cuyahoga. Since they were now removed, at least temporarily, from the British sphere, the migrants sounded out French authorities at Detroit about establishing trade relationships. The French responded by sending an experienced fur trader, Francois Saguin, to the Cuyahoga (what they called the White River).

In 1742 Saguin erected a "French House" on the river's west side across from the mouth of Tinkers Creek. It was an excellent location, serving a hinterland rich in furs. Saguin got along well with his customers, but he was hampered from the beginning by Detroit's inability, or unwillingness, to furnish him adequate trade goods when just two canoe loads (large, freight carrying canoes) would suffice for a year of trading. Possibly, he

Historic sites discussed in Chapter 5. *Maps by Charles Ayers.*

Key for sites on facing page map.

1. Ohio Iroquois site c. 1740s
2. Joseph DuShattar trading post, 1791–1794
3. Ottawa village – later Pilgerruh, 1786
4. George Croghan trading post, 1744
5. Francois Saguin "French House," 1742
6. Ohio Iroquois Town, 1755
7. Ponty's Town, 1750–1760s
8. Ottawa village, c. 1800
9. Ohio Iroquois village, later Hale Farm, c. 1800
10. Hopocan town, c. 1777
11. Netawatwees Town, also known as Cuyahoga Town, 1759
    [later the location of a British trading post, 1775]
12. Stigwanish/Ottawa village, c. 1800
13. Big Falls of the Cuyahoga River, site of Old Maid's Kitchen

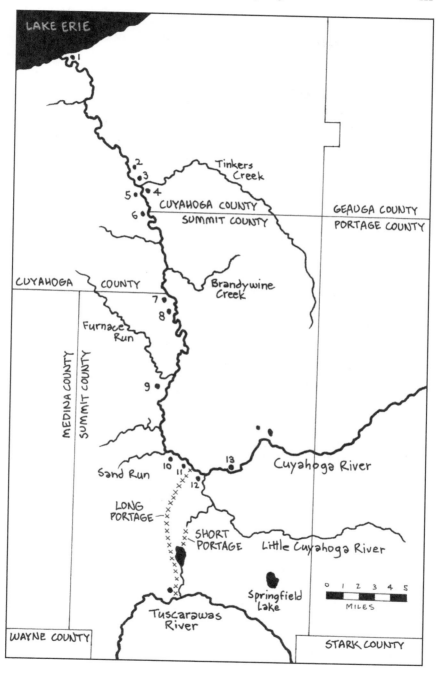

did not know that even before the formal onset of war, British cruisers in the Atlantic were seizing French ships carrying trade goods, thus creating an acute shortage for French traders in the field.

In 1744 Britain's most experienced trader, a colonial named George Croghan, opened a post not far from Saguin's but on the other side of the river. Even before this, some British colonials had cut into Saguin's trade by working the Native Americans' hunting camps. The Indigenous residents in turn welcomed this competition, for now they had some bargaining leverage. As news of this happy condition spread, people from other Indigenous groups were attracted to the Cuyahoga. In 1743 Detroit's commandant sent the Intendant (civil administrator) Robert Navarre to report on Saguin's operation. Navarre's report listed some ten tribes represented along the river or nearby. He estimated the number of villagers at 2,000 to 2,400 persons, an extraordinary concentration for the time.

The most important newcomers were Ottawas (also called Odawas) and Wyandots (the British name for the Wendat branch of the Huron nation). Both had split off from their larger groups which remained under French hegemony in the Detroit region. They were seeking new hunting grounds, opportunities to trade with the British, and a chance to hide from their French creditors at Detroit. As early as 1743 Ottawas were reported planting cornfields along the Cuyahoga. Wyandots arrived a few years later, led by an anti-French war chief named Orontony (also called Nicholas). Wyandots considered northern Ohio lands as far east as the Cuyahoga to be theirs. For decades they had hunted along the river, but they did not establish any substantial villages in the valley, just temporary encampments.

Saguin had been in business less than two years when he realized he could not compete with British rivals. He closed his post and returned to Detroit, but the French commercial retreat was temporary. By the mid-1740s French authorities had determined to overrun the Cuyahoga and drive out British traders. This was part of a larger plan that led, in 1753, to the construction of forts along the Upper Ohio (Allegheny) designed to frustrate British encroachment into Ohio lands claimed by France. The French also erected a new trading post in 1751 on the site of Saguin's post. Shortly thereafter they built a fortified post sixty miles to the west at Sandusky.

Intensified French aggression caused many Native Americans to leave Cuyahoga for safer locations to the east. Some Ohio Iroquois moved to a group of villages known as the Kuskuskies, located on the Beaver River near modern New Castle, Pennsylvania, where Seneca and Cayugas had villages with access to British traders. We have no idea how many remained in the Cuyahoga Valley, but they had at least a modest presence in the 1750s and beyond. One Ohio Iroquois town appears on a 1755 map, located on the river's west side, a short distance upstream (south) from the old French House location, that is to say not far above the mouth of Tinkers Creek. They were present in modest numbers in later decades, although after the American War for Independence we read less about them in the Valley, and more of Senecas and Cayugas. This indicates, perhaps, that the postwar Iroquois arrived more or less directly from tribal lands in New York and remained at least somewhat loyal to Six Nation's leadership.

Wyandots also defected from the Cuyahoga. Orontony's group followed the Ohio Iroquois to the Kuskuskies, but shortly left to establish a new town, which they named Conchake, at the forks of the Muskingum (near modern Coshocton). After smallpox reduced their numbers, the Wyandots abandoned Conchake for new villages on the upper Scioto, and then most moved on to the waters of the Sandusky, where their principal villages would finally lie.

Ottawas were perhaps the most persistent occupiers of the Cuyahoga Valley. From the early 1740s until after European-American settlement sixty years later, they maintained small villages and encampments near which they planted their cornfields and, occasionally, orchards. Like many Indigenous groups at that time, they moved with the seasons, accounting for much confusion among later students trying to determine village sites.

For several reasons it is difficult to trace movements of Indigenous groups. Non-natives often tend to think of tribes as coherent wholes with tribal members acting in concert and speak of the Ottawas or the Lenapes (also known as Delawares) as though all members were of a like mind. Most Ohio groups, however, were composed of divisions that often acted independently of decisions made by the larger "nation." Civil chiefs and war chiefs might exert influence, but they could not dictate. Ohio Iroquois, for example, represent a fragment separated from and acting independently of the Six Nations Council and their own tribal relatives.

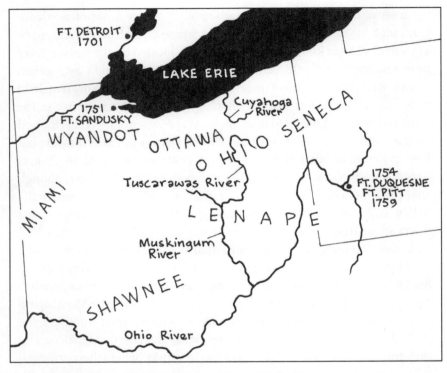

General Tribal Locations, c. mid-late 1700s. *Map by Charles Ayers.*

Similarly Wyandots and Ottawas residing in the Valley were independent fragments of tribes or nations still living under French influence at Detroit.

Divisions among the Lenape, who came into the Valley from the east and south in the mid-eighteenth century, figured large in Cuyahoga Valley affairs. That nation had three major divisions: the Unami (Turtle), Unalachtigo (Turkey), and Munsee (Wolf). Each had its own leadership, although all recognized one principal chief whose role was essentially advisory. The Munsee acted with such independence that some contemporaries, and later historians, considered them a separate tribe. Despite their self-directed ways, the Munsees remained under the Lenape nation's cultural umbrella.

There is little hard evidence to sharpen our understanding of the Indigenous presence in the Valley during the tumultuous 1750s. The frontier was aflame as French and British competition evolved into the so-called French and Indian War (the North American manifestation of the European Seven Years' War). In the war's early phases (1754–58), French victories, many of them close by in western Pennsylvania, brought nearly all Ohio Native groups into their camp. After 1758 fortunes changed, and most Indigenous groups either became neutral or shifted allegiance to the conquering British. This was not devious behavior; it was common sense. These groups were primarily concerned with preserving their own autonomy and control of their homelands, and they acted accordingly as the conditions changed. Furthermore, they had to be on good terms with winners, since they provided important trade and power relationships.

Cuyahoga Indigenous groups were active in the French cause until the very late 1750s for a very good reason: the British seemed to pose a more immediate threat to them. While the French were also an imperial power that sought to control them, theirs was primarily a trading empire that relied on alliances with various Indigenous groups rather than establishing large and expanding settlements of French people. The British, on the other hand, were an empire that relied on settler colonialism—the movement of large numbers of people who came with the intent of taking and settling on Indigenous lands. As British settlers began to pour over the Appalachians, allying with the French seem to be the best hope Native groups had of protecting their homelands from theses intruders. Accordingly, Ohio Iroquois, Lenapes, Ottawas, Wyandots, and Chippewas (also called Ojibwe) raided lonely outposts and isolated cabins in western and central Pennsylvania. Their numbers were not large; they did not have to be, for small war parties and roving bands could have a considerable effect in the sparsely settled borderlands. The Valley route was also one segment of the war path followed by the Great Lakes Indians as they made their way to supplies at the forks of the Ohio.

These raids succeeded in achieving their primary goal. Wishing to bring about an end to the raids, British colonists sought to negotiate peace with the Native groups, resulting in the Treaty of Easton in October 1758. Representatives from Pennsylvania and New Jersey met with representatives from Indigenous groups with claims to lands in the Ohio Country. In return for ceasing to fight with the French and giving up claims to lands in New Jersey, Native groups received pledges from the colonists to return large tracts of land further west to them, acknowledge their claims to the Ohio Country, and keep from creating any new settlements or forts west of the Appalachians after the war. Having thus secured their homeland, these groups declared their neutrality in the conflict, which was disastrous to the French effort in the lower Great Lakes. Without the help of their Native American allies, the French were forced to withdraw from their posts protecting the Ohio Country.

The Seven Years' War ended on the Great Lakes by 1760. In that year, Montreal, France's supply center for her western posts, capitulated to a British army. The capitulation required France to surrender all her military posts in the west. British forces, including American colonials, promptly occupied Detroit and Fort Duquesne (which they renamed Fort Pitt). Yet, thinking these insufficient, they also constructed a tiny new post near present-day Sandusky in what Ohio Indigenous groups saw as a flagrant violation of the Treaty of Easton. French trading posts also came under British control and, after 1764, could operate only under British license. The definitive Peace of Paris (1763) excluded France totally from continental North America. The British believed the Cuyahoga Indigenous groups were now subject to British policies. However, the Indigenous groups of the east Ohio Country were not included in negotiations leading to the Peace of Paris, nor had the British defeated them militarily. Indeed, having negotiated peace on their own terms with the Treaty of Easton, they believed they had established control of their homelands and their own self-determination. It was a recipe for further conflict.

~~~~~~~~

What villages did the Cuyahoga warriors come from? There is no definitive answer, but we can make reasonable assumptions. Two famous maps published in 1755 give limited information. The Mitchell Map, drawn in 1750 (but not published until 1755), was based on second-hand information. It shows an (Ohio) Iroquois town on the east side of the Cuyahoga, perhaps twenty miles upstream from Lake Erie. This might have been a remnant of the larger Ohio Iroquois presence during the 1740s when that tribe had a village on the east side of the Cuyahoga's mouth and other encampments located upstream.

The Lewis Evans map of 1755 identifies the "French House" at the old Saguin site. Although that post closed ca. 1744, the French had erected a new post on the site in 1751. The Evans map also shows an Ohio Iroquois town located on the river's west side a short distance upstream from the French post. The map also shows an Ottawa town on the river's east side, most likely the Ottawa village just north of where Tinkers Creek joins the Cuyahoga. This village was occupied longer than most, and though it appears on the 1778 map drawn by Thomas Hutchins, some students question its existence at that time.

Ponty's Camp (Ponty's Town) was probably established in the 1750s and endured into the 1760s. It was an Ottawa town located on the river's west side, at or near the present intersection of Riverview and Columbia roads. This village had no assured link to the famous Pontiac, an Ottawa war chief. He was not born there, but his birth in about 1720 may have been nearby at the Cuyahoga's mouth. This is where, in later years, he is said to have parleyed with Major Robert Rogers, a colonial then leading British forces en route to occupy Detroit.

Many Valley warriors were Lenapes. They first settled northeast Ohio about 1757–59, establishing towns along the Mahoning before moving westward into the Cuyahoga Valley. The first, and most enduring Lenape location was Netawatwees Town, named for the chief of the Unami division. Netawatwees Town became better known as Cuyahoga Town, or simply Cuyahoga. Most, but not all students of the Valley place it at the northern terminus of the Portage Path. Some misplace it at a site much closer to the "big falls" of the river.[4]

Cuyahoga Town could well have extended a good distance upstream from its central cluster. Lenape towns along navigable rivers often spread out, sometimes for miles, with cornfields on the rich, easily cleared bottomland, huts and cabins nearby on high ground.

In 1759, Lenapes from Cuyahoga Town, including perhaps Netawatwees himself, raided the Pennsylvania frontier and took captives, among them a seven-year-old girl named Mary Campbell and an older woman, Mrs. Stewart, with her infant. The captors pushed westward at a rapid pace, hoping to outdistance any pursuers. It is this event that created the legend of "Mary Campbell's Cave" (see Chapter 8). The captives were brought to Netawatwees Town (Cuyahoga Town) where Netawatwees reportedly adopted Mary and treated her well. Mary remained with Netawatwees at Cuyahoga Town until 1764, when he abandoned it and led his people to the Muskingum. In November Mary was reunited with her family during the return of prisoners mandated by Colonel Henry Bouquet as punishment for participation in the Resistance of 1763. Mary's name appears on the list of repatriated prisoners.[5]

Violence in the Great Lakes borderlands did not end with the conclusion of the Seven Years' War. After Montreal's capitulation, Ohio Native groups had to rely on the British for trade goods and for gifts they required to meet their needs. British Indian policy, however, was penurious and restrictive, creating much hardship and anger in Indigenous communities. These British practices and their repeated violations of the terms of the Treaty of Easton brought the resentment of Great Lakes group to a boiling point.

Pontiac, an Ottawa war chief, was among the most famous Indigenous leaders who traded on this anger to foment armed rebellion against British posts in the west. In this, he was aided by the visions of the Lenape prophet Neolin, who preached rejection of European goods and resistance to their encroachment on Indigenous lands. Pontiac found much support, but despite threats from Pontiac's followers, most Unami and Unalachtigo Lenapes tried to remain uncommitted. These threats were enough to send traders on the Cuyahoga and elsewhere in Ohio in search of safer fields to exploit.

In the summer of 1763, a massive Native American resistance against the British broke out throughout the Great Lakes region. Older histories recounting this Resistance of 1763 often refer to it as "Pontiac's War" or "Pontiac's Rebellion," but these designations are problematic. First, they ascribe more control and influence to Pontiac than he actually had in this widespread resistance. Second, a "rebellion" suggests revolting against legitimate political authority, but British claims of authority were tenuous at best. Because the Indigenous groups around the Great Lakes were not parties to the Treaty of Paris and never formally submitted to British authority, they viewed their resistance as an entirely justified response to the provocative behavior of the British. Almost symbolically, Fort Sandusky—which the Ohio groups viewed as a clear violation of the Treaty of Easton—was the first British fort to fall. Pontiac led warriors from many western Great Lakes tribes in a siege of Detroit. Though it failed by a narrow margin, other Indigenous groups overran all of Britain's western posts except Detroit, Fort Pitt, and Niagara. Most often, as with the thirteen-man garrison at Sandusky, British soldiers were killed and the post burned to the ground. Unable at first to break the sieges at their remaining posts, the British responded with an early and infamous act of biological warfare. Under the guise of a negotiating parley at Fort Pitt, Colonel Henry Bouquet ordered the distribution of blankets and a handkerchief known to be exposed to smallpox to the besieging Indian forces in hopes spreading the disease to them.

While the sieges of the British forts eventually ended in the fall as Indian warriors returned to their villages at harvest time, the resistance did not. The British authorities, realizing that they needed to create peace with the Great Lakes groups, rethought their Indian Policy. On the one hand, the Royal Proclamation of 1763 forbade British colonial settlement in the Trans-Appalachian region, leaving that area as an Indian Reserve. On the other, though, the British raised two armies, one at Niagara, and the other at Fort Pitt, designed to force the Ohio groups to sue for peace. Colonel John Bradstreet and the northern army moved west from Niagara in the summer of 1764, sailing along the Lake Erie shore, past the mouth of the Cuyahoga, without taking any action against the Cuyahoga Valley groups. Later that season, Colonel Henry Bouquet led 1,200 men westward from Fort Pitt to the forks of the Muskingum (near Coshocton). There he imposed terms on the assembled warriors, one condition being that all prisoners, white and Black, be turned in, no matter how long their captivity, no matter how close the attachment with their adoptive families. This was the mandate that sent Mary Campbell back to her Pennsylvania family after five years of captivity. We do not know Mary's reaction, but we are told that her adoptive father, Netawatwees, mourned his loss.

Neither Bradstreet nor Bouquet invaded the Cuyahoga Valley, but their proximity fueled rumors of imminent destruction, providing a powerful stimulus for Netawatwees to move his village close to the support of other Unami and Unalachtigo villages. Ironically, by moving briefly to the Muskingum, he put his people directly in Bouquet's path. Fortunately for him, Bouquet was bent on peace, not on war.

For a decade following Bouquet's expedition into the Ohio country, little mention can be found of activity along the Cuyahoga. At some point during this period, Cuyahoga Town was reoccupied. Tegasah (Digasu), probably a village chief, was its head man. The remainder of the Valley's southern end was dominated by the Lenapes. Wyandots dominated the northern end and maintained temporary encampments on the west side of the river's mouth.

British traders were again active. In 1775 they erected a new trading post at Cuyahoga Town and supplied it from Fort Pitt, with strings of pack horses carrying goods across the Mahoning Trail. Trade goods also moved from Fort Pitt to Detroit via the Mahoning Trail's northern branch. These goods were stashed at the Cuyahoga's mouth, awaiting shipment across Lake Erie to Detroit.

Beyond the Cuyahoga orbit, tensions were building in the early 1770s as Shawnee and Ohio Iroquois raiders harried would-be settlers coming to parts of western Pennsylvania and lands south of the Ohio River. The Iroquois had ceded these lands to the British without the consent of Ohio Indigenous groups, who saw these settlers as invaders of their territory. Kentucky, recently opened to adventurous, land-hungry British colonists, was attracting settlers. Boats carrying them down the river were favorite targets for Native American forces.[6] In 1774 Virginia's royal governor, John Murray, Earl of Dunmore, devised a plan to stop the Indigenous attacks. Two colonial armies were to converge at the Shawnee towns on the Scioto. Dunmore led one force from Fort Pitt to that vicinity, where he established Camp Charlotte south of modern Columbus. The second force, composed of frontiersmen and led by Andrew Lewis, moved down the Kanawha Valley and fought Shawnees and their allies in an inconclusive battle at Point Pleasant, located at the confluence of the Kanawha and the Ohio, before moving on to join Dunmore at Camp Charlotte. There the Shawnees agreed that Native Americans would stay north of the Ohio River, and new British settlers south of the river.

"Dunmore's War" provided but a prelude to vicious warfare in the borderlands that reached full flower after 1777. By that time, the American War for Independence was well underway, and both Euro-American settlers and Ohio Native Americans had to choose sides.

Nearly all Ohio Indigenous groups chose to fight on Britain's side. Britain's trade ambitions threatened them less than the Americans who came to settle on their land. Pennsylvanians, Marylanders, Carolinians, Virginians, and Kentuckians were now the enemies of the Lenapes,

Ottawas, Ohio Iroquois, Wyandots, and Chippewas, who still had a presence in the Cuyahoga Valley. The British trading post at Cuyahoga Town was well supplied with the articles of war, making it a premier attraction for Indigenous warriors. The Cuyahoga was also conveniently located as a staging area for raids against western US settlements, especially those in western Pennsylvania.

Surely that helps explain why, in the Fall of 1777, Hopocan (also known as Konieschquanoheel or Captain Pipe), the new chief of the Munsee Lenapes, led his people to Cuyahoga. In 1776 Hopocan had succeeded his uncle, Custaloga (Packanke) as chief of the Munsee, and since that time had lived briefly at the Kuskuskies and along the Walhonding. Although Hopocan had initially befriended Americans, a series of American atrocities against Indians drove him into the British camp.[7]

Hopocan's town was located on the south side of the Cuyahoga River where it veered northwestward, about eight-tenths of a mile west by north of the Portage Path's northern terminus. It is likely, therefore, that the town was on the site of, or very near to, Chestnut Lodge (formerly Mingo Lodge) in Sand Run Metro Park. Native American artifacts have been found there as they have in nearby locations along Sand Run Parkway and at the eastern end of Smith Road.

While Hopocan was contemplating his move to the Cuyahoga, Gen. Edward Hand, commanding American forces at Fort Pitt, decided to destroy British military stores reputed to be gathered at the Cuyahoga's mouth. In February 1778, in abysmal weather, he led five hundred Pennsylvania militiamen up the Beaver and Mahoning rivers. At two places, one of them about forty miles east of the Cuyahoga, his ragtag army encountered groups of Indigenous people. There were no warriors among them. That did not deter the trigger-happy troops, as they shot and killed one man, one boy, and four women before the disconsolate general led them back to Fort Pitt. Forever after, Hand was stigmatized for his "Squaw Campaign."[8]

Hopocan maintained his town on the Cuyahoga for about eighteen months, during which time he rejected Lenape offers to join their villages along the Muskingum. Things changed late in 1778, when the new commandant at Fort Pitt, General Lachlan McIntosh, led 1,200 soldiers westward over Bouquet's trail to the Tuscarawas. His men erected a stronghold named Fort Laurens along the river at modern Bolivar. It was to be a jumping off place for a proposed attack on British-held Detroit and to protect nearby Lenapes still friendly toward Americans. Hopocan regarded Fort Laurens as a grave threat. It stood directly between his town on the Cuyahoga and the main Lenape towns on the Muskingum. To avoid being isolated, he solicited help from the Wyandots, who sent horses to move Munsee baggage to a new village site near the Wyandots at Sandusky. Hopocan's Cuyahoga village was never reoccupied.

Within four months of Hopocan's departure for the Sandusky, Fort Laurens was abandoned. The Cuyahoga remained a precarious place for Indigenous people, however, since American military activity increased around Fort Pitt. Spies and scouts like Captain Samuel Brady kept an eye on the region. The British trading post had been neutralized, leaving Cuyahoga Town in limbo. Thomas Hutchins's 1778 map clearly shows the town located at the northern terminus of the Portage Path but it is doubtful that it was still an important gathering place. Atrocities like the "Squaw Campaign" and the infamous 1782 massacre perpetrated by Pennsylvania militia against Moravian Lenapes at Gnadenhutten on the Tuscarawas River certainly did not encourage other groups to settle in the region. Indeed, in the early 1780s, Moravian missionaries reported the entire Valley to be devoid of Indigenous towns.

The American War for Independence ended in the Peace of Paris (1783). In it, Britain recognized the independence of her thirteen colonies and—once again without the participation, representation, or assent of Indigenous groups in the negotiations—ceded to the struggling new nation a princely realm stretching from the Appalachians to the Mississippi, from British Canada to Spanish Florida. The British refused to evacuate Detroit even though it was on United States soil. They wanted Detroit as a base from which to supply and encourage (unofficially) the western Great Lakes Indigenous groups in their struggle against encroachment on their Ohio lands. Lenapes, Shawnees, and Ohio Iroquois had been forced to move villages westward to the vicinity of the Auglaize and the Maumee. The Cuyahoga remained well out of the mainstream as American settlers, supported by the military, started their unrelenting push into Trans-Appalachian lands.

Native Americans who remained along the Cuyahoga were now beholden largely to American settlers for the trade and presents so necessary to them. Joseph DuShattar maintained a trading post from 1791 to 1794 about nine miles upstream from the river's mouth. He served a transient population of Ottawas, Massasaugas (a local branch of the Chippewa), Senecas (now distinct from Ohio Iroquois), and a handful of others including occasional Lenapes and Wyandots. The latter seem to have patronized a storehouse at or near the Cuyahoga's mouth. A sketch map drawn by a land scout about 1791 shows an encampment in that location, and another about ten miles upstream, which would place it near DuShattar's trading post. Chippewas remained active, and in 1791 their warriors killed some settlers living in eastern Pennsylvania. It may have been this action that accounted for the thirty American militiamen reported at the river's mouth that same year.

In 1786 Moravian missionaries David Zeisberger and John Heckewelder temporarily located about a hundred of their Native American converts on or near the site of the Ottawa village once occupying land east of the river and just north of Tinkers Creek. Named Pilgerruh (Pilgrim's Rest), the site was abandoned within ten months as the Moravians moved on to other locations. During their brief stay, the missionaries reported Indians coming to Pilgerruh singly or in small groups, but they maintained no villages in the Valley.

There was little Native American activity to report on the Cuyahoga at the end of the eighteenth and beginning of the nineteenth centuries. Elsewhere in Ohio, this was a critical time as Great Lakes Indigenous groups formed a loose confederation they called the United Indian Nations (also known as the Northwestern Indian Confederacy) to more effectively oppose the settlers encroaching on their Ohio lands. Prior to 1788 such settlers were unauthorized squatters, but in that year authorized settlement in Ohio began at Marietta and Cincinnati. The United States assumed that these people had a legal right to settle in what had been Indian country because it had acquired these eastern and southern Ohio lands from tribal claimants through the Treaty of Fort McIntosh (1785). The treaty opened to settlement vast areas of Indian land north of the Ohio River, drawing a line separating lands to be open for US settlement from lands reserved to the Native Americans. As part of that line, the Cuyahoga-Portage Path-Tuscarawas section helped constitute what became the effective western boundary of the United States (1784–1805).

However, the treaty's land claims had been signed away by Lenape, Wyandot, Ottawa, and Chippewa sub-chiefs who lacked authority to make such a deal, and the Shawnee and Miami, who claimed much of the ceded lands, were not represented at all. While US authorities claimed legitimacy for the treaty, most Indigenous leaders regarded it as fraudulent and refused to abide by its terms, sending their warriors to attack settlers north of the Ohio for encroaching on their lands.

In resisting this encroachment, the Northwestern Indian Confederacy was initially successful in inhibiting further US settlement. This prompted the new President George Washington and Congress—who wanted to encourage settlement and enrich the US Treasury through sales of Western lands—to defeat the Confederacy militarily. From 1790 to 1794 the United States sent three major expeditions against it. The first two—under Josiah Harmar and Arthur St. Clair—ended in disaster for the US forces, in large part because of the extremely skillful strategic and tactical leadership of Miami Chief Michikinikwa (Little Turtle). However, Anthony Wayne's huge expedition outnumbered and overwhelmed the Confederacy's forces, breaking Indian resistance at the Battle of Fallen Timbers (1794). The next year, tribal leaders signed the Treaty of Greenville, which redrew the McIntosh line separating Indians and US settlers. Ohio Indians largely honored this treaty and adhered to the new line which, like its predecessor, included the Cuyahoga-Portage Path-Tuscarawas segment as part of the federal union's effective western boundary. In 1805 the Treaty of Fort Industry moved the line of separation many miles westward.

The transition in the lower Cuyahoga Valley from Indigenous occupancy to that of US settlers was eased by the slow pace of settlement following on the heels of the 1796–97 survey of Western Reserve lands (east of the Cuyahoga only) by the Connecticut Land Company, a private venture. The surveyors and the first settlers encountered individual Senecas and Ottawas, or small Indigenous families, but they found no villages of consequence. These Indigenous people relied on itinerant traders like James Hillman who operated out of Pittsburgh after 1786. Trade was slow since the Cuyahoga was no longer the prime fur region that had attracted Iroquois and others to it some fifty years earlier.

In the nineteenth century's first decade more farmers from New England and the east appeared in the Valley. They too encountered

Treaty of Greenville Medal. Oak Native American Ethnographic Collection. *Courtesy of Institute for Human Science and Culture, The University of Akron.* "Peace medals" were awarded to Native American leaders by the federal government throughout early US history. Their intent was to further US/Native relationships and give access to the benefits of the dominant white society. Today, such medals are viewed with some controversy as contemporaries question the role of the medals in light of ensuing decades of broken diplomacy.

individual Indians, and they could identify sites once occupied by villages or encampments. An Ottawa village, for example, was located on the river's west side at Boston, perhaps on the present-day parking lot of the Boston Mills ski resort. Ottawa orchards were located north of that site toward today's Summit-Cuyahoga county line. Judge William Wetmore, later founder of Cuyahoga Falls, reported both a Lenape and a Seneca village near the land on the river to which he moved in 1804. Some claim that an Ottawa village was located at the mouth of the Little Cuyahoga (near the confluence of the Little Cuyahoga and main Cuyahoga River in the Big Bend area of Sand Run Metro Park), with a chief variously known as Stig-wanish, or Seneca, heading it. Most likely the Native American presence reported at the mouth of the Little Cuyahoga was an encampment rather than a village of consequence. Indeed, Stigwanish has been claimed by other locations in or near the Valley. Substantial Native American villages at Silver Lake and near the waters of the Cuyahoga upstream from the "big falls" in what is now Portage County have been reported by local investigators.

General Lucius Bierce, an avid local investigator working in the first half of the nineteenth century, reported that Jonathan Hale's farm on the river's west side contained remnants of an Ohio Iroquois village. These were thought to be Cayugas, a circumstance that led local enthusiasts to claim that it was associated with the famous Ohio chief, Logan. It is possible that sometime before 1774 Logan visited this village, but his main towns were located in eastern and south-central Ohio. From 1774, when he achieved notoriety, until his death in 1780, Logan's whereabouts have been rather well documented, and the records do not suggest a connection with the Cuyahoga Valley.

Whatever the Native American population in the Lower Cuyahoga Valley may have been after the mid-1790s, it is clear that it was small, mobile, and incapable of concerted action. All sources, including eyewitnesses, agree that just prior to the outbreak of the War of 1812, virtually all local Native American peoples disappeared, presumably moving westward away from encroaching whites and toward British support and protection. By the time of the 1860s census, only thirty residents of Ohio were listed as Indian, only seven of which lived in the Cuyahoga Valley. Thus, like the precontact first peoples before, the historic independent Indigenous groups of the Cuyahoga had largely passed into memory.

Annotated Bibliography

While few first-hand written accounts exist regarding the pre-Revolutionary period in the Cuyahoga Valley, some primary sources focused on other parts of Ohio refer to the area. These include James Smith, *Scoouwa: James Smith's Indian Captivity Narrative* (Columbus: Ohio Historical Society, 1976) and Eugene Bliss, ed., *Diary of David Zeisberger, a Moravian Missionary Among the Indians of Ohio* (Cincinnati: The Historical and Philosophical Society of Ohio, 1885). Paul Wallace's *The Travels of John Heckewelder in Frontier America* (Pittsburgh: University of Pittsburgh Press, 1958) is not technically a primary source, but quotes extensively from the journals and writings of Heckewelder and gives valuable insight into this time period. Some late-nineteenth and early twentieth-century accounts of this period collect oral histories of this period, including Charles Augustus Hanna, *The Wilderness Trail* (New York: G. P. Putnam's Sons, 1911) and Belle McKinney Hays Swope, *History of the Families of McKinney-Brady-Quigley* (Chambersburg, PA: Franklin Repository Printery, 1905).

Richard White's *The Middle Ground: Indians, Empires, and Republics in the Great Lakes Region, 1650–1815* (Cambridge: Cambridge University Press, 1991) not only presents a comprehensive view on Indian, French, British, and US relations in the Great Lakes region, but also gives significant attention to how these interactions manifested themselves in Northern Ohio. More targeted studies include Daniel P. Barr, *Unconquered: The Iroquois League at War in Colonial America* (Westport, CT: Praeger Publishers, 2006); several essays in Daniel Barr, ed., *The Boundaries Between Us: Natives and Newcomers along the Frontiers of the Old Northwest Territory, 1750–1850* (Kent: Kent State University Press, 2006); Paul R. Misencik and Sally E. Misencik, *American Indians of the Ohio Country in the 18th Century* (Jefferson, NC: McFarland & Co., 2020); and Michael N. McConnell, *A Country Between: The Upper Ohio Valley and Its Peoples, 1724–1774* (Lincoln: University of Nebraska Press, 1992). A more general treatment of Indigenous peoples of Ohio during this period can be found in Kevin Kern and Gregory Wilson, *Ohio: A History of the Buckeye State, 2nd Edition* (Hoboken, New Jersey: John Wiley & Sons, 2023), Chapters 3–5 and 8.

Finally, there is a new generation of historical scholarship that seeks to refocus and recenter the narrative of Indigenous/Euro-American relations

in US History away from its traditional, implicitly Eurocentric histo-
riography. Ned Blackhawk's *The Rediscovery of America: Native Peoples
and the Unmaking of U.S. History* (New Haven: Yale University Press,
2023)—which won the 2023 National Book Award for Nonfiction—is a
recent synthesis in this tradition which puts the events and encounters
described in this chapter into a larger and fuller historical context.

6 Path Finding

Maps That Document Native Americans in
Northeast Ohio

Linda G. Whitman and Peg Bobel

In the late 1800s and early 1900s, a few avocational historians and archaeologists in northeast Ohio took an interest in what they believed to be the
disappearing traces of Ohio's Native American past. By the 1850s, after
decades of conflict, the last of the Native American groups in Ohio had
been forcibly removed. Therefore, in the minds of these early historians,
the lives and cultures of the Indigenous peoples existed only in the past,
a history simply to be documented. Their search for paths, village sites,
and burial mounds took place around the same time as archaeology
began to develop into a profession. The avocational and professional
work progressed and developed through the 1900s and continues to this
day. Over time the meaning and intents of the various researchers have
shifted—from preservation of observations and recollections, to marking
paths and boundaries from a white settler perspective, to acknowledging
and honoring the paths and sites from the original Native American
point of view.

Beginning around the 1980s, archaeologists and historians began looking at how Native Americans made and used maps to make sense of their
terrestrial and cosmographic worlds. As G. Malcolm Lewis notes in *The
History of Cartography*, "Indigenous maps were based on different assumptions than European maps and created for different functions. They were
born of experience and oral tradition, not on inscribed archival history

in the Western sense."[1] Native American worldviews and belief systems that "relied on human memory to transfer sophisticated knowledge from one generation to the next" are expressed by oral traditions, storytellers, pictographs such as the one in Independence, Ohio, monumental earthworks like the Hopewell ceremonial sites in central Ohio, and woodhenges such as the one at Sunwatch Village site in Dayton, Ohio.[2] While Indigenous and white understandings of geography and cartography differ, what follows here is a discussion of the Euro-American history of mapping and documenting Native American sites in Ohio. One early twentieth-century group known as the Indian Pathfinders illustrates the interest in preserving and documenting what they believed was important to Ohio's history.

While by the late 1900s the work of the Indian Pathfinders had largely faded from memory, one member of a local archaeology club, Joe Jesensky, had, as a young man, made acquaintance with one of the group's founders. In his later years Jesensky developed a keen interest in local history, specifically Native American history as it related to the Cuyahoga Valley, collecting documents and recording all he could find along the way. In the 1980s Jesensky met another local historian, Jean Kainsinger, and finding that their interests overlapped, set off on a mutual pursuit together. On a pleasant late summer morning in 1986, Joe and his friend Jean rode to Kirtland, Ohio, on a quest to find historic documents that could be of great interest to them both. They had made contact with Betsy Baker, granddaughter of Elmer B. Wight, who had in her possession some papers of Mr. Wight's and his close friend and associate Virgil Allen. Wight and Allen had both lived in Walton Hills, Ohio, and their personal histories could be of great help to Kainsinger, who was writing up the history of Walton Hills. As for Jesensky—he was in search of items he had remembered from decades before when, as a young artist exploring the Tinkers Creek Valley, he made acquaintance with Mr. Wight, who allowed Jesensky and his friends to build a cabin on his farm above the wooded creek valley. Of further interest, Wight and Allen were cofounders of the Indian Pathfinders Association Number 1, a group whose papers from the early 1900s just might be in Mrs. Baker's garage.

Although Jesensky did not find what he was hoping to find, like early aerial photos of the Tinkers Creek Valley that Wight had commissioned, Joe and his friend Jean were not disappointed. Out in the Bakers' barn, they pried open two file cabinets, dusted off the spider webs and mouse droppings, and began delving into file after file of Allen and Wight's research. "We went through those old drawers and files like a child opening up Christmas presents on Christmas morning!!," Joe recalled in his notes he recorded about the find. He went on: "What a treasure trove we discovered that day!" They photocopied some of the letters, trip notes, and maps, which Jesensky carefully retained. For us today, that treasure trove is a link to a group of Cleveland-area men who in the early 1900s systematically researched trails and sites related to Native American occupation of what is now northeast Ohio.[3]

According to Jesensky's recollections, the Indian Pathfinders Association's main mission was to create a map of Ohio that would show all the known trails, villages, and other sites related to Native American occupation. The constitution of the group confirms this goal, stating, "The Indian Pathfinders' Association of Cleveland is organized for the purpose of locating, monumenting and recording these paths and the historic incidents connected to them." The preamble in the constitution sheds some light on what motivated these gentlemen. They lay out their case that "a knowledge of these paths is of first importance to the student of early Ohio history," and based on their belief that the paths dated to precontact times, "all the events connected with the passing of the Indian and the coming of the white man were controlled by the paths," and that military expeditions of both "the Indian and 1812 wars" followed these paths. They concluded that no map of Ohio existed at that time that shows "with any degree of accuracy the location of these paths, Indian villages, route of military expeditions and fort sites." It was their mission to research and produce such a map.[4]

The group's preamble reveals the dominant belief and perspectives of even well-educated men of this time: that the age of "the Indian" had passed (a euphemistic way to describe the forced removal of Indigenous groups) and "White Man" now prevailed and now dominated the region. It likely did not occur to them as they pursued their mapping that Native peoples themselves were mapmakers, conceptualizing geography and routes in a different way.[5]

Jesensky believed the Pathfinders group was never able to complete its mission, but their extensive research gives us great insight into where the scholarship stood at that time and what historic maps were available to aid in their research. By looking at their sources we can gain an understanding of how professional archaeology and documentation developed in the state of Ohio. But first, who were these men, what drew them to their mission, and to what extent did their knowledge of or attitudes towards Native Americans reflect or differ from prevailing thinking in those times? The Indian Pathfinders (also at times spelled as two words, Path Finders) was formed in 1914. In a letter dated June 19, 1914, from Russell K. Pelton, of Cleveland, to P. P. Cherry, in Akron, Ohio, Mr. Pelton explains that he and several other gentlemen (who he names as Virgil D. Allen, Fred. M. Barton, Chas. Orr, and Elmer B. Wight) had read Mr. Cherry's treatise on the Portage Path and "being much interested, instructed and stimulated thereby" have formed the "Indian Path Finders Association No. 1, Cleveland, Ohio." The letter states that the group had already located the site of the 1786 Moravian Christian Indian settlement near Tinkers Creek and was working on preparing as accurate a map as possible of all the Indian trails in northeastern Ohio.[6]

But why Association No. 1? Pelton explains that to fulfill their mission, they had contacted men in other counties, encouraging others to form additional chapters. For instance, five men in Youngstown had formed Association No. 2, a friend in Portage County, W. S. Kent, of Kent, Ohio, was interested in forming a group, and Mr. Pelton was hopeful Mr. Cherry would form Association No. 3 in Akron. Pelton assured Cherry that "five men who are active, congenial and mutually interested are enough for any County association." Mr. Pelton goes on to offer aid to Mr. Cherry by noting that his friend Mr. Cash might help form the Akron group, and John Hovey of Akron might also be helpful, if he had not already "passed over the Great Divide." He notes that Mr. Hovey was mentioned in a footnote in Archer Butler Hulbert's *Indian Thoroughfares*, published in Cleveland in 1902, material the Pathfinders had been studying.[7]

It is not clear whether or not these other groups ever formed, but by 1916 the Cleveland group had been active enough to gain the attention of a reporter from a society magazine, who profiled the group in an August 5, 1916, article entitled "Clevelanders Mark Old Indian Trails." The article offers some hints as to what brought these men to their mission and to each other. It could have been as simple as the nearly universal appeal of finding an ancient point, or "arrowhead." Mr. Pelton was known to wear "an arrowhead fob of Tennessee jasper, found at Brecksville." According to the magazine article, Pelton's friend and cofounder of the Association, Virgil D. Allen, picked up a number of "specimens" all around a tree in Northfield and attached an identifying marker noting it was along one of the Native American paths.[8]

The article also notes that at first these pathfinders "delved individually into the extraordinary love of early American and Ohio history, merely as a personal hobby." But over time, they found each other "brother travelers on the highways of Indian history and history of Indian highways," banding together for the sake of research and discovery. They believed that civilization (white, Euro-American civilization) developed along the paths, and that a study of them would reveal not only what has come since, but "much that has gone before."[9]

According to Pelton, the original group in 1914 consisted of five professional men, all Clevelanders: Elmer B. Wight, president, a Cleveland surveyor, landscape designer, and civil engineer; Virgil D. Allen Sr., secretary of the group, civil engineer, and president of the Allen-Osborn Co.; Charles Orr, former director of Cleveland Public Schools; Fred Barton, publisher; and Russell K. Pelton, agent in charge of the Benjamin Rose Estate. The 1916 article lists the five charter members slightly differently, as Wight, Allen, Barton, Pelton, and Mr. De Lo E. Mook, attorney and Boy Scout commissioner.[10]

Besides being professionals and sharing a common interest in local history, some of these men also had offices in the same downtown Cleveland building, the Rose Building at East 9th Street and Prospect Avenue, today a Cleveland Landmark. By the early 1900s Benjamin Rose had become a wealthy man through his meatpacking industry, and around 1900 invested a good bit of his capital into building a ten-story office building several blocks east of the downtown district. Mr. Rose—today remembered for his philanthropy and interest in care for the aged that led to the creation of the Benjamin Rose Institute—passed away in 1908, and Russell Pelton was made manager of his multi-million-dollar estate. Pelton's office was in the Rose Building, as was Virgil Allen's and Elmer Wight's. Mr. Barton's business was located just around the corner from the Rose Building in the Caxton Building, the same building that housed the Cleveland Society magazine, *Cleveland Town Topics*.[11]

Wight's and Allen's lives were quite intertwined: not only were they good friends, but they also became in-laws when Virgil Allen's son, Virgil Allen Jr., married Wight's daughter Margaret. The younger Allen couple built a home next door to Elmer Wight's, then after Elmer died, they moved to Wight's country home, the Cleaveland Hill Farm in Walton Hills, Ohio. Elmer Wight had purchased the farm in 1917 and used it as a summer place until the 1940s. At that farm, Joe Jesensky first became acquainted with Elmer Wight, who allowed Joe and his friends to build their artists' cabin on the property. Wight shared his love of local history and Native American history with Joe, who passed it along to the authors of this chapter. The Wight descendants eventually sold Cleaveland Hill Farm to Cleveland Metroparks, and while the buildings are all gone, the land is now part of Bedford Reservation.[12]

The writer of the *Cleveland Topics* article notes that the Pathfinder men derived both pleasure and educational benefit from their studies, and it is clear that they took their endeavor seriously. They met monthly and committed themselves to each studying earlier histories of Cleveland, other particular books, or relevant manuscripts, diaries, or letters. They would then write abstracts on their finds and file reports in the Pathfinders' collection. They wrote letters, many of them penned by Virgil Allen, contacting county engineers and others throughout the state who they thought might have knowledge about Native American trails or sites, and even received an encouraging response from the Smithsonian Institution. Sometimes they gave talks about their research, and civil engineer Allen penned an article for *Dependable Highways* periodical, in which he connects his engineering interests with his curiosity about "aboriginal thought on the subject of highway making and town building."[13]

And they explored. The men apparently enjoyed hiking and exploring and kept notes of their excursions, talking to farmers who had collections of points or believed an ancient trail traversed their land. One member even studied original notes of Connecticut Land Company surveyors, looking for instances where surveyors found evidence of an "Indian path." They also perused and took notes from the Annals of the Early Settlers' Association, an organization of citizens who came together to preserve the early history of Cuyahoga County and the Western Reserve. The engineers in the group had skills in drafting and map-making, and some had connections to other professionals beyond Cuyahoga County, with whom they corresponded.[14]

By 1916 their membership roster listed thirty-eight names. One gentleman they knew and who may have joined their group was P. H. Kaiser, an Oberlin College graduate, attorney, and former superintendent of Elyria Public Schools. Kaiser was well-respected in Elyria and moved to Cleveland after marrying the daughter of the Honorable John H. Boynton. Kaiser became interested in local history and held memberships in both the GAR (Grand Army of the Republic, an organization of Union Civil War veterans) and the Early Settlers Association. He was much older than the other Pathfinder founders—in 1914 he would have been seventy-three, while Allen was only forty-five. The younger men likely looked to him as an elder who shared their interest in local history.[15]

But what may have drawn the Pathfinders most to Kaiser was his address, "The Moravians on the Cuyahoga," a paper presented to and published by The Western Reserve Historical Society in 1894. Kaiser's interest in the Moravian missionaries and their Native American converts was personal as well as academic. His parents were members of the Moravian Church, a Protestant sect dating to about the middle of the fifteenth century. Fleeing from persecution in Europe, Moravians settled in Colonial America in the 1700s, first in the colony of Georgia and later at Bethlehem, Pennsylvania. There a young Moravian named David Zeisberger became interested in the plight of the Native Americans he encountered and "resolved to devote his life to Christian work among them."[16]

Kaiser's address is a thoughtful, detailed account of the activities of missionaries David Zeisberger and his assistant John Heckewelder as they lived and worked among the Lenape (also known as Delaware) Native Americans in Ohio from 1771 to 1791. Relying on detailed Moravian diaries and letters as source material, Kaiser describes specific places, people, and events, including the temporary settlement in the Cuyahoga River Valley known as Pilgerruh and the 1782 massacre of Christian Natives at Gnadenhutten on the Tuscarawas River. His treatise reveals both the care and aid given the Lenape by the peace-loving Moravians, but also shows a prevailing attitude of the day as he describes the Native

Americans as "untaught red men of the American forests."[17] The white European Moravians were legitimately concerned about the living conditions of the Native population, and Zeisberger approached his would-be converts by living among them and attempting to learn native languages. The missionaries' and Kaiser's accounts provide a window into white/ Native relationships that differed significantly from other more aggressive, conquering, and militaristic interactions.

Kaiser also provided his listeners and readers—some of whom were Pathfinders—with a map drawn by Reverend John Heckewelder that shows rivers, Native American sites, and the routes that connected them. Kaiser describes the map as "rudely sketched" and explains that it "was found among the papers of General Moses Cleaveland and presented to the Western Reserve Historical Society, of Cleveland, by his daughter." The historical society later published the map along with a description written by Heckewelder of "that part of the Western Country comprehended in my map," an area in today's Ohio now known as the Connecticut Western Reserve. The map dates to 1796, the year that Moses Cleaveland led the first survey of the Western Reserve for the Connecticut Land Company. It was apparently used by the surveyors, but it is not known whether or not Heckewelder drew the map while in this area or from memory, nor is it known whether or not Moses Cleaveland had the map before he arrived to begin his survey.[18] Nor is it known if he obtained any information for his map from local Native informants.

Heckewelder's description of what is now northeast Ohio deals mostly with comments on the value of the natural resources as far as their suitability for farming and grazing. He praises the attributes of the Cuyahoga River, including that it affords boats a good harbor, and is navigable by canoes upstream as far as the falls (at today's city of Cuyahoga Falls). He also notes "Indian Country" as being west of the Cuyahoga River and the Muskingum River, with the inscriptions on the map noting that each river is the "Territorial Line between the Ind. & the United States."[19]

The Heckewelder map and description would have been of great interest to the Pathfinders. Typical of many maps of this time, text was handwritten, going in many directions with no real scale, and word spellings representing the prevailing orthography of the day. Paths were named as connectors between cities, towns, rivers, or other landmarks. This early map was so significant that, in 1963, the Western Reserve Historical Society published a booklet describing the Heckewelder map and contracted cartographer James Bier to create a modern version of the 1796 map drawn accurately to scale. Modern political and geographic features were added that allow for a better understanding of the relationships between them and the eighteenth-century Moravian and Native American towns and trails.[20]

By the beginning of the twentieth century, several early maps and manuscripts were available to the Pathfinders to begin their quest. We know from an extant letter of the Pathfinders that they were studying the works of Archer Butler Hulbert.[21] We also know that the 1796 Heckewelder map was published in Hulbert's *Indian Thoroughfares of Ohio* (1900) and *Indian Thoroughfares* (1902). Hulbert also contains additional maps titled "Indian Thoroughfares of Ohio based on Hutchins" (1900) and "Indian Thoroughfares of Eastern Ohio and Western Pennsylvania, Based on Hutchins" (1902). These maps are virtually identical, detailing rivers, streams, forts, and Native American trails, towns, and tribal territories. A few trails are labeled with names connecting destinations, while others have names that were probably given by settlers, obliterating the origin, function, or destination.

Who was Hutchins? With a checkered career, Thomas Hutchins (1730–1789) became the first geographer of the United States. Born in New Jersey, he served with the British Army in the French and Indian and Revolutionary wars. The British charged him with treason in 1779, prompting him to resign his commission. Then in 1781 Congress appointed him as the first geographer of the United States. Some years before that, while still working with the British, he participated in Colonel Henry Bouquet's 1764 Expedition, during which Hutchins mapped portions of what is now eastern Ohio.[22] The map drawn while on Bouquet's Expedition showed forts and Bouquet's sixteen campsites and Native American towns, as well as details of rivers and streams. His strategic interest was reflected in the title of the map: "A general map of the country of the Ohio and Muskingum showing the situation of the Indian towns with respect to the Army under the Command of Colonel Bouquet."[23]

Hutchins' mapping experience with Bouquet may have helped earn him his appointment as United States geographer despite his history as a turncoat. As the US geographer Hutchins continued surveying and mapmaking, producing maps of the Northwest Territory. This mapping facilitated the settling of the territory, resulting in much bloodshed as Native Americans were pushed west. As a result of westward expansion, Ohio became the first state formed from the Northwest Territory.

Another resource available to the Pathfinders would have been the work of Charles W. Whittlesey. He conducted one of the earliest professional projects of documenting precontact archaeological sites and Native American trails in Ohio. Whittlesey was appointed assistant state geologist in 1837 and conducted the first state geological surveys. After the Civil War, now Colonel Whittlesey became a historian and helped found the Western Reserve Historical Society in Cleveland. As its president he began documenting aboriginal trails and sites on a twelve-by-fourteen-foot wall map. He published a chapter in *New Topographic Atlas of the State of Ohio* titled "Topographical and Historical Sketch of the State of Ohio," which included a map. The "Historical Map of the State of Ohio" depicts the location of ancient earthwork archaeological sites; Native American villages, trails, and territories between 1750 to 1780; and military expedition routes, forts, and battle sites during the same time period. His map included county boundaries and river drainages. Indian trails, indicated in dashed lines, are not named. Military trails are shown as hatched lines and are dated.[24]

At the same time that the Pathfinders were diligently researching Native American trails, a group of professional archaeologists at the Ohio Archaeological and Historical Society (now the Ohio History Connection) in Columbus were working in a similar direction documenting precontact Native American archaeological sites, towns, and trails. The result of these efforts is the landmark *Archeological Atlas of Ohio* by William C. Mills (1914). The atlas was primarily concerned with compiling and documenting the location of archaeological sites by county but also included a chapter and map of Indian trails emphasizing that the trails were very significant for the settlement and development of the State. Along with Indian trails and towns, the map included major rivers, lakes, county borders, and contemporary cities. Mills noted that the trails were located in both open country, and more importantly, on high ground between waterways and on hills and ridges adjacent to streams. These trails and streams provided entry for white settlers and traders north and west into the state from the Ohio River, influencing the location of settlements and towns.[25]

In 1984 archaeologist William Dancey provided the first review of Mills' *Atlas* and a look into its production. He notes that Warren K. Moorehead, the Society's first Curator of Archaeology between 1895 and 1897, was charged by the Society's executive committee to create a map of Ohio's archaeological sites. An undertaking of this scale had not been attempted in the United States to date. England, France, and Germany had already documented the location of their archaeological sites, and Moorehead felt that Ohio's archaeological sites were just as important. Even at this time, Moorehead recognized that Ohio's sites were quickly being destroyed, emphasizing the urgent need for them to be documented.[26]

Moorehead initially searched through site reports and other documents, marking their findings on a wall map measuring six feet square. He sent tracings of these county maps to amateur and avocational archaeologists requesting that they add the location of sites they knew. However, he felt that the Society should conduct the surveys with trained archaeologists to verify sites' existence and locations. Sites reported by amateurs were only field-checked if their existence was questioned.

William Mills, curator from 1898 through 1921, acquired the mapping project after he was hired.[27] However, progress on the project waxed and waned. By 1909 the executive board requested that the project be continued and allocated funds for its completion. Henry C. Shetrone, Mills' assistant, spent his first year (1913) field-checking site locations for the *Atlas*. Ultimately Mills compiled the *Atlas* using data from Moorehead's research, informant interviews and maps, site maps of earthworks published by Ephraim G. Squier and Edwin H. Davis in 1848, Whittlesey's 1872 map, and Shetrone's 1913 fieldwork.[28] Mills systematically updated the master map county by county with this data and published the *Atlas* in 1914. Mills went on to become director of the Society from 1920 through 1928. Shetrone succeeded Mills as curator from 1921 to 1929, when he became director.

In 1918 Shetrone published "The Indian in Ohio with a Map of the Ohio Country" in *The Ohio State Archaeological and Historical Society Quarterly*. This article included a map titled "The Ohio Country of the Historic Indian Period" compiled by Shetrone and drawn by R. B. Sherman. The map, which looks a lot like the Mills (1914) *Atlas* trail map, included rivers, Native American trails, towns and territories, early American cities/towns, military forts and battles, and the Greenville Treaty Line. However, only major Native American trails that traversed the state were included.[29]

The Ohio Historical Society (now Ohio History Connection) reprinted this map in the 1970s as "Indians in Ohio History: A Map of Ohio Indian Villages Sites and Trails with a Chronological Listing of Important Dates and Events in the History of Early Ohio Tribes." All the Native American trails shown on the Mills 1914 map are included in this version and they are all referenced as Indian Trails. A list of historic events from 1669 to 1842 is printed on both sides of the map. Both the Mills (1914) and Shetrone and Sherman (1970s) maps are referenced by today's archaeologists as they conduct background research to identify if any Native American sites or trails are present in their research area before archaeological investigations are conducted.

Shortly after Mills' *Atlas* was printed, Virgil Allen began compiling the Indian Pathfinders "Map of State of Ohio Showing Indian Trails, Towns, Missions, Block Houses and Military Forts and Routes." The base map, likely drawn in 1916, consists of Ohio's counties, major drainages, and unnamed paths. We think this map was likely discovered by Jesensky and Kainsinger among Elmer Wight's papers. Both the Whittlesey 1872 map and Mills's 1914 map would have been available to the Pathfinders at this time, but it is unknown whether or not each knew of the other's work. It is likely that work on the Pathfinders' map ceased after the publication of Mills's *Atlas*—Jesensky believed their project was never completed, and we have not found a later version of their map.[30]

While this may suggest that the Pathfinders no longer pursued documenting Native American trails in Ohio, the inquiry itself did not cease. For example, Frank. N. Wilcox went on to publish *Ohio Indian Trails* in 1933.[31] He wrote about and illustrated the trails with a clear sense of history and geographic instinct that led him to grasp how these trails "were bound to vary in character, situation and purpose." He is likely the first to document how each trail was named and how they were used and usurped by explorers, traders, settlers, and the military. *Ohio Indian Trails* included a small map showing unnamed trails and small-scale topography of Ohio. In his interpretation, Wilcox describes the importance of each

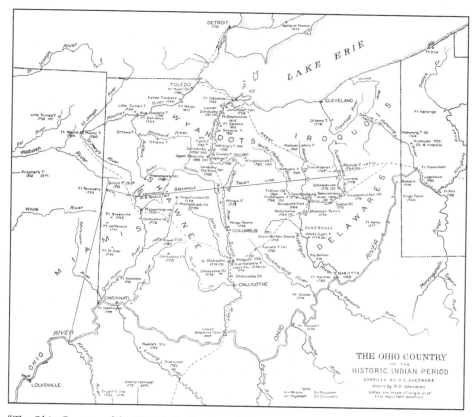

"The Ohio Country of the Historic Indian Period," 1918 map by Shetrone and Sherman.
Reproduced by permission from The Ohio History Connection

trail along with how and why it uses certain landforms. Today's transportation routes in northeast Ohio still bear faint connections to those used hundreds of years ago by Indigenous peoples. Wilcox was fascinated by the concept of route continuity in geographic patterns and attempted to catch the visual spirit of the paths through his artistic illustrations.[32]

In 1970 Kent State University Press reprinted Wilcox's *Ohio Indian Trails*, edited by William A. McGill. The preface by McGill notes that this edition includes heretofore unpublished drawings and paintings by Wilcox. This 1970 edition also includes two maps of Ohio on the endpapers: one shows the relation of "old trails" to modern towns and the topography of the state, while the other is entitled "Indian Trails & Towns circa 1776."[33]

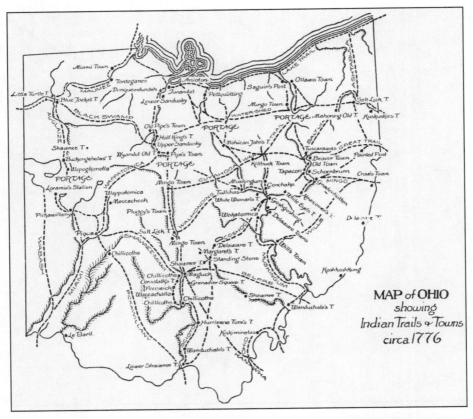

Wilcox's map from the 1970 edition of *Ohio Indian Trails. From Frank N. Wilcox's* Ohio Indian Trails, *Kent State University Press,* ©1970. *Reprinted by permission from Kent State University Press*

Joe Jesensky continued this tradition of research and illustration by focusing on Native Americans and other inhabitants in the Cuyahoga River area. Found among his personal papers is a more contemporary map, compiled by James Daniel Lee, that shows known history of what is now Ohio as it was in 1799, including trails, forts, villages, treaty lines, and other political boundaries based on many sources.[34]

A 1984 map drawn by Jesensky shows a compilation of some of the research he conducted. It portrays a portion of northeast Ohio from Lake Erie at Cleveland following the Cuyahoga River to where the Portage Path connects to the Tuscarawas River. It includes Native American paths

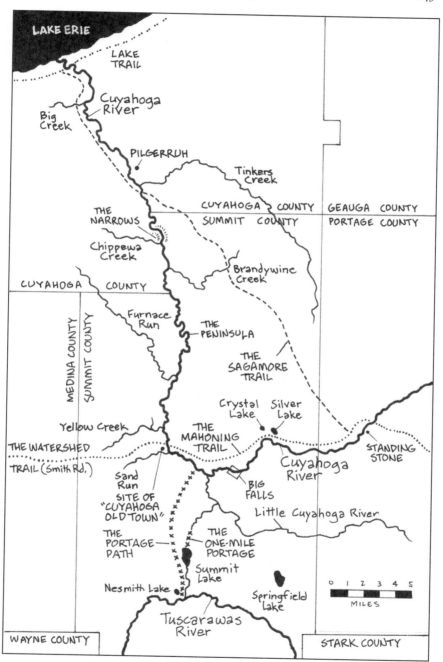

Major Indian Trails in the Cuyahoga Valley. *Map by Charles Ayers, 2022, adapted from original untitled map by Joe Jesensky, 1984*

and towns along with named streams, falls, and lakes. Jean Kainsinger's 2006 map reels us in even closer by depicting Native American trails that cross or became modern roads through Cuyahoga Valley National Park and Bedford Reservation of Cleveland Metroparks, with references to modern roads.[35]

One particular path is on Jesensky's map marked "Portage Path," denoting the "carrying place" where natives could transport canoes and belongings across the watershed divide between the navigable reaches of the Cuyahoga River and the navigable sections of the Tuscarawas River. A road and an elementary school are named after it, historical markers explain its significance, and thousands of cars drive its general route daily. Unlike the longer trails that connected distant points, such as the so-called Great Trail from Fort Pitt (today's Pittsburgh) to Detroit, the Portage Path was much shorter, only eight miles in low water and even shorter in high water. It was vital to the natives, as it was the shortest and best route for crossing the divide, allowing transport between Lake Erie and all points south to the Ohio River and beyond. But the Portage Path story is also an example of how Euro-American surveyors, land speculators, frontiersmen, and settlers adopted and adapted the native trails to their own purposes.

This portage is shown on a map as early as 1755, simply as "Portage 1 m." Later, in 1788, George Washington expressed interest in finding a passage from Lake Erie to the Ohio River and recognized that the Cuyahoga and Muskingum Rivers (the Tuscarawas River being part of the Muskingum) came closest together of all the rivers flowing north and south from the watershed divide. In 1796, Moravian missionary John Heckewelder also touted the advantages of the area, especially the Cuyahoga River, noting that boats could navigate upstream to just short of a major waterfall, at which point "there is the best prospect of Water communication from Lake Erie into the Ohio, by way of Cuyahoga & Muskingum Rivers; The carrying place being the shortest of all carrying places." He goes on to describe all the abundant resources which would be accessible to settlers—the fertile soils, vast stands of oaks, hickories, poplars, maples, and many others, and he describes the area around "old Cuyahoga Town" as being "a remarkable fine Situation for a Town." He was right—today's Portage Path road leads uphill to Akron from that very spot.[36]

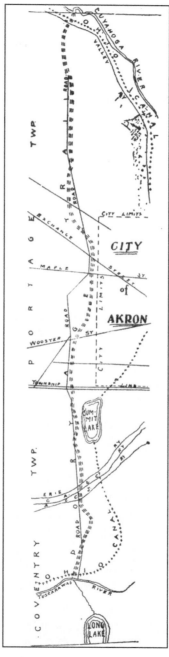

Portage Path in context by Arthur Butler Hulbert. *Ohio Archaeological and Historical Quarterly* 8, no. 3 (1900): 291. *Reprinted by permission from The Ohio History Connection*

One reason we can pinpoint so precisely the location of this particular Native American path is that it temporarily served as a portion of the boundary line between lands to the east, which were ceded by Native peoples to the United States, and lands to the west controlled by Native peoples, as per the 1785 Treaty of Fort McIntosh. Most Native Americans questioned the validity of this treaty, and continuing conflicts between white settlers and Native peoples led to the Treaty of Greenville, signed in 1795. That treaty also used the Portage Path as part of the boundary, the Greenville Treaty Line. Shortly thereafter the Connecticut Land Company's surveyors arrived, measuring and laying out parcels for private land speculators to sell to Easterners ready to migrate to what is now northeast Ohio. Because they could only survey lands east of the Greenville Treaty Line, surveyors needed to survey the Portage Path itself, and surveyor Moses Warren's 1797 survey notes exist yet today in the archives of the Western Reserve Historical Society.[37]

Over the years the path was used and altered, with roads eventually built upon and near it. As traces of it disappeared, several attempts were made to mark it accurately for history's sake. In 1911, Summit County Engineer Joseph Gehres drew a map of the Portage Path based on the survey, showing where modern roads were relative to the path. The 1936 *Atlas of the City of Akron* also showed the path superimposed on the modern street pattern within the city, the route of the path again based on historic surveys. Again in the 1950s, surveyors from the firm of Gehres & Kingsley located the north terminus of the trail. Then in the 1990s, historians and Akron leaders decided it was time to commemorate the 200th anniversary of Moses Warren's survey. Leading up to the 1997 commemoration, the Summit County Historical Society, the City of Akron, Summit Metro Parks, and others set out to mark the path using Warren's notes and previous investigations. To do so they employed the services of the land survey firm Campbell & Associates, Inc., of Cuyahoga Falls. Also, as part of the project, the north and south termini was marked with bronze statues and the entire path marked with bronze broad blade monuments, so anyone could trace the route Native Americans used prior to Euro-American settlement.[38]

The effort to mark the path was championed and funded by a private citizen, William S. Yeck of Dayton, Ohio, an Akron native who grew up along the path. On July 20, 1997, several events were held to celebrate the 200th anniversary of the survey, including a hike and bus tour along its path, dedication of the northern terminus and launching of the trail-marking project, and a Native American powwow in Akron. Several years later, in 2002, the modern survey was completed. Two bronze statues of an Indian lifting a bark canoe, created by Peter Jones, an artist and citizen of the Onondaga Tribe of western New York, now stand, one at the north terminus and one at the south, and the bronze monuments mark the path's route through Akron. The Portage Path also plays a prominent role in the more recent annual celebration of "North American First People's Day" in Akron.[39]

The commemoration of this path is both a tribute to the Native Americans who lived here in times past and an acknowledgment of how their paths were then used and adapted for the purposes of the dominant Euro-American culture swiftly developing the borderland. As George Washington and Heckewelder suggested, ultimately that very divide that the portage crossed would be traversed by water via the Ohio & Erie Canal. The Portage Path that once separated Native lands from those claimed by the United States only briefly held back the tide of western expansion.

Many of the references above provide extensive descriptions of the various Native American trails. However, our intent is to tell the story of the significance of the trails and the people who worked to document them and to touch on how current scholarship explores the differences between Native American and Euro-American cartography. These trails were traveled on foot, by horse, maybe along with carts or wagons, and eventually tractors, trucks, cars, buses and semis. Some say they were originally created by deer and bison (which may or not be the case). They were undoubtedly used by Native Americans for hunting and gathering, visiting, trade, exploration, conflict, and conflict resolution. They connected people and villages to one another, allowed for obtaining or trading of food resources such as game, fish and shellfish, and mineral resources like salt, flint, pipestone, clay pits, and hematite, and even more importantly, information necessary for their physical and spiritual existence. Their exact locations inevitably changed through time as they are the result of thousands of years of Native Americans' interactions with each other, animals and plants, tribal migration, forced relocations, and population shifts and lifestyle changes due to European contact in the form of explorers, missionaries, traders, settlers, soldiers, and us. At the same time evidence is being lost, we continue to refine our understanding of the significance of these early paths to earlier inhabitants and the part they played through history.

7 Indians in an Urban World

Federal Government Policy during the
1950s–70s and the Cleveland American
Indian Center

Lynn R. Metzger, revised and completed by Peg Bobel

Northeast Ohio is home to thousands of Native Americans living and working in communities large and small. These individuals and families, mostly first- or second-generation residents of Ohio, represent many different tribal affiliations. Their stories are unique, but all reflect on nationwide policies and programs emerging in the United States in the 1950s. To understand their stories, we first have to look back over two hundred years.[1]

While today there are no federally recognized Indian reservations in Ohio, there was a short period in Ohio when small, isolated groups of Native Americans lived in areas designated as "reserves" or "reservations," mostly in the northwest part of the state. In the first decades of Ohio statehood, from around 1807–1842, various treaties, acts of Congress, and executive orders governed cessions of land held by various tribes, at the same time noting areas "reserved" in which specific Native groups could remain. The reservation movement was in part an attempt to resolve the conflict between an increasing surge of white settlers and the Native people residing in the region. While seeking peace, assimilation of the Native population was one of its goals. For instance, historian Helen Hornbeck Tanner explains that in 1819 the US Congress "set up a 'civilization fund' expended through Protestant missionary programs," including, notably, for the Wyandot reservation at Upper Sandusky, Ohio. Tanner notes that when possible, treaties between the United States and Native Americans included provisions that promoted Christianity, the English language, and farming, all things practiced at Upper Sandusky and elsewhere.[2]

The Wyandot reservation and other reserves were but a prelude to the policy of complete removal of the Native groups in the late 1830s, and by 1842 the last of these "reserved" lands had also been ceded. By the mid-1800s, the few Native Americans who had remained in Ohio following years of conflict had been forced to move west, leaving the land in this region to the European settlers from the eastern states and new immigrants arriving from across the Atlantic.[3] The last Native people to leave Ohio were the Wyandot. By 1843 the Wyandot, who were mostly farmers, perhaps the most "assimilated" and politically savvy of the Native groups in Ohio, were forced to move to a reservation in Kansas, and so became the last Native Americans to leave as a group from Ohio. The Wyandot were forced to sell their Ohio lands at less than market value, an injustice that was not addressed until over a hundred years later in 1985 when the US government awarded Wyandot descendants $5.5 million in partial compensation.[4] They also deeded to the Methodist Church three acres on which sat the Methodists' mission church and cemetery, for protection of their house of worship and the place where many Wyandot were buried. In the fall of 2019, partly as "an act of repentance," the United Methodist Church formally returned ownership of the land, church, and a portion of the Old Mission Cemetery, to the Wyandotte Nation of Oklahoma. The Wyandotte hope to have the site protected through a trust arrangement with the US government and be recognized as a National Historic Landmark.[5]

The Native Americans who remained in Ohio after the mid-1800s were scattered and isolated, often in family groups, many of which had a combined Native and European heritage. By the early 1900s, since Northeast Ohio was close to the Allegany Seneca reservation in New York State, some Senecas and members of other Iroquois (Haudenosaunee) Confederacy tribes moved to nearby Ohio for industrial jobs. At the time, Akron and Cleveland industries were also actively recruiting laborers from West Virginia and Kentucky, resulting in the influx of workers who were of Cherokee descent. The Cherokee as a group had been forced by the United States government to move from the whole region of the southern Appalachians to Oklahoma in the 1838–39 mass migration now known as the Trail of Tears. Some Cherokee, however, had intermarried with other groups, largely Scots and Irish, who had settled in the Appalachian Mountains region. These Cherokee who moved to Northeast Ohio became the largest group of Native Americans to resettle in this region in the early 1900s.

The population of Native Americans in Northeast Ohio in the early twentieth century was therefore mixed and scattered, and the numbers of Native Americans in Ohio at the time is difficult to estimate or track. In the 1940 and 1950 population censuses, the census takers were asked to guess whether or not an individual was of Native American descent. Adding to the murkiness of census numbers, some individuals did not identify themselves as Indian, melting into the non-Native population, and the US Census Bureau did not ask individuals if they were Native American until 1960.[6]

By the late 1950s there was a new type of migration of Natives to the area that brought individuals and families from western reservations to the region. This was the result of the federal government's Bureau of Indian Affairs (BIA) program that came to be known simply as "Relocation." The program, also known as the Employment Assistance Program, operated from 1948 to 1970, relocating individuals from many different western tribes to certain host cities, including Cleveland, Ohio, where the migrants could find employment and improve their economic condition.[7] The migration to Cleveland eventually spread into neighboring cities where jobs could be found, such as Akron, Canton, Lorain, and Elyria.

The BIA's goals were to train individual Native Americans to be self-sufficient in an urban and industrial nation and assimilate them into the dominant white culture through that process. Relocation was an important program nationally and for this region. Many Native Americans who moved to urban areas in the Relocation program regard it with mixed feelings, and the policy is still considered controversial in the Native American community. Some felt it gave them opportunities well beyond the reservation while allowing them to still maintain tribal ties. Others felt the move to urban areas was very damaging to their cultural heritage. It was, however, a voluntary program that provided employment and ultimately helped to develop a sense of unity among members of different tribes, reinforcing a sense of Pan-Indian identity, which ironically was *not* a goal of the BIA.[8]

The background of Relocation explains not just the regional Native American population, but the national Indian scene and the resulting national Indian movements as well. The story begins in the late 1940s. During World War II, about twenty-five thousand Native Americans served in the military, and another forty thousand worked in war-related industries. The most famous military men were the Navajo Code Talkers, whose talents helped in the war against Japan. The Code Talkers developed a way for the US Marines to communicate in code based on the Navajo language. When the war was over, those working in war industries, just like many non-Native women, were told they no longer had jobs. The armed services veterans returning to the reservations were also unemployed. There was great poverty and few economic resources on the reservations, and to add to the economic stresses, the population's birth rate increased, as did that of the non-Native population. Most of the nation was busy with the post-war economic boom that was taking place elsewhere in the country and paid little or no attention to Indian reservations until the winter of 1947–48 when a catastrophic blizzard isolated the Navajo and Hopi reservations and people were starving. The terrible conditions were reported by the press, and subsequent public outcry pushed the government to immediately begin airlifting food to those vast and rugged reservations. This crisis brought the poverty of the reservations to the public eye and created pressure on the Bureau of Indian Affairs to provide more opportunity and assistance to the Native population.[9] (It should be noted that all tribal reservations have treaties with the federal government that stipulate government responsibilities to the tribes in compensation for taking their lands. The federal government is required to provide specific services for the tribes, under the direction of the BIA.)

Several programs designed mostly by non-Natives were supposed to help the reservation populations. The relocation program began by offering the opportunity for Navajo men and women to voluntarily move to Denver and enroll in job training programs. Not all of the training programs were considered very useful. For instance, many Native Americans were trained to reupholster furniture. The program was a starting point in alleviating some economic hardship; however, the BIA did not factor in the loneliness of the relocated Natives and cultural differences between the vast Navajo reservation and urban Denver. Even after many individuals returned to the reservation with few new skills, the BIA still decided to expand the program and changed the name to Employment Assistance Program. By 1963 the BIA had established offices in eight cities across the country, designating them "relocation cities." The cities chosen were believed to have high employment opportunities and were places where migrants could receive job training. In addition to Denver, the cities included Los Angeles, San José, and Oakland in California; Chicago, Illinois; Minneapolis, Minnesota; Dallas, Texas; and Cleveland, Ohio. Cleveland was the most eastern of the relocation cities and the farthest from the western reservations.[10]

The application process for the relocation program was at first fairly casual and simple: the individuals, at first mostly males, went to the BIA office on the reservation and applied to migrate or "go on relocation." They could choose their destination, and if there was an opening in the city of their choice, they were sent there. If not, they had to choose a city with an opening. Different factors played into choosing a city; for example, a mild climate and previously relocated friends or family were seen as advantages. California was a favorite destination, and Los Angeles, the most popular city, often ran out of available slots, while Chicago and Cleveland often had openings. Tribal background also affected the choice of city. Some Native Americans were willing to relocate far from the reservation, while others preferred to maintain closer contact with the reservation. Navajos relocated throughout the country, while Chippewa preferred the Midwest cities of Chicago and Minneapolis. Cherokee migrated throughout the country as well, and were the most represented in the initial wave of migration to Cleveland.[11]

Once the relocation city was chosen, the BIA assisted the applicant by arranging transportation, usually by bus, assigning housing in the receiving city, and shipping household goods. The applicant was then enrolled in a training program or placed in a job. After about a month, there was very little help from the BIA, as it was assumed the applicants could make it on their own in their new location. In retrospect, some administrators of the program, like Bob Delaware, administrator of the BIA's Employment Assistance Program in Washington, DC, felt they could have done things differently. When interviewed in the 1980s about the program, Delaware commented, "We did a few things backwards in the big relocation years. We should have screened the applicants better and we should have offered them more training on how to live in the city."[12]

The number of individuals who went on relocation is difficult to determine, partly because many went more than once. For example, an Apache tribal member told of relocating first to Los Angeles, then returning to the reservation for a period, then relocating to Cleveland. He ended up relocating three times, going back to the reservation for some months in between. In his case he also held the same job in both areas each time. Compounding the problem, the BIA was inconsistent in reporting movements of Native Americans from area offices to field offices, and researchers have found that some statistics simply do not match. One BIA record noted a number of people who left their homes in 1967 and apparently never arrived at their destinations. Elaine Neils, who wrote a study on the migration, commented, "One sadly wonders what happened to 296 persons who left their home area for direct employment in 1967 and never arrived at a destination; apparently three families with 117 children among them were lost along the way."[13]

The first Native Americans who were relocated to Cleveland in the program arrived in 1958 under the direct employment provision of the Employment Assistance Program.[14] This first group consisted of 62 individuals and 139 accompanying family members. In 1959, 191 individuals came via the direct employment provision and 36 through the adult vocational training program. From 1958 through 1971, a total of 4,150 Native Americans were relocated to Cleveland through both arms of the program. At the peak of the program these individuals represented thirty-three different tribes. But that is only part of the migrant story. Because Cleveland, Akron, and other regional cities had employment opportunities and fairly good wages to offer, many of the relocated natives wrote or called siblings and other relatives, urging them to come to Cleveland to join them. The first to relocate were usually the younger men and women, many who had had work experience in the military or off the reservation, after which their relatives and young families followed. Often called the "piggyback" effect, many researchers believe it accounted for more Natives moving to the area than those who came just via the official relocation program.[15]

In Cleveland and other cities in Northeast Ohio, relocation provided training and jobs. For example, initially many men were trained as welders and worked in the automotive parts industries, and women were trained as nurses' aides and hairdressers. Early on in the program a number of Natives were employed at American Greetings Co., some as artists. Since the goal for the relocated Native Americans was for them to assimilate into the wider population, there were no social support systems offered once they reached the host city, and they found that they had to negotiate the urban scene on their own. To complicate matters, sometimes the relocated Native Americans were caught in a Catch-22: they were denied services by local social service agencies on the grounds that their special status under the BIA and other federal services made them ineligible.[16]

Living in the urban area was dramatically different from reservation life and was often difficult and lonely for the newcomers. The population of Native Americans in Cleveland, at its peak, was about five thousand, but this was still a small minority within the overall population. As the number of newcomers grew there evolved social gathering places, the first of these being known as "Indian Bars," places where the men gathered after work. There were also informal bowling and softball teams. The BIA initially settled the relocatees on the near east side, the center of the urban African American population. Many western Indians had rarely seen African Americans, which heightened the tension of adjusting to urban life. This situation led some to associate their adjustment problems with the presence of urban African Americans in that area. As more women began to arrive and families grew larger, the newcomers began to move from the near east side to the near west side in the Lorain, Detroit, and Denison Road areas, in neighborhoods that tended to be ethnically mixed. There, Native Americans founded a new gathering center, a concrete sign that they were creating their own community without ties to the federal government or the BIA.[17]

The Cleveland American Indian Center (CAIC) first began in the basement of St. Johns Episcopal Church, with an $18,000 grant from the Council of Economic Opportunities of Greater Cleveland. The development of this center was rooted in national Indian politics of the time as well as the social reform mood of President Lyndon Johnson's War on Poverty. The center's founding director was Russell Means, who served as director from 1969 to 1972. Means was a dynamic director, whose later political activities brought him into the national spotlight. Means had a degree in accounting from Arizona State University and was working as an accountant for Cleveland's Council of Economic Opportunities when he and Sarge Old Horn, along with other members of a small informal Indian club, began working on a project that led to the incorporation of the Indian Center on April 28, 1969. Means also founded the second chapter of the American Indian Movement (AIM) in Cleveland and traveled and spoke widely on behalf of Indian issues. His political activities drew the Cleveland Indian community into awareness of and participation in national Indian issues, but before Means moved on to the national limelight he helped to establish the CAIC as a public voice for Native Americans living in the area.[18]

Means was also highly aware of how white society appropriates Native American terms and symbols. He found the use of Chief Wahoo, a grinning caricature with exaggerated features and a single feather, to be especially demeaning. To Means, this distorted caricature of a Native American degraded all Native Americans and reinforced the public's stilted view of Native Americans as relics of the past. While at the CAIC, Means filed a $9 million lawsuit against the Cleveland Indians to protest the Chief Wahoo logo. Years passed without settlement as attorneys for the baseball team succeeded in stalling the case. It was settled quietly in 1985 for $35,000 and a slightly modified Chief Wahoo, but advocates kept the issue in the public's awareness for the following decades, prompting vigorous debate between those wanting to abolish what they viewed as a racist logo and those wishing to keep it. After much public and private debate, in 2018 the Cleveland Indians owners and the commissioner of Major League Baseball announced their decision to abandon the logo on uniforms beginning in the 2019 season, and then in 2020 the team's owner Paul Dolan announced the team would drop the name "Indians." In 2021 Dolan announced the team's new name: "The Guardians."[19]

The first years of the Cleveland American Indian Center witnessed considerable turmoil as the Native American population grew and the center struggled to represent multiple different tribes with different cultural practices. The center's primary mission was to assist Native Americans in adapting to the urban setting, but it also represented them in the larger political and social arena, often in contrast to the assimilation goals of the BIA. At first the center provided help with basic needs of the relocatees: used clothing, food, and advice on all matters of urban living. Relocation was difficult for most arrivals, as most had little experience of off-reservation life or life in a large city.

Since policies regarding Native Americans are always tied to the attitudes and climate of the national government and public opinion, Native groups across the country and in urban areas were affected and influenced by the great social change wrought during the 1960s. As more federal funds were poured into President Johnson's War on Poverty various federal departments created "Indian desks," or special segments of departments assigned to include Native American populations as never before. The emphasis was largely on education, employment, and health. The Cleveland American Indian Center was able to secure funding to sponsor many different kinds of programs in the above areas, but they also chose to sponsor educational and community outreach programs to reinforce American Indian cultural concepts.[20]

Herbert Johnson followed Russell Means as director of the CAIC, and in 1972 he explained the center's programs in a letter to a non-Native attorney:

> You asked me about the Indian people and if we were separatists. I shall try to explain. The Indian is torn between the white society and the Indian lifestyle he has been brought up in. The youth especially suffers because he is being taught to get into the mainstream of society, but at the same time he isn't being accepted. From the beginning of U. S. history, whiteman has tried and made it difficult for us to continue to live as Indians. Whiteman has taken away our means of living as Indians, giving us a different choice—to live like a whiteman, or not at all. But we still refuse. It is discourteous and aggressive and not good Indian behavior if we come out and tell you that we cannot and will not be like you. Just within the past three years we have been getting recognition as Indian people. People in Cleveland and surrounding Ohio cities are becoming aware of Indians in Ohio and Cleveland.[21]

The CAIC was not alone in sponsoring programs to lead to greater cultural awareness for the public: similar centers existed in cities across the nation. The center played a part in a national movement generated by Native Americans themselves to collaborate and recognize their heritage beyond their tribal identifications. The movement encompassed recognition of a shared heritage, fundamental Native values, centuries of oppression, and the knowledge that by working together they could improve their lives. Some of this drive was a product of education, with more Native Americans completing high school, college, and specialty schools. This Pan-Indian movement embraced a wider worldview and a new strategy for survival and growth based on one Native American ethnic group comprised of many tribal peoples.[22]

Ironically, most of the early work done via the Native American centers was the result of government programs designed to help Native Americans assimilate into mainstream American society, not to preserve Native American culture. But these Native communities were also caught up in the vast cultural changes of the 1970s, and the Red Power movement evolved along with the Civil Rights movement. Cleveland's Native American community continued to follow Russell Means's activities after he left the leadership of the CAIC. He traveled extensively, advocating on behalf of American Indian causes, and was involved in two major confrontations between Native Americans and the federal government: the Trail of Broken Treaties and takeover of the Bureau of Indian Affairs building in Washington, DC, in November 1972, at which time the Native Americans presented a twenty-point solution paper to President Nixon, and the confrontation at Wounded Knee, South Dakota, on February 27, 1973. Means's activism nationally tied the local Native American community more closely to the American Indian Movement and nationwide issues. Even if some in the local Native American community disagreed with his actions or speeches, they nonetheless found him exciting and his ideas challenging.[23]

Cleveland, by way of its location, was a convenient stopping point on the route between politically active South Dakota tribes and tribal protestors' destination of Washington, DC. As a result, protestors heading to DC often spent time in Cleveland, and the CAIC sponsored dinners for the travelers and the center's community. As a result, many Cleveland Natives joined in the national protests, such as the occupation of the Washington, DC, Bureau of Indian Affairs building noted above, the 1970 protests at Plymouth Rock, and the Longest Walk, a five-month-long march from San Francisco to Washington, DC, in 1978 to protest and successfully defeat proposed legislation calling for the abrogation of treaties.[24]

Locally, many Natives and non-Natives did not agree with Russell Means's negotiated settlement with the Cleveland Indians regarding the use of the Chief Wahoo logo, continuing to protest the symbol, but such actions did not help bolster the credibility of the CAIC and its leadership in the greater Cleveland community. Even more damaging to the center's position in the community was the notorious Moses Cleaveland affair. In 1971, Clevelanders were planning a reenactment of the landing of Moses Cleaveland at the mouth of the Cuyahoga River as part of its 175th anniversary. In an example of white ignorance or insensitivity, the CAIC was "invited to attend dressed in dance and warrior garb." The center's members did participate, but not as the event planners anticipated. As the Cleaveland boat approached the shore it was met by a boat containing a number of Native Americans from the CAIC, led by Dennis Bowan, the youth director at the center. The costumed Native Americans told the landing party that they could not land because this land belonged to the Natives. This was not met well by the officials and organizers of the event, resulting in anger, scuffling, and arrests. From the Native perspective, the celebration was an opportunity to remind the public that Native Americans had occupied this land long before Europeans arrived. Opinions reflected in the newspapers, however, criticized the CAIC group as "overfed warriors and loud mouth clowns."[25]

Over time, protests and lawsuits have led to many changes in Native American status. The return of some lands, protection of religious freedom, protection of sacred sites and burials, and permission to operate casinos are all results of political activism. In addition, such activism continues to reinforce Native American identity on both the regional and national scale. More recent protests concern a range of environmental, economic, human rights, and social issues. In the twenty-first century, protests continue regarding natural gas pipeline projects, development projects, mining on tribal lands and land with spiritual and cultural significance, and the persistence of culturally offensive sports team names.

By the 1970s, the Cleveland center, then directed by Jerome Warcloud, sponsored many social, cultural, and educational programs using the available federal funding for urban poverty relief and outreach programs. From a study the center conducted in the mid-1970s, staff identified four major problems within the community and tailored services to address them. These challenges included a high rate of unemployment, poor housing, high incidence of health problems, and educational deficiencies in the children.[26]

The education programs were aimed at both the Native community and the wider community. Many cultural values bumped into the expectations of the school systems at all levels. One of the hardest issues for the youth was being taunted as a "wahoo." Many tribal values, such as not responding in class and trying not to stand out, along with enduring poverty, often pushed the young members of the community to the fringes of their classes and schools. Many parents worked with the school systems to improve attitudes, especially for the teachers. Still, for the parents the public schools were a vast change from the boarding schools that many had attended, where students were forbidden to speak the tribal language, were forced to cut their hair, wear non-Native clothes, and learn primarily manual labor skills. By this time, many schools on the reservations were controlled by the tribe, and in at least one instance, some Cleveland youth were sent to South Dakota to attend high school, a reverse practice in one generation.[27]

The youth programs of the CAIC, besides sports, outings, and classes, included two multi-day cultural road trips. In 1979 and 1980 center staff took youth to the Plains states and to Sioux Indian reservations—Cheyenne River, Pine Ridge, and Rosebud. There the young people camped, participated in powwows, met activists in the American Indian Movement, and visited sites associated with significant historical events, such as the Wounded Knee cemetery at Pine Ridge. The impact of the trips was deep. From being a minority in Cleveland the youth were now among their own, where "Indianess" did not separate them from the dominant culture but was the lived reality of the people on the reservations. At the same time, they saw first-hand the economic poverty and isolation of the reservations. Those experiences reaffirmed their unity as an exploited minority with a unique history.[28]

The center also sought to serve the spiritual aspects of the Native American community, using posters, poems, and gatherings to support "the Indian way" and to recognize oneness with Mother Earth and each other. Gatherings were held at a lake near Ravenna, Ohio, to help renew the spirit of the community, heal conflict, and reinforce community bonds and cultural identity. These gatherings usually included ritual ceremonies, prayer, and instruction in Native American spiritual ideas.[29]

The CAIC managed to stretch its nonprofit funds well into the 1980s, shrinking programs as the Reagan administration began to cut funding for urban programs. By the early 1990s the center's work began to focus more on cultural programs. In addition to there being less funding available, the need was no longer as great for social services: many of the early relocated Native Americans understood the urban and government system or had retired and moved back home to the reservation, rejoining their fellow tribespeople and contributing their skills to tribal life. The younger generation became bicultural—more comfortable in the non-Native world but still very much involved in Indian cultural affairs. They became truly pan-Indian, participating in cultural events such as powwows around the region and nationally.

Although Cleveland had the first Indian center in the Northeast Ohio region, the CAIC established an outreach center in Akron in 1975, served by the Cleveland center's Robert Hosick. By 1978, Hosick created his own separate center in Akron, the North American Indian Cultural Center (NAICC). Robert Hosick was born in Cordova, Alaska, and had never lived on a reservation. His mother was Tlingit and his father Scottish, so he grew up bridging the two cultures. Robert served in World War II and moved to Akron around 1950. While he was serving as a job counselor for the Cleveland center, he also ran a privately owned craft shop and cultural center in Cuyahoga Falls and was generally more active within the white community than the director at the Cleveland center was. A third center opened in Ohio in Xenia at the same time that the Akron center opened, and there was competition and some conflict as the various centers vied for funding.[30]

The initial funding for the NAICC came via a federal grant of $110,000, a Comprehensive Employment and Training Act (CETA) grant, and the center was to serve the needs of American Indians in a thirty-county area. With the Xenia center serving fifty-three counties, and the Akron center serving thirty, that left only five counties for the Cleveland office to serve, dramatically decreasing their funding. In Akron, Hosick oversaw the program aimed at placing 250 unemployed Native Americans into jobs within the first year of the funding. The 1970 census showed 6,654 American Indians in Ohio, but Hosick and others estimated the number was probably higher. He was keenly aware of the hesitancy among some Natives to identify themselves as American Indian, and believed, as he stated in a newspaper interview in 1978, that "It's important to know who you are, and once you know that, it's easier to live." Hosick had already had experience in placing American Indians into jobs, but found that job retention was a challenge. As he said in the same interview in 1978, "Indians are not used to going by the clock." Along with employment services, the NAICC also provided cultural programs, youth activities, referral services, and emergency food and clothing.[31]

After Robert Hosick's death in 1985 his son H. Clark Hosick took over as director of the North American Indian Cultural Center in Akron. The younger Hosick, a Vietnam War veteran, expanded the scope of programs at the center and became involved in outreach activities at the state level. He spent many years educating the non-Native population about legal issues such as The Indian Child Welfare Act of 1978 that regulates adoptions from reservations, the Indian Gaming Regulatory Act of 1988 that regulates gaming (casinos) on American Indian land, and the American Indian Religious Freedom Act, signed into law by President Jimmy Carter in 1978.[32] The American Indian Religious Freedom Act legalizes traditional practices and ceremonies, overturning laws that had banned American Indian spiritual practices. Unfortunately, the Religious Freedom Act passed without penalty provisions.

The Akron center continued to receive US Department of Labor grants for job training and placement and over the years expanded its services to include non-Native low-income people. By 1986 it had also expanded into other arenas of activity. With the national push for energy conservation during the 1980s, the center was able to secure large federal grants for home weatherization for low-income clients. Both the Cleveland and Akron centers were active in the home weatherization program, which provided jobs for American Indians and other low-income applicants while providing much-needed weatherization on older, non-insulated housing. Over a period of about five years of the weatherization program the center added insulation and made repairs to more than 2,500 homes in Summit County alone.[33]

In Cleveland, the Housing Resource Center, founded by Jim LaRue and two partners, advised and trained others on rehabilitating older houses, including installing plumbing and insulation. Their resource center was on W. 48th Street, near where many of the relocated Native Americans were living in the late 1970s and early '80s. The Native Americans tended to live in an area around W. 65th Street and north towards Lake Erie. Through the Housing Resource Center, LaRue and others consulted with and trained people on techniques for rehabbing houses, and began a tool loan program, often working in conjunction with the Native Americans in the weatherization job-training program, as well as helping to rehabilitate the housing in the Native American neighborhood.[34]

Besides the Native American cultural centers in Cleveland and Akron, other field offices or services sprang up in outlying counties. In 1978 the Akron center opened an office in Canton, but soon moved it to Youngstown, believing the Canton office was too close to the Akron center. In 1979, William Kennedy Jr., and his brother Sam opened the Allegheny Nation Indian Center in Canton, run mainly by the Kennedys and volunteers. That center aimed to assist American Indians in Stark County with a hot meal program, clothing and household goods, and drug, alcohol, and legal counseling. The Akron center gave some financial assistance to the Canton organization and also cooperated on efforts to find jobs for clients of the center.[35]

In addition to social services, Clark Hosick and others engaged in issues in the region that affected Native Americans. On several occasions they became involved in instances where they believed precontact Native American sites were being desecrated or destroyed. In 1988, Clark Hosick and Mel Fletcher, a counselor at the NAICC, decried the plan to excavate soil from a known precontact site in Independence to be used as cover soil on a proposed landfill. The site (South Park) had been included within the boundaries of Cuyahoga Valley National Park and as news of the landfill proposal spread, a major fight ensued between the private landowner and those opposing the landfill. Much of the opposition was simply against having a major landfill within the national park, while separately, but related, others sought for protection of the precontact site. In visiting the site, Fletcher discovered that it had already been looted over the years by pothunters seeking artifacts, and in fact it may be the most looted site in Cuyahoga Valley National Park. Archaeological investigations from as early as 1930, and later salvage excavations conducted by the Cleveland Museum of Natural History in the early 1980s confirmed the site to be a significant Whittlesey Tradition village site. Although it is believed that the site is essentially destroyed by past activities, it is still regarded as needing protection. In 1995, the site's private owner granted the National Park Service a preservation easement over what remains of the original site. Additionally, a marker on the Ohio & Erie Canal Towpath Trail describes the significance of the site.[36]

In the late 1970s, the North American Indian Cultural Center also petitioned the federal government to create a center, or reservation, in Northeast Ohio, a designated place for local American Indians to gather and celebrate their culture. The group was looking for two hundred or more acres and eyed both the newly created Cuyahoga Valley National Recreation Area (now named Cuyahoga Valley National Park) and the Ravenna Arsenal, a closed complex that manufactured shells and bombs during World War II. Much of the arsenal land is still considered environmentally contaminated. Although there was some interest in, and sympathy with, the desire to create a reservation, the American Indians' efforts were unsuccessful.[37]

Overall, reviews of the success of the BIA's relocation, job training, and employment programs and policies remain mixed. In the late 1960s American Indians in the relocation program had the opportunity to critique the BIA's policies during hearings held by the National Council on Indian Opportunity in several US cities. The hearings identified a number of problems that included a lack of adequate orientation when relocating from reservation to city, cultural barriers, and low quality of work opportunities, issues also encountered by those arriving in Cleveland. Bucking the BIA's goal of assimilation, American Indians in the cities to some degree maintained their cultural roots and identities while adjusting to city life.

National Park Service wayside of South Park on the Ohio & Erie Canal Towpath Trail, Cuyahoga Valley National Park. *Photo by Charlotte Gintert/Captured Glimpses Photography*

While the economic and social effects of Relocation can be debated, one clear result was the dispersal of Native Americans from western reservations to locations across the United States. This diaspora is illustrated by the 2010 US Census, which notes that the top ten places with the highest number of individuals identifying as American Indian and Alaska Native (alone or in combination with one or more other races) were cities that ranged from the East Coast to California, with New York City having the largest number and Los Angeles the second largest. Cleveland is not on the top-ten list, but Chicago, another of the relocation cities, ranks number eight. Of the overall population identifying as American Indian or Alaska Native, 78 percent lived outside American Indian or Alaska Native areas (federal reservations, off-reservation trust lands, etc.). Even of those identifying as only American Indian or Alaska Native (not combined with other races), 67 percent lived outside Native areas.[38]

The 2020 population census reports that in Ohio 234,389 persons identified as American Indian or Alaska Native alone or in combination with other races making up 2 percent of Ohio's total population.

To meet the needs of Native Americans in Northeast Ohio, some of the local assistance and advocacy programs that began in the 1950s have continued in one form or another, administered by small nonprofits. In addition, cultural events such as First Peoples days, powwows, and educational events elsewhere in the state continue the efforts to combat racist stereotypes and accurately present and interpret Native American values and culture to the majority non-Native population.

8 White Visions of "Red Men"

Native Americans in Northeast Ohio Memory

Kevin F. Kern

In the early 1900s, the Saranac Tribe, Number 141 of The Improved Order of Red Men (IORM), met on Tuesdays at its "Wigwam" in Wilcox Hall at 130 South Main Street in Akron (This was also the "Teepee" of its women's auxiliary, The Degree of Pocahontas, Ogarita Tribe No. 29, which met on alternate Thursdays).[1] One of the many fraternal organizations that proliferated in the United States in the 1800s, the IORM claimed to trace its origin to the Sons of Liberty, who famously dressed as "Indians" when they staged the Boston Tea Party. The group appropriated Indigenous terminology for its organization and ceremonialism. Each chapter was a "Tribe" presided over by a "Sachem," and members ascended through the degrees of "Adoption," "Warrior," and "Chief." The state-level organization was called the "Reservation" headed by a "Great Sachem," and the National Organization was the "Great Council of the United States" headed by such officers as the "Great Incohonee," the "Great Senior Sagamore," and the "Great Keeper of the Wampum." National Councils were held every "Great Sun" (annually) during the "Corn Moon" (September). At its peak, the organization boasted more than half a million members, including presidents Warren Harding and Theodore Roosevelt. However, none of those members actually were Indians—the Improved Order of Red Men restricted its membership to whites until 1974.

The case of Akron's Saranac Tribe illustrates the problematic way Northeast Ohioans and the larger American society have chosen to perceive and remember American Indians. A fascination with Native Americans has pervaded Euro-American culture since its earliest days, yet throughout US history white Americans have persisted in seeing them through various cultural lenses: envisioning them variously as "mysterious forebears," "uncivilized barbarians," a "disappearing race," "noble savages," or often some combination of these (and other) stereotypes. The ways in which American society has appropriated Native Americans and their cultures (a phenomenon that historian Robert Berkhofer Jr. called "The White Man's Indian") has in many ways helped to define American national identity. In this sense, these memories say much more about the non-Natives of Northeast Ohio than they say about the Native Americans themselves.[2]

One early conception related to the Native American heritage of the area was the trope of the "mysterious forebears." As Europeans began to venture past the Appalachian Mountains into the Ohio River Valley, they encountered evidence of ancient constructions—mounds and earthworks—that seemed to be unrelated to any current Indigenous group. One of the earliest Europeans to comment on these was David Zeisberger, a Moravian missionary. On his way to establish a mission among the Lenape in 1772, he became the first European to comment on the ancient earthworks of Ohio Indigenous people:

> Long ago, perhaps more than a century ago, Indians must have lived here who fortified themselves against the attacks of their enemies. The ramparts are still plainly to be seen. We found three forts in a distance of a couple of miles. The whole town must have been fortified, but the site is now covered with a thick wood. No one knows to what nation these Indians belonged. It is plain, however, that they were a warlike race.[3]

Zeisberger's (incorrect) assumption that the earthworks were fortifications is understandable, given their similarity to the kinds of earthen fortifications and breastworks common in Europe. Yet his assumption betrays an inherent belief that the "mysterious forebears" of Ohio's Indigenous people were warlike, a characteristic frequently attributed to the Native Americans of the time.

Zeisberger was right in one important respect, though: Indigenous people built these earthworks. The same cannot be said of many later writers. Most observers of the late eighteenth and early nineteenth centuries

"Improved Order of Red Men" ribbon.
*Illustration by Charles Ayers, based on
historic photograph.*

attributed these large and complex earthworks to anyone *but* the ancestors of the Native people they knew. Various writers suggested that the
Marietta Earthworks, for example, were the products of the Toltecs of
Central America, the ancient Scythians of Asia, or even the Spaniard
Hernando DeSoto's expedition of the 1540s. Even Ephraim Squier and
Edwin Davis—whose epic 1848 work *Ancient Monuments of the Mississippi Valley* became the definitive work on the subject until superseded
by later, more scientific excavations—favored a theory that the mound
builders represented "a state of society essentially different from that of
the modern race of Indians north of the tropic," drawing ties to groups
in Central and South America and referring to them as "an extinct race."⁴

In Northeast Ohio, this trope persisted for many years through the
(mis)interpretation of sites like "Fort Island." This glacially formed hill
rising from a once-swampy area in present-day Fairlawn drew speculation
regarding its ties to precontact peoples from the earliest days of Akron's
history. General Lucius Bierce, one of Akron's early mayors and the author

Mound at Marietta.   *1847.*

The Mound at Marietta. *Illustration by Henry Howe,* Historical Collections of Ohio in Two Volumes, *Vol. 11 (Ohio, 1896), 791*

of the earliest history of Akron and Summit County, was the first to write that this site was a fortification, suggesting that it and nearby Beech Island were defensive works built by the "mysterious moundbuilder race" against the threat posed by the ancestors of present-day Native Americans.[5]

Over the following decades, subsequent writers transformed and elaborated upon Bierce's conjecture. In the 1870s, famed local geologist and amateur archaeologist Charles Whittlesey attributed Cuyahoga Valley earthworks to the poorly understood Erie tribe, and by the early twentieth century the legend accordingly had changed to a dramatic and tragic denouement of the Beaver Wars of the mid-1600s. These battles between the powerful Iroquois (also known as Haudenosaunee) Confederacy and other Great Lakes groups for supremacy in the fur trade happened after European settlement on the continent but before there were any European eyewitness accounts of the region, leaving the particulars of the conflict ripe for speculation. Thus, according to local lore, a remnant of the Erie group that was defeated on the eastern edge of Lake Erie fled to this natural hill surrounded by an impassable swamp, then dug a ditch and threw up a palisade around its perimeter for further protection. Finding these

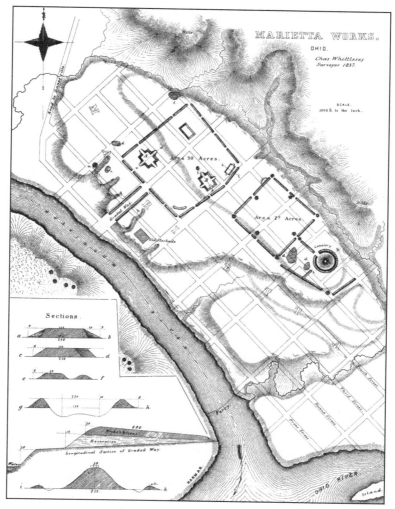

Marietta Works. *E. G. Squier and E. H. Davis,* Ancient Monuments of the Mississippi Valley, 1847. *Edited and with an introduction by David J. Meltzer (Smithsonian Institution, 1998), Plate XXVI following p. 72*

refugees in an unassailable position, the Iroquois waited patiently until the swamp froze in winter to cross the natural moat and overwhelm the outnumbered Erie defenders, making this site the "Last Stand of the Erie."[6]

A point of pride among local residents, Fort Island became a field trip destination for generations of schoolchildren and the namesake of a local primary school. The "last stand" legend—not too different from the doomed "mysterious forebears" narrative of the presumed "moundbuilder race"—continued to be repeated in various publications and even sanctioned by local historical authorities. When the Summit County Historical Society published a study of the legend in 1958, its author could find no documentable or published evidence of the story before 1921. Yet this fairly thorough study still equivocated at the end, saying that the "last stand" theory for the site was "entirely plausible and possible." Even when renowned Ohio archaeologist Raymond Baby pronounced in the early 1960s that the site was of Late Woodland vintage (roughly 1,500 to 1,000 years ago), a reprint of the pamphlet added that this new evidence did not "preclude the fact that a remnant of the Eries, in one of their last-ditch stands against the Senecas later, may have strengthened it with palisades..."[7] Thus the legend continued until the late twentieth century, when scientific investigations revealed that it was almost entirely incorrect.

Despite decades of archaeological investigations in the region, there is no evidence at all that the Erie resided anywhere farther west than what is now Erie, Pennsylvania. Archaeological surveys of Fort Island in 1988 and 1989 only supported this conclusion—archaeologists found few artifacts, and none at all from the period of the Beaver Wars. In fact, radiocarbon dates from the site (c. 1050–1375 CE) fell into the early Late Precontact Period, hundreds of years earlier than the Beaver Wars and hundreds of years later than the Adena and Hopewell moundbuilding groups. Beyond this site in particular, decades of excavations throughout Ohio and surrounding regions have revealed that Late Woodland and Late Precontact peoples routinely placed palisades around villages, encampments, and sacred spaces, making the "fortifications" of this particular site less unusual that they may have seemed when early observers first described the site. Even the idea that any group used this site as a settlement is suspect—the dearth of artifacts suggests that the mound was not used as a habitation for any significant length of time by the Erie or anyone else. While the Fairlawn Parks and Recreation department has officially recognized that the story is a legend, the site is still called Fort Island.[8]

Related to the "mysterious forebears" concept, the "uncivilized barbarian" trope was also common throughout much of early Colonial and US history, perpetuated by numerous tales of conflicts between white American settlers and Indigenous Americans and by "captivity narratives"—one of the most popular types of American literature in the eighteenth and early nineteenth centuries. These were the accounts of settlers who had been captured and held by native groups for various lengths of time, who later described what happened during their captivity, often in lurid detail. Such memoirs and biographies routinely portray the American Indian captors as barbaric and dangerous, and/or desirous of pressuring captives to abandon their "civilized" upbringing and conform to (presumably inferior) Indigenous culture—disparagingly referred to as "going native."

Several legendary figures in Northeast Ohio history reflect the "uncivilized barbarian" memory of local Native groups. Probably the most famous captive associated with the area is Mary Campbell, a young girl captured in Pennsylvania by Lenape and held for several years in what is now Ohio during the so-called French and Indian War of the 1750s–1760s. Although by most accounts the Lenape treated Campbell well and adopted her into a family, the memory of her experience reflected the idea of "going native"— by some accounts she was so thoroughly assimilated upon her return at the end of the war that her own parents did not even recognize her at first. Described in a number of early accounts of the area, she spawned enough local interest to achieve posthumous fame as "The first white child on the Western Reserve."[9]

Summit Metro Park's Gorge Metro Park is the location of the "Mary Campbell Cave," a place where local legend holds that Lenape held Mary Campbell for a while during her captivity, and where the local chapter of the Mary Campbell Society Children of the American Revolution dedicated a plaque to her in 1934. Formerly known as Old Maid's Kitchen, the rock shelter was officially renamed Mary Campbell Cave only in 1935; and like the Fort Island legend, generations of local schoolchildren learned the Mary Campbell Cave story. Also like the Fort Island legend, though, there is little to no substance to it. No contemporaneous written evidence exists linking Campbell to this particular rock shelter, and an archaeological excavation in 2019 did not turn up any material evidence, either. In 2019, Summit Metro Parks changed the name of the familiar landmark back to Old Maid's Kitchen.[10]

The barbaric or savage image of Ohio Indigenous groups was often perpetuated through stories and legends about early white Americans. One

Postcard of Old Maid's Kitchen, c. 1910

of the area's most noted—and notorious—Indian fighters of the late 1700s was Captain Samuel Brady. A Revolutionary War officer from Pennsylvania, Brady left his mark on Northeast Ohio through his exploits fighting in the American Revolution and beyond. An often-told story focused on Brady's near-miraculous 1780 escape from his capture by Indians— usually described as "blood-thirsty" and/or "savage." Chased to the edge of a gorge overlooking the Cuyahoga River in what is now Kent, Brady claimed to have leaped the twenty-two-foot gap (now much wider), buying himself time to find a hiding place while his pursuers were forced to take an alternate route. He survived by submerging himself in a nearby small lake and breathing through a reed while his captors searched for him. Local residents memorialized him in a number of ways: Brady's Leap is the name of a park in Kent; and the lake where he hid is called Brady Lake, as was the nearby village. The Brady's Leap Ohio Turnpike Service Plaza stands at mile 197, quite some distance from the spot of the episode. For many years, Captain Brady's was a popular café at the corner of Main and Lincoln Streets just across from the Kent State University campus.[11]

A local hero for as long as the trope was popular, Brady and his memory have not fared well in recent years. Historiographical and cultural changes have tempered the previously uncritical images of Captain Brady and other famous Indian fighters. An examination of what prompted the celebrated leap reveals that Brady—driven by vengeance for family members killed while fighting Native Americans—had sworn "never to be at peace with Indians" and had only recently led his Rangers in an ambush that killed a Sandusky band before a retaliatory expedition captured him. He unapologetically continued to kill Native Americans well after the war was over, even boasting about it during a trial for the murder of twelve Lenape in 1791 by laying their scalps on the bar and saying simply, "There they are, I killed them" (the jury made up of frontiersmen acquitted him, charging him only with court costs). By the late twentieth century some residents of the area began to question the heroic status of a man who committed atrocities on Natives who were defending their homeland against invaders like Brady. In this way the "uncivilized barbarian" trope was turned on its head, with Brady now filling the role. His mark on the landscape has begun to fade. Citizens of Brady Lake voted to dissolve the village in 2017. Captain Brady's restaurant in Kent for a while renamed itself as just "Brady's Café" in part to avoid the stigma. Today, not even the Brady name survives there—in the early 2000s the location became a Starbucks, and as of this writing it is the Cleveland Bagel Cafe.[12]

Even as the "uncivilized barbarian" image was still very much in vogue in the nineteenth century, a new image of the American Indian began to emerge. The "vanishing American"—the idea that Native Americans were fated for extinction—is a trope that began in the early 1800s, promoted in such works as the popular play *Metamora; or, The Last of the Wampanoags* and James Fenimore Cooper's *The Last of the Mohicans*. This idea flourished during the late 1800s and early 1900s in the wake of a couple of different trends of the period. First, the decades-long series of conflicts between Indigenous people and the US government for control of Western lands was drawing to a close, and the government placed nearly all remaining Native American groups of the West into reservations. Here they suffered from deprivation, malnutrition, and disease, which decimated their populations. At the same time, the idea of "Social Darwinism" was becoming more popular, positing that there were superior and inferior groups of humans, and that the superior groups were bound—by scientific principle—to prevail. As noted clergyman Josiah Strong wrote in 1885, the world was entering a new stage of its history—*the final competition of races, for which the Anglo-Saxon is being schooled.* . . . And can any one doubt that the result of this competition of races will be the "survival of the fittest?" . . . Whether the extinction of inferior races before the advancing Anglo-Saxon seems to the reader sad or otherwise, it certainly appears probable.[13]

As the numbers of American Indians dwindled rapidly and intellectual authorities asserted that the extinction of "inferior races" was inevitable, many Americans began to view Native Americans with a combination of pity and resignation. Their supposed coming extinction prompted some people to feel nostalgic or even wistful, prompting individuals and groups to memorialize the First Ohioans in different ways.

This memorialization is literally all over the map. Of Ohio's eighty-eight counties, the names of nearly a quarter (twenty) come from either Indigenous groups or Indigenous words (as does the name Ohio itself). Several more come from the names of men whose fame derived mostly or in part from fighting Native Americans in or around Ohio. On the local level, most of the older monuments and markers concerning Native Americans around the Akron/Summit County area arose either directly or indirectly from this "vanishing Indian" motif. The idea that Native American landmarks (as well as the Native Americans themselves) were passing away motivated some residents of the area to preserve knowledge and sites of the region's Indigenous past. One such group, the Pathfinders, worked diligently to find and map out old Indian trails (see "Path Finding," Chapter 6). Local landmarks traced to Indigenous forebears include the Portage Path in Akron, and some of its few remaining, presumably authentic, artifacts. One of the more famous of these is the so-called "Signal Tree" in Cascade Valley Metro Park. This Bur Oak thought to be at least three hundred years old prompted locals to assume someone had manipulated it into its distinctive three-pronged fork shape as a sapling, perhaps an Indian marking a terminus of the Portage Path. Yet even this tangible artifact is not necessarily what local legend holds. Its unconfirmed vintage is an educated guess; and even if it were shaped by Native Americans in the 1700s, there is no way of knowing exactly what its shapers were endeavoring to signal. Still, the local affection it holds and extensive community efforts toward its preservation stand as potent evidence of its continuing importance in local memory.[14]

Others sought to memorialize the already-vanished local Native Americans through place names, monuments, and statuary. Although former Ohio Indigenous groups continued to exist on western reservations, their lack of a significant presence in the state since the removal of the Wyandots in the 1840s underscored their perceived "vanishing" nature, and people began to give greater attention to preserving their memory. When Portage Township trustees renamed the Portage Path "Cobb Avenue" in the late 1800s, former Akron mayor and local historian Samuel Lane publicly fulminated that it was "the most flagrant monstrosity in the way of street nomenclature," and that officials had no right to "arbitrarily destroy" the path's identity. "Let the historic and venerated old name, Portage Path, stand forever," he proclaimed in a letter to the editor. When Akron annexed the area from Portage Township in 1900, a petition to change the name back quickly garnered thousands of signatures and prompted the City Council to do just that. In the wake of this popular groundswell, in 1901 local developer Gus Kasch placed an eight-foot arrow near Marvin Avenue where the original Portage Path crossed Market Street, and four years later he placed a six-foot bronze statue of a Native American at the site. A victim of vandalism and car accidents, this statue has since been refurbished twice and moved to the front of the PNC Bank located at the corner of Market and Portage Path in Akron's Highland Square neighborhood.[15]

Yet the Portage Path statue is only one of a number of late nineteenth/early twentieth-century tributes to the vanished Native Americans of Northeast Ohio. In fact, it is only one of three virtually identical statues in the region: both Lodi and Barberton also purchased the same figure from the same place: J. L. Mott Iron Works in Bronx, NY (cast from a mold the foundry purchased from William Demuth and Co. called "No. 53 Indian Chief" in its catalogue). Barberton's bears the name of famed revolutionary-era Lenape Chief Hopocan (Konieschquanoheel, also known as Captain Pipe), who once resided in the area (yet another "No. 53" stands as Tecumseh in a Cincinnati park). Other "vanishing American" memorials include the first property donated to what became the Summit Metro Parks. To commemorate Akron's centennial in 1925, the local chapter of the Daughters of the American Revolution dedicated a boulder with a bronze plaque depicting a Native American with a canoe at Courtney Park—a small triangle of land at the corner of Portage Path and

Bronze statue, "No. 53 Indian Chief," in Akron. *Photo by Charlotte Gintert/ Captured Glimpses Photography*

Bronze statue, "No. 53 Indian Chief," in Barberton. *Photo by Charlotte Gintert/Captured Glimpses Photography*

Merriman Road—marking the northern terminus of the Portage Path. They dedicated another boulder the same day at a point on Manchester Road marking the southern terminus.[16]

While these and other still-extant, well-intentioned memorials to Northeast Ohio Native Americans proliferated in the late 1800s and early 1900s, the most common Indian imagery that greeted most residents of the area at this time were representations appropriated by the contemporary American popular culture that are only rarely seen now. Many of the earliest silent films shown in Nickelodeons were "westerns" featuring (usually savage) Native American warriors as the antagonists of the heroic cowboys or pioneers. A carved wooden Indian was a standard sight in front of tobacco stores throughout the United States, representing the association between Native Americans and tobacco. Indian imagery also became attached to a wide variety of other products: brands like Calumet Baking Powder, Argo Corn Starch, and Land O' Lakes butter are only a few of the many products that used Native American imagery in their advertising. Akron's own Mohawk Rubber Company used not only a tribal name, but also idealized images of Indigenous people on their advertising and stock certificates. Chippewa Lake Park in Medina County similarly used a generic Indian profile in full war-bonnet as a logo. Many other companies used Indian motifs in the trading cards that were a popular form of advertising during the period. To buy the tobacco, coffee, gum, or other products that used the lure of these trading cards to draw customers, store patrons would pay with perhaps the most ubiquitous Native American image of all: the "Indian Head" penny minted by the US government until 1908. Those nickelodeon patrons would similarly purchase entrance to those Western movies with the Indian-headed "Buffalo" nickels.[17]

The commercialization of Native American imagery was sometimes associated with another conception of Indigenous people that gained influence throughout the twentieth century: an updating of the much older "noble savage" trope of the Enlightenment Era of the seventeenth and eighteenth centuries. In Enlightenment literature and philosophical works, the "noble savage" lived in a state of nature and was consequently considered to be pure and uncorrupted by the worst aspects of civilization. He thus stood in contrast to—and often in critique of—the excesses of prevailing European society. While Native American groups still posed a tangible threat to US westward movement, this conception was not very popular in the United States; but once the government successfully used wars and treaties to remove them from most of the landscape, more and more people began to consider Native Americans as authentic, natural, and sometimes even mystic keepers of ancient wisdom. In a rapidly industrializing and urbanizing society, the "natural Indian" represented an admirable simplicity and purity which advertisers could use to evoke confidence in certain products. While many manufacturers have since changed their advertising imagery, even now consumers can still purchase things like "Indian Head Old Fashioned Stone Ground Yellow Corn Meal" and "Natural American Spirit" cigarettes—the latter in a box adorned with the image of a Native American smoking a peace pipe.[18]

Ironically, playing to the revived "noble savage" image actually allowed a few Native Americans to exhibit some degree of agency in their own lives and even public policy. A prime local example of this can be found in the experience of the early twentieth-century Cleveland public figure Oghema Niagara, more commonly known as "Chief Thunderwater." Born in 1865 on the Tuscarora Reservation in Upstate New York, his father was a Seneca healer named Jee Wan Ga and his mother was the Osaukee daughter of Chief Keokuk, Aw Pau Chee Kaw Paw Qua Keokuk. When he was ten years old, the upcoming Centennial Exposition in Philadelphia recruited his family to be part of one of the US Government exhibits there. Afterward, he and his family traveled with Buffalo Bill's spectacularly successful Wild West Show for a number of years. Returning to upstate New York in the 1880s, he married and became a chieftain of the Seneca Turtle Clan before moving his family to Cleveland in the early 1900s, where he became president of the Preservative Cleaner Company.[19]

Niagara was a savvy entrepreneur often quoted as saying "the White Man only worships money." Using his experience from touring with Buffalo Bill's show and embracing his identity as Chief Thunderwater (and sometimes "Big Chief Medicine Man"), he exploited the white image of the authentic/mystical Indian in marketing his own herbal medicines drawn from the traditional ingredients and recipes of his father. Claiming that they "cured his people back in the days when bison trampled the prairie flowers in the dust," he successfully sold a range of remedies including "Thunderwater Tonic Bitters," "Mohawk Oil Liniment," "Seminole Sweet Gum Salve," and "Jee-Wan-Ga Herb Tea." For public appearances he often dressed in what most white people imagined was "authentic" Native American apparel, including a buckskin jacket, moccasins, and a feathered war bonnet. Between his work with his oil and polish company and the Thunderwater and Rose herbal medicine business, Niagara made enough money to buy a seventeen-room mansion that was not just a home to his family, but also a haven for transient Native Americans who were down on their luck.[20]

Yet as Chief Thunderwater, Niagara was also a savvy politician who used his name and image to promote Indigenous-related causes. He joined The Business Men's Taft Club, and met both Presidents Taft and Wilson to promote policies beneficial to Native Americans. He also partnered with the Early Settlers Association of the Western Reserve to create the Pioneers Memorial Association in an effort to preserve the Erie Street Cemetery, threatened with removal by Cleveland urban planners in the early 1900s. Niagara seized upon the fact that the cemetery was the final resting place of Meskwaki Chief Joc-O-Sot, an early nineteenth-century correlate to Chief Thunderwater: wounded fighting against US troops in the Black Hawk War, he later moved to Cleveland and achieved fame portraying stylized Indians with a traveling theatrical company. In Chief Thunderwater regalia, Niagara held an annual ceremony at Joc-O-Sot's grave, declaring the spot sacred ground and prophesying that calamity would befall the city if his body were to be touched. Niagara also became an international leader in the early Indian Rights Movement, lecturing widely and using his status as a Chieftain of the Iroquois Nations and the founder and leader of the Supreme Council of Indian Tribes of the United States and Canada to advocate for improved conditions on reservations and greater autonomy for Indian Nations. After he died at age eighty-five in 1950, he was buried next to Joc-O-Sot in the Erie Street Cemetery he had done so much to preserve.[21]

Yet beyond the idiosyncratic examples of Joc-O-Sot and Chief Thunderwater, nearly all of the memory of Native Americans in Northeast Ohio over the past two hundred years has been perceived through the filter of cultural appropriation by non-Indigenous people. The Improved Order of Red Men is only one example of a group that embraced appropriated Native American ideas and terminology. While IORM members officially saw one function of their group as the preservation of Native American traditions, they ultimately meant the appropriation of Native American ideas, imagery, and terminology to serve the ends of perpetuating a fraternal organization of Euro-Americans. Far more Northeast Ohioans appropriated Indigenous culture and internalized the "noble savage" trope in a structured and officially sanctioned way through generations of Boy Scout, Girl Scout, and Camp Fire Girl traditions and activities. The Boy Scouts of America, for example, arose in part from a previous movement called the Woodcraft Indians founded by Ernest Thompson Seton. The Order of the Arrow, the BSA's National Honor Society, is replete with faux-Indigenous ceremony, nomenclature, and ritual which has more to do with James Fenimore Cooper's fictional work than it does with

Graves of Chiefs Joc-O-Sot (right) and Thunderwater (left) in Erie Street Cemetery, Cleveland. *Photo by Charlotte Gintert/Captured Glimpses Photography*

authentic Native American tradition. But the Boy Scouts were not alone: The Camp Fire Girls and the Girl Scouts also appropriated Indigenous traditions and nomenclature in service to their youth education ends. This left an impression not only on tens of thousands of local youths, but also on the Northeast Ohio landscape in the names of the camps that were such a large part of these movements. The Boy Scouts, for example, had Camp Chickagami in Parkman, Camp Stigwandish in Madison, and Camp Manatoc in Peninsula; the Girl Scouts had Camp Hannawatha in Hopedale, Camp Kiloqua in Marblehead, and Camp Hilaka in Richfield. Although some of these camps took their names from authentic Indigenous words or people, many were English words just made to sound like supposed Indian names (perhaps the most on-the-nose example of the latter was Camp Wanacomback in Amherst).[22]

Beyond the major scouting groups, the YMCA had its own suite of "Indian"-themed camps and groups. In 1911, even before the newly formed Boy Scouts had established its earliest camping infrastructure, the Akron YMCA created Camp Mudjekeewis (from the Anishinaabe word meaning "first-born," it is now known as Camp Y-Noah in Green). A YMCA director in St. Louis started the Indian Guides program in the 1920s to foster father/son bonding, based on what he perceived as the "qualities of American Indian culture and life: Dignity, Patience, Endurance, Spirituality, Feeling for the earth, and Concern for the family."[23] It became a national institution after World War II, and was joined by the similarly themed Y-sponsored groups Indian Maidens (mother/daughter) and Indian Princesses (father/daughter) in the 1950s, and the Indian Braves (mother/son) in the 1970s. All of these groups used the same kind of appropriated and imagined Indigenous traditions in service to their goal of bringing families closer together. Now known as Adventure Guides, these groups are still active in the Akron area.

Perhaps the most deeply entrenched example of cultural appropriation in Northeast Ohio, though, is the use of Indigenous-themed names for sports teams. This tradition extends back to the very beginnings of organized sports in Ohio. Some of the earliest Ohio high school state football champions included the Oberlin Indians (1899, 1900) and the Fostoria Redmen (1902, 1906–1907, 1910–1912, 1914–1915); and Ohio still has the dubious distinction of having more schools with Indigenous-themed mascots than any other state. A 2014 survey revealed that over 200 Ohio K-12 schools used some form of Native American-inspired mascots, far outdistancing the number of much larger states like California and Texas. More than 11 percent of Ohio high schools have mascots related to Native American imagery, and Ohio also leads the nation in schools using the most patently offensive of these terms: "Redskins." Even after Miami University in Oxford dropped "Redskins" in favor of "Redhawks" in 1997, Ohio still had a dozen high school teams bearing this name, more than 10 percent of all such teams nationwide. In August of 2021, state representatives Adam Miller and Jessica Miranda introduced a resolution encouraging Ohio schools to retire such mascots in consultation with Native American groups.[24]

The most high-profile Native-American-themed Ohio team of all was the Cleveland Indians baseball team; but it was far from the only professional athletic team that used that name in Ohio. Akron's first professional football team was called the Akron Indians from 1908 until 1920, when it became a charter member of the nascent National Football League as the Akron Pros. With that name no longer in use, the charter member Cleveland Tigers changed its name to the Indians in 1921. Cleveland also had an International Hockey League franchise named the Indians from 1929–1934. Perhaps the most colorful example of this—and perhaps the most colorful team ever in any American professional sport—was the Oorang Indians founded in LaRue, Ohio (outside of Marion), the site of a former Wyandot settlement. Famed athlete Jim Thorpe—the first president of what became the NFL and a veteran of its early champion Canton Bulldogs—was manager, coach, and a player for the all-Indian team, which played all but one of its games in its brief two-year existence on the road. Like Chief Thunderwater, Thorpe and his teammates exhibited some agency by playing on "White Man's Indian" stereotypes to achieve their own ends. To drive paid attendance to their games, Thorpe and his team essentially invented the halftime show, which sometimes included "Indian dances" and knife- and tomahawk-throwing throwing exhibitions.[25]

Yet it is the Cleveland Indians that long claimed the spotlight as the most omnipresent example of Native American imagery in Northeast Ohio, with references to "The Indians" or "The Tribe" for decades filling the airwaves and newspaper pages from spring through fall, and team jerseys and jackets a pervasive presence year-round. Although defenders of the nickname argued that it honored Louis Sockalexis—the first Native American professional baseball player—the truth is that the earliest use of the term in reference to the team was not a tribute, but rather to make fun of the then-Cleveland Spiders' use of a minority player at a time when professional baseball was almost exclusively played by white men. Although there was little debate regarding the name through most of the twentieth century (even Chief Thunderwater was a vocal supporter of the team), the organization faced increasing public pressure in recent years over its name and imagery. In response, the team announced in 2018 that it would be retiring the cartoonish mascot Chief Wahoo—both the image and name of which most Native American groups found offensive. After nation-wide protests sparked by the killing of George Floyd in 2020 expanded to include demands to redress the legacy of colonialism, the team held a series of meetings with representatives from various communities, including Native American groups. As a result of these talks, the team's owner Paul Dolan announced in December of that year that the team would drop the "Indians" name, and in July of 2021, he announced officially that the team's new name would be "The Guardians." This marked the beginning of a new partnership with the local Indigenous community. On August 7, 2023, the Guardians welcomed members of the Lake Erie Native American Council (LENAC) to their first Guardians game, and B. T. Rambeau—a long-time LENAC activist and youth baseball coach—threw out the first pitch. Rambeau hoped the event would facilitate more conversations between Guardians fans and the Indigenous community, saying "It's an opportunity to embrace the change."[26]

The public debate over the Cleveland Indians sheds some light on how memory of Native Americans in Northeast Ohio has evolved in the late twentieth and early twenty-first centuries. A greater sensitivity to Indigenous culture is evident in the challenges posed to stereotypes in the media. Accepted public imagery has changed, too. One local example of this is the work of Peter Toth. A Hungarian American sculptor, Toth has carved more than seventy large statues of Native Americans—nearly all from massive tree trunks—in a series he calls "Trail of the Whispering Giants." He has placed at least one of these statues in all fifty states and a couple of Canadian Provinces, always for free. A former resident of the Akron area, Toth made Akron home to two of his giants, including "Tomahawk," one of the earliest of the series. Made from a dead elm trunk in the Lone Spruce area of Sand Run Metro Park during the summer of 1972, this one fell victim to vandalism in 1977 and no longer exists. The other one, number 51 in the series and named "Rotaynah" (from the Tuscarora word for "Chief"), stood thirty-six feet tall and was placed in front of Fairlawn Elementary School (now Resnik Community Learning Center) in 1985. This red oak statue fell victim to the elements. Decay and insect damage made its sixteen-foot-tall feather headdress unstable, and Akron Public Schools chose to remove this piece in 2011. Although Toth and others made attempts to repair the damage to the rest with foam, fiberglass, polyurethane, and steel poles, school district officials eventually deemed the rest of the statue to be a hazard, and it has joined its headdress in storage.[27]

Sculptor Peter Toth (second from left) and workers with sculpture, September 11, 1972. *Photo by Don Prack, Courtesy of Summit Metro Parks*

Toth's Whispering Giants in some ways represent an amalgam of multiple tropes and the continued complex legacy of Native American memory in Northeast Ohio. His imagery and even the name of the series evokes at the same time the "mysterious forebears," the "vanishing American," and the "noble/mystic/authentic Indian" tropes. These sculptures are not the mass-produced, generic "No. 53 Indian Chief" statues from the turn of the twentieth century: Each one is unique and meant to represent the Indigenous peoples of the particular areas where they stand. They (and other similar works like Joe Frohnapfel's sculpture of Chief Netawatwees on Front Street in Cuyahoga Falls, Chief Logan at Bath Community Park, or Chief Wagmong near the village offices of Silver

Lake) have often been lovingly embraced by the communities in which they reside as acknowledgments of original Indigenous populations and their subsequent shameful treatment by European-Americans. As Toth once succinctly summed up the goal of his life's work, "I am just a person trying to honor maligned people."[28]

Yet Toth's Whispering Giants, however well-intentioned, also represent a lingering ambiguity in how white Americans remember Indigenous Peoples. Some Native American groups have criticized Toth's statues as playing on physical stereotypes and even caricature. While he meant them to be sincere tributes to the First Americans and has not profited off of them, some could say that they still echo the "White Man's Indian." Toth has said that his personal history as a childhood refugee from Communist Hungary in the 1950s informed his inspiration to memorialize a similarly oppressed people. In this way, the sculptures still represent Berkhofer's definition of "The White Man's Indian," in which even white attempts to see the "real" Native Americans are still "framed in terms of White values and needs, White ideologies and creative uses."[29]

Yet while recognizing these continuing ambiguities, Northeast Ohio has come a long way from hosting the Saranac Tribe of the Improved Order of Red Men in the early 1900s. For example, in the 1990s Akron community leaders took up an initiative to memorialize the Portage Path as a culturally significant landmark. Finished in 2001, the Path is now marked by fifty bronze replicas of traditional stone points (often called "arrowheads") with a statue of a Native American carrying a canoe at each terminus. Significantly, these 3,200-pound bronze statues are realistic images of a Miami man in authentic garb created by Onondaga/Seneca artist Peter Jones. When the foundry tried to turn his clay model into a traditional Indian caricature with puffy hair and bulging muscles, Jones corrected it, saying "I had to remove about twenty pounds of clay from the buttocks. We didn't have that. We still don't."[30] The resulting statues for the first time gave a meaningful, authentic Indigenous voice to the way the area memorializes Native Americans. Similarly, in 2018 The Portage Path Collaborative—an initiative of a number of local historical and educational groups, including the Lippman School—successfully lobbied the Akron City Council to declare the first annual "North American First Peoples Day" to honor Indigenous history, life, and culture. Native

Bronze sculpture on the Portage Path in Akron by Peter Jones. *Photo by Charlotte Gintert/Captured Glimpses Photography*

Americans played a focal part of the festivities, with representatives from the Northern Cheyenne Nation of Montana leading a walk of the Portage Path and Peter Jones exhibiting and discussing his artwork.[31]

No one can say that contemporary Northeast Ohio is free from lingering examples of "The White Man's Indian." Yet—from renaming Mary Campbell Cave, to downplaying figures like Captain Brady, to abandoning Chief Wahoo and the name "Indians," to officially recognizing North American First Peoples Day, to literally following the lead of Native Americans in a walk down the Portage Path—perhaps a new phase of Native Americans in Northeast Ohio memory is beginning: turning the pages of "the mysterious forebears," "the uncivilized barbarian," "the vanishing race," and "the noble/authentic/mystic Indian," to find a new, shared page of memory of historic and contemporary Indigenous people on their own terms.

Contributors

Chuck Ayers is an Akron native and holds a BFA in graphic design from Kent State University. He was an artist at the *Akron Beacon Journal* for twenty-six years, and for thirteen of those years he was the *Beacon*'s editorial cartoonist. Chuck was the cocreator of the comic strip *Crankshaft* (since 1987) and the pencil artist for *Funky Winkerbean* comic (since 1994).

Peg Bobel is a freelance writer and former Cultural Resource Specialist for Summit Metro Parks. Peg holds a Master of Science in Social Administration degree from Case Western Reserve University and was a social worker in public agencies for nearly twenty years. Later, while serving as Executive Director of the Cuyahoga Valley Association, she and her husband Rob edited the book *Trail Guide Handbook: Cuyahoga Valley National Park*, as well as the popular *Towpath Companion*. In 2009, Peg and her colleague Lynn Metzger edited and contributed to *Canal Fever: The Ohio & Erie Canal from Waterway to Canalway*.

Charlotte Gintert is an archaeologist for Summit Metro Parks. She has also written numerous articles for the former *The Devil Strip* magazine on Akron's history and architecture and occasionally leads historical walking tours with Akron2Akron. In addition to her heritage work, she operates Captured Glimpses, a scenic photography business. She and her husband live in Akron, Ohio.

Dr. Kevin F. Kern is an Associate Professor of History at The University of Akron. He received his PhD from Bowling Green State University in 1997 and specializes in Ohio History, late nineteenth- and early twentieth-century US History, and the History of Science and Technology. He is coauthor of the book *Ohio: A History of the Buckeye State* and is currently working on a book titled *State of the Game: Ohio and the Creation of a Football Culture.*

Dr. George W. Knepper was Distinguished Professor of History Emeritus at The University of Akron when he passed away in 2018. Over his long and illustrious career, he penned numerous works on the histories of The University of Akron, the city of Akron, and Ohio. He was best known as the author of the book *Ohio and Its People.*

Dr. Lynn Metzger was Professor Emerita in the Department of Anthropology at The University of Akron, where she taught cultural anthropology courses and conducted many community-based research projects. In addition, she coedited *Canal Fever: The Ohio & Erie Canal from Waterway to Canalway* and coordinated two exhibitions from the Oak Native American Ethnographic Collection on permanent loan to the Cummings Center Institute for Human Science and Culture at The University of Akron.

Dr. Brian G. Redmond is Curator Emeritus of Archaeology, Cleveland Museum of Natural History. His research has made major contributions to our understanding of prehistory of Northern Ohio. His expertise extends from investigations at Paleoindian period sites dating from 11,000 to 10,500 BC through the archaeology of later prehistory, AD 500 to 1650. He is an Adjunct Associate Professor in the Department of Anthropology, Case Western Reserve University.

Dr. Michael Shott is Professor Emeritus in the Department of Anthropology at The University of Akron. His research focuses on stone-tool analysis and how the archaeological record formed, based on fieldwork in the American Midcontinent, Great Basin, Mexico, and South America. Shott's last major project catalogued large private collections of artifacts from south-central Ohio for detailed scientific analysis.

Francisca Ugalde is currently an instructor in museology for the Foundations of Museums and Archives certificate program at The University of Akron. Since 2010, she has been the object and information manager of a private Native American ethnographic collection. She assisted in research and development of two exhibitions: *Connecting Objects to their People: From the Arctic to Arizona* (2011) and *Drums, Tomahawks, and the Horse: Native American Cultural Tools* (2013). She received her MA in Arts Administration—Collections Management from The University of Akron in 2012.

Linda Whitman, MS, is a Visiting Research Scholar and an Emerita Instructor of Archaeology and former Director of the Community Archaeology program in the Department of Anthropology at The University of Akron and a retired Cultural Resource Specialist at Summit Metro Parks. Before coming to the university, she conducted cultural resource management projects for thirteen years. Her research area is precontact and historic archaeology in the Midwest. She is author of numerous archaeological reports and journal articles.

 Notes

Chapter 1

1. This number reflects individuals who self-identify in the 2020 US Population Census as either Native American and Alaska Native alone or in combination with other groups. US Census Bureau, 2020 Census Demographic Data map viewer, https://www.census.gov/library/visualizations/2021/geo/demographicmapviewer.html.

2. Peter Jones, interview by Linda Whitman and Peg Bobel, July 23, 2020.

3. "Changing the Narrative About Native Americans: A Guide for Allies," First Nations Development Institute and Echo Hawk Consulting, for Reclaiming Native Truth, A Project to Dispel America's Myths and Misconceptions, https://www.firstnations.org/publications/changing-the-narrative-about-native-americans-a-guide-for-allies/.

4. "Changing the Narrative," First Nations Development Institute and Echo Hawk Consulting.

5. Tina Norris, Paula L. Vines, and Elizabeth M. Hoeffel, US Department of Commerce, Bureau of the Census, *The American Indian and Alaska Native Population: 2010* (Washington, DC, 2012); National Indian Council on Aging, "Census Shows Increase in Native Population," accessed November 17, 2021, https://www.nicoa.org/census-shows-increase-in-native-population/; Nicole Chavez and Harmeet Kaur, "Why the Jump in Native American Population May Be One of the Hardest to Explain," CNN, https://www.cnn.com/2021/08/19/us/census-native-americans-rise-population/index.html.

6. National Conference of State Legislatures, "An Issue of Sovereignty," January 2013, https://www.ncsl.org/legislators/quad-caucus/on-issue-of-sovereignty.aspx. See also US Department of the Interior, Indian Affairs, "Frequently Asked Questions."

7. US Department of the Interior, Indian Affairs, "Frequently Asked Questions."

8. Regarding citizenship: The Snyder Act of 1924 gave full US citizenship to all Native Americans born in the US, however, per the Constitution, it was up to the states to

determine who could vote. It took forty years for all states to allow Native Americans to vote, and even then Native Americans faced (and in some instances still face) obstacles to voting, such as poll taxes, intimidation, distance from polling places, or rules that are difficult to abide by, for instance being required to have a street address when many reservations have no, or nontraditional, addresses. See Library of Congress, "Voting Rights for Native Americans," https://www.loc.gov/classroom-materials/elections/right-to-vote/voting-rights-for-native-americans/; Democracy Docket, "Barriers to the Ballot for Native Americans," October 12, 2021, https://www.democracydocket.com/news/barriers-to-the-ballot-for-native-americans/.

9. "Changing the Narrative," First Nations Development Institute and Echo Hawk Consulting.

10. Ohio Department of Education Model Curriculum for Social Studies, https://education.ohio.gov/Topics/Learning-in-Ohio/Social-Studies/Model-Curriculum-for-Social-Studies.

11. Claire Heldman, interview by Linda Whitman, Peg Bobel, and Fran Ugalde, August 15, 2020.

12. Marlys Rambeau, interview by Linda Whitman and Peg Bobel, October 7, 2020.

13. Sam Chestnut's father, Steve Chestnut, was a partner in the Seattle law firm Ziontz Chestnut, where for more than forty years he argued on behalf of numerous western tribes, especially in the area of mineral rights.

14. Sam Chestnut, interview by Linda Whitman and Peg Bobel, with Matt Russ, Thomas Shoulderblade, and Dawnielle Shoulderblade, June 21, 2021.

15. Chestnut, interview.

16. Chestnut, interview.

17. Thomas Shoulderblade, interview by Linda Whitman and Peg Bobel, with Dawnielle Shoulderblade, Sam Chestnut, and Matt Russ, June 21, 2021. Editors' note: the incident is more complicated than the statement suggests regarding the executions and Lincoln's response to the 1862 conflict. See https://apnews.com/article/archive-fact-checking-2786870059.

18. Matt Russ, interview by Linda Whitman and Peg Bobel, with Sam Chestnut, Thomas Shoulderblade, and Dawnielle Shoulderblade, June 21, 2021.

19. David Treuer, interview by Alia Wong, "The Schools That Tried—But Failed—to Make Native Americans Obsolete," *The Atlantic*, March 5, 2019, https://www.theatlantic.com/education/archive/2019/03/failed-assimilation-native-american-boarding-schools/584017/.

20. Northern Plains Reservation Aid, a Program of Partnership With Native Americans, "Boarding Schools," http://www.nativepartnership.org/site/PageServer?pagename=PWNA_Native_History_boardingschoolsNP.

21. Northern Plains Reservation Aid, "Boarding Schools."

22. David Treuer, *The Heartbeat of Wounded Knee: Native America from 1890 to the Present* (New York: Riverhead Books, 2019), 135.

23. Northern Plains Reservation Aid, "Boarding Schools."

24. Sam Yellowhorse Kesler, "Indian Boarding Schools' Traumatic Legacy, and the Fight to Get Native Ancestors Back," *National Public Radio*, Saturday August 23, 2021, https://

www.krwg.org/2021-08-28/indian-boarding-schools-traumatic-legacy-and-the-fight-to-get-native-ancestors-back; Ivey DeJesus, "With family ties to Carlisle Indian School, US official investigates boarding centers and their painful legacy," *PENN Live Patriot News*, June 30, 2001, https://www.pennlive.com/news/2021/06/with-family-ties-to-carlisle-indian-school-interior-secretary-deb-haaland-investigates-boarding-schools-and-their-painful-legacy.html. The remains of the following children were returned: Lucy Take the Tail (Pretty Eagle); Rose Long Face (Little Hawk); Ernest Knocks Off (White Thunder); Dennis Strikes First (Blue Tomahawk); Maud Little Girl (Swift Bear); Friend Hollow Horn Bear; Warren Painter (Bear Paints Dirt); Alvan (Kills Seven Horses); Dora Her Pipe (Brave Bull). Visitors to the US Army Heritage and Education Center at Carlisle Barracks can take a self-guided walking tour of the Carlisle Indian Industrial School Grounds. For more information on the Carlisle Indian School Project that aims to honor the legacy of the Carlisle students, see: https://carlisleindianschoolproject.com.

25. Northern Plains Reservation Aid, "Boarding Schools." For a further understanding of the rights of Native parents in this regard, see: Indian Child Welfare Act of 1978, Public Law 95-608, *U.S. Statutes at Large* 92 Stat. 3069.

26. Opinion, Deb Haaland, "My grandparents were stolen from their families as children. We must learn about this history," *Washington Post*, June 11, 2021, https://www.washingtonpost.com/opinions/2021/06/11/deb-haaland-indigenous-boarding-schools/.

27. National Native American Boarding School Healing Coalition, "NABS Supports Federal Indian Boarding School Investigation and Calls for Federal Truth Commission," June 2, 2012, https://boardingschoolhealing.org/kill-the-indian-save-the-man-an-introduction-to-the-history-of-boarding-schools/.

28. US Department of the Interior, "Department of the Interior Releases Investigative Report, Outlines Next Steps in Federal Indian Boarding School Initiative," news release, May 11, 2022. To access Volume 1 of the report go to: https://www.bia.gov/sites/default/files/dup/inline-files/bsi_investigative_report_may_2022_508.pdf.

29. US Department of the Interior, "Interior Department Launches Effort to Preserve Federal Indian Boarding School Oral History," news release, September 26, 2023.

30. Bryan Newland, Assistant Secretary, Indian Affairs, *Federal Indian Boarding School Initiative Investigative Report, May 2022,* special report prepared at the request of Deb Haaland, Secretary of the Interior, June 22, 2021, cover letter.

31. David Treuer, interview by Jeffrey Brown, "Author David Treuer on Rewriting the Native American Narrative," *PBS NewsHour*, PBS, May 2, 2019, https://www.pbs.org/newshour/show/author-david-treuer-on-rewriting-the-native-american-narrative.

32. Heldman, interview.

33. Rambeau, interview.

34. LaDonna BlueEye, interview by Linda Whitman and Peg Bobel, March 13, 2021.

35. Asylums Projects, Oklahoma, "Wheelock Academy," https://www.asylumprojects.org/index.php/Wheelock_Academy.

36. Roberta Estes, "Thomas Asylum for Orphan and Destitute Indian Children," June 12, 2013, Native Heritage Project, https://nativeheritageproject.com/2013/06/12/thomas-asylum-for-orphan-and-destitute-indian-children/.

37. Dan Herbeck, "The Lessons of Pain: the Terrible Legacy of the Thomas Indian School Remains All Too Fresh," *The Buffalo News*, October 1, 2006, https://buffalonews.com/news/lessons-of-pain-the-terrible-legacy-of-the-thomas-indian-school-remains-all-too-fresh/article_a8c13fd7-2e34-5f96-ba30-c89108140a8f.html.

38. Peter Jones, interview.

39. Hansel Ndumbe Eyoh, "Language as Carrier of People's Culture: An interview with Ngugi Wa Thiongo," *Ufahamu: A Journal of African Studies*, UCLA, March 30, 1985, eScholarship, https://escholarship.org/uc/item/32j2p716.

40. Ellen L. Lutz, "Saving America's Endangered Languages," *Cultural Survival Quarterly Magazine*, June 2007, https://www.culturalsurvival.org/publications/cultural-survival-quarterly/saving-americas-endangered-languages.

41. Michael Jones, interview by Linda Whitman, January 12, 2022.

42. An example of a land acknowledgement is this one from Case Western Reserve University, Cleveland, Ohio: "In recognizing the land upon which we reside, we express our gratitude and appreciation to those who lived and worked here before us; those whose stewardship and resilient spirit makes our residence possible on this traditional homeland of the Lenape (Delaware), Shawnee, Wyandot, Miami, Ottawa, Potawatomi, and other Great Lakes tribes (Chippewa, Kickapoo, Wea, Piankishaw, and Kaskaskia). We also acknowledge the thousands of Native Americans who now call Northeast Ohio home. Case Western Reserve University and the greater Cleveland area occupy land officially ceded by 1100 chiefs and warriors signing the Treaty of Greenville in 1795." https://case.edu/socialjustice/sites/case.edu.socialjustice/files/2019-07/Land%20Acknowledgement.pdf

43. "Covid Relief Bill Includes Support for Native American Languages," *Language Magazine*, March 16, 2021, https://www.languagemagazine.com/2021/03/16/covid-relief-bill-includes-support-for-native-american-languages/.

44. Mark Walker and Emily Cochrane, "Tribal Communities Set to Receive Big New Infusion of Aid," *The New York Times*, March 18, 2021, updated October 27, 2021, https://www.nytimes.com/2021/03/18/us/politics/tribal-communities-stimulus-cornonavirus.html.

45. Indian Health Service, Fact Sheet "Disparities," accessed January 22, 2022, https://www.ihs.gov/newsroom/factsheets/disparities/.

46. Rupa Marya and Raj Patel, *Inflamed: Deep Medicine and the Anatomy of Injustice* (New York: Farrar, Straus and Giroux, 2021), 201–202.

47. LaDonna BlueEye interview; Tim Pierce, UM Legislative News Service, "Hanna's Act Passes Montana Legislature, Intensifying Search for Missing Indigenous Women," April 23, 2019; Jazzlyn Johnson, "Struggle for Justice: The women behind Hanna's Act," *Native News Journal*, May 6, 2019, http://nativenews.jour.umt.edu.

48. Marya and Patel, *Inflamed*, 210, 289–292.

49. Lecia Bushak, "Cleveland's Native Americans Face Heart Disease, Stroke Disparities," Ideastream Public media, July 3, 2019, https://www.ideastream.org/news/clevelands-native-americans-face-heart-disease-stroke-health-disparities; Marya and Patel, *Inflamed*, 349–352. For an example of a wellness program that includes traditional ways and knowledge, see Marya and Patel's discussion of the Mni Wiconi Clinic and Farm in Dakhota/Lakhota territory, in *Inflamed*, 345–348.

50. LaDonna BlueEye interview; Public News Service, "Tribes in Need of Different Anti-Smoking Programs," *El Paso Herald-Post*, August 12, 2016, https://elpasoheraldpost.com/tribes-need-different-anti-smoking-programs/.

51. James Workman, interview by Linda Whitman and Peg Bobel, July 23, 2020.

52. Azusa Ono, "The Relocation and Employment Assistance Programs, 1948–1970: Federal Indian Policy and the Early Development of the Denver Indian Community," *Indigenous Nations Journal* 5, no. 1 (Spring, 2004): 30–32; Wikipedia contributors, Wikipedia, The Free Encyclopedia, "Indian Termination Policy," https://en.wikipedia.org/w/index.php?title=Indian_termination_policy&oldid=1066947452. See also Donald Lee Fixico, *Termination and Relocation: Federal Indian Policy, 1945–1960* (Albuquerque, NM: University of New Mexico Press, 1990).

53. National Council of Urban Indian Health, Outreach Materials, "Relocation," www.ncuih.org, 2018_0519_Relocation.pdf. (Accessed March 9, 2018; page now discontinued).

54. Workman, interview.

55. Heldman, interview.

56. Heldman, interview.

57. Heldman, interview.

58. Rambeau, interview.

59. Rambeau, interview.

60. Bushak, "Cleveland's Native Americans Face Heart Disease, Stroke Health Disparities."

61. George Horse Capture, foreword to *North American Indian Art*, by David W. Penney (New York: Thames & Hudson, Inc., 2004), 8.

62. David W. Penney, *North American Indian Art* (New York: Thames & Hudson, Inc., 2004), 10.

63. Peter Jones, interview.

64. Peter Jones, interview.

65. First Peoples Fund Community Spirit Award Honorees, Peter B. Jones, firstpeoplesfund.org.

66. Peter Jones, interview.

67. Peter Jones, interview.

68. Peter Jones, interview.

69. Phil Keren, "Grant would display river's history through artwork," *Akron Beacon Journal*, July 23, 2021.

70. Edwin George Artist Statement, for "Edwin George, Cherokee Painter and Storyteller Art Exhibition," shown at the North Water Street Gallery, Kent, Ohio, April 24-May 23, 2004, standingrock.net; Tanya Ackerman, "Myths of the Cherokee find way to canvas for artist," *The Daily Kent Stater*, November 25, 1998 (digitized copies of the newspaper can be found at dks.library.kent.edu.); Edwin George biography, The Ohio State University Center for Folk Lore Studies, Ohio Heritage Fellows Collection, https://cfs.osu.edu/archives/collections/ohio-heritage-fellows-collection/edwin-george.

71. George, Artist Statement.

72. George, Artist Statement.

73. The Cherokee syllabary was developed by Sequoyah, a Cherokee originator who, in the early 1800s, developed a system of writing that the Cherokee people could use for communication and documentation. His accomplishment was remarkable, and though this form of written language was at first greeted with suspicion by the Cherokee people, its usefulness was soon recognized, and the syllabary adopted and learned by nearly all Cherokee by 1830, making the Cherokee one of the first Indigenous groups to have a written language. During the time of the Indian Removal Act of 1830, when the US government forcibly moved Native Americans from eastern lands to western territories, the Cherokee language and syllabary was one thing they were able to hold onto in the midst of great loss. Their newspaper and other written works helped maintain unity during a time when the tribe was dispersed geographically and divided politically. Today the Cherokee Nation is committed to preserving and growing the language, offering language classes, a translation service, resource materials for teachers, and development and support of the language for digital devices. "Sequoyah and the Creation of the Cherokee Syllabary," National Geographic Resource Library article, nationalgeographic.org, accessed 11/2/2021; "Cherokee Language," language.cherokee.org.

74. Janis Wunderlich, e-mail message to authors, August 22, 2021.

75. Rambeau, interview.

76. Rambeau, interview.

77. Claire Heldman Artist Statement and video interview, for "The Art of Claire Heldman: Lakota Wia Exhibition," shown at the Lynn Rodeman Metzger Galleries of The Institute for Human Science and Culture, The University of Akron, Akron, Ohio, October 1, 2021, through March 5, 2022; Claire Heldman interview.

78. Heldman, Artist Statement and video interview.

79. David Giffels, "Totem's Restoration Yields Story," *Akron Beacon Journal*, May 13, 2004.

80. The University of Akron, "The Art of Claire Heldman: Lakota Wia," exhibition flyer, https://www.uakron.edu/chp/whats-on/lakota-wia.

81. Valerie Evans, interview by Linda Whitman and Peg Bobel, October 8, 2020.

82. Evans, interview.

83. Evans, interview.

84. Julia Edwards, interview by Linda Whitman and Peg Bobel, August 19, 2021.

85. Edwards, interview.

86. Edwards, interview.

87. We encourage readers to seek out the works of the artists who are introduced in this chapter, as well as other Native American artists and exhibits of arts and crafts. In considering purchasing art, please be aware of The Indian Arts and Crafts Act of 1990. This law prohibits misrepresentation in the marketing of arts and crafts products in the United States, making it illegal to falsely claim that a work of art or craft is "Indian-made." For instance, items claiming to be "Indian jewelry" would be a violation of the law if the jewelry were produced by someone who was not a member of an Indian tribe or a certified

Indian artisan. In deference to legitimate Native American artists, before buying art online or at events, one should check the authenticity of the items being offered for sale.

Chapter 2

1. "Statement on Anthropology, Colonialism and Racism," University of Pennsylvania, Department of Anthropology, https://anthropology.sas.upenn.edu/news/2021/04/28/statement-anthropology-colonialism-and-racism.

2. "Statement on Anthropology," University of Pennsylvania.

3. Joe Watkins, *Indigenous Archaeology: American Indian Values and Scientific Practices* (Walnut Creek, CA: Alta Mira Press, 2000); Sonya Atalay, "Indigenous Archaeology as Decolonizing Practice," *American Indian Quarterly* 30, no. 3/4, 2006, https://www.jstor.org/stable/pdf/4139016.pdf; George P. Nicholas, "Indigenous Archaeology," Oxford Bibliographies, Oxford University Press, 2020, https://www.oxfordbibliographies.com/view/document/obo-9780199766567/obo-9780199766567-0073.xml; Kisha Supernant, Jane Eva Baxter, Natasha Lyons, Sonya Atalay, eds., *Archaeologies of the Heart* (Charn Switzerland: Springer Nature Switzerland AG, 2020)

4. See *Sapiens*, a digital magazine aimed at transforming how the public understands anthropology/archaeology and the other subfields of anthropology with an eye on making it accessible, relevant, and diverse. https://www.sapiens.org/archaeology/archaeology-diversity/.

5. "What is Anthropology?," American Anthropological Association, https://americananthro.org/learn-teach/what-is-anthropology/.

6. Barbara Little, *Historical Archaeology: Why the Past Matters* (Walnut Creek, CA: Left Coast Press, 2007), 13–17.

7. Scott G. Ortman, "A New Kind of Relevance for Archaeology," *Frontiers in Digital Humanities, Digital Archaeology*, October 17, 2019, https://www.frontiersin.org/articles/10.3389/fdigh.2019.00016/full.

8. Little, *Historical Archaeology*, 42–46.

9. "What Do Archaeologists Do?" Society for American Archaeology, https://www.saa.org/about-archaeology/what-do-archaeologists-do.

10. "What do Archaeologists Do?," Society for American Archaeology.

11. Some of the ideas expressed here are borrowed from my colleague Dr. Timothy Matney in his Introduction to Archaeology PowerPoint, The University of Akron.

12. "Archeology Program: Archeology for Interpreters, A Guide to Knowledge of the Resource," National Park Service, US Department of Interior, https://www.nps.gov/archeology/afori/howfig_print.htm.

13. "Archaeology Laws & Ethics," Society for American Archaeology, https://www.saa.org/about-archaeology/archaeology-law-ethics.

14. For a more detailed explanation of these laws and how they affect Native American tribes, see Joe Watkins, *Indigenous Archaeology*, 37–68.

15. "National Historic Preservation Act of 1966," National Park Service, US Department of the Interior, https://www.nps.gov/subjects/archeology/archaeological-resources-protection-act.htm.

16. Watkins, *Indigenous Archaeology*, 41.

17. Watkins, *Indigenous Archaeology*, 42–43.

18. Watkins, *Indigenous Archaeology*, 42–43; "Laws, Regulations and Guidelines, Native American Graves Protection and Repatriation Act of 1990," National Park Service, US Department of the Interior, https://www.nps.gov/subjects/archeology/nagpra.htm.

19. For a good book on visiting archaeological sites in Ohio see: Susan L. Woodward and Jerry N. McDonald, *Indian Mounds of the Middle Ohio Valley: A Guide to Mounds and Earthworks of the Adena, Hopewell, Cole, and Fort Ancient People* (Blacksburg, VA: McDonald & Woodward Publishing Company, 2002); for information on volunteering in National Parks see: "Volunteering," National Park Service, US Department of the Interior, https://www.nps.gov/subjects/archeology/volunteering.htm; for information on Archaeology in Ohio and Ohio Archaeology Month see the Ohio History Connection website, https://ohiohistory.org.

20. Bradley T. Lepper, *Ohio Archaeology: An Illustrated Chronicle of Ohio's Ancient American Indian Cultures* (Wilmington, OH: Orange Frazer Press, 2005).

21. Donald Henson, "Avocational Archaeology," *Encyclopedia of Global Archaeology* (New York: Springer, 2014), https://link.springer.com/referenceworkentry/10.1007/978-1-4419-0465-2_2061#springerlink-search.

Chapter 3

1. In this chapter, all dates are calendrical or "real-time" ages (BP: Before the Present) derived from calibrated radiocarbon dates, and, by convention, the "Present" is set at AD 1950.

2. David S. Brose, "Penumbral Protohistory on Lake Erie's South Shore," in *Societies in Eclipse: Archaeology of the Eastern Woodlands Indians, AD* (2001): 1400–1700, eds. David S. Brose, C. Wesley Cowan, and Robert C. Mainfort Jr. (Washington, DC: Smithsonian Institution Press, 2001), 64–65.

3. Metin I. Eren, Brian G. Redmond, G. Logan Miller, Briggs Buchanan, Matthew T. Boulanger, Brooke M. Morgan, and Michael J. O'Brien, "Paleo Crossing (33ME274): A Clovis Site in Northeastern Ohio," in *In the Eastern Fluted Point Tradition, Volume 2*, ed. Joseph Gingrich (Salt Lake City: University of Utah Press, 2018), 189.

4. Brian G. Redmond and Kenneth B. Tankersley, "Evidence of Early Paleoindian Bone Modification and Use at the Sheriden Cave Site (33WY252), Wyandot County, Ohio," *American Antiquity* 70, no. 3 (2005): 503–526. https://doi.org/10.2307/40035311.

5. Cheryl Claassen, "Reevaluating Cave Records: The Case for Ritual Caves in the Eastern United States," in *Sacred Darkness: A Global Perspective on the Ritual Use of Caves,* ed. Holley Moyes (Denver: University Press of Colorado, 2012), 211–224.

6. Fred Finney, *Calumet, Canal, and Cuyahoga: an Archaeological Overview and Assessment of the Cuyahoga Valley National Park* (St Paul: Upper Midwest Archaeology, 2002), 183–184.

7. Eren, "Paleo Crossing (33ME274): A Clovis Site in Northeastern Ohio," 187.

8. Matthew T. Boulanger, Briggs Buchanan, Michael J. O'Brien, Brian G. Redmond, Michael D. Glascock, and Metin I. Eren, "Neutron Activation Analysis of 12,900-Year-Old Stone Artifacts Confirms 450–510+ Km Clovis Tool-Stone Acquisition at Paleo Crossing (33ME274), Northeast Ohio, USA," *Journal of Archaeological Science* 53 (2015): 550–558. http://dx.doi.org/10.1016/j.jas.2014.11.005.

9. Mark F. Seeman, "Intercluster Lithic Patterning at Nobles Pond: A Case for 'Disembedded' Procurement among Early Paleoindian Societies," *American Antiquity* 59, no. 2 (1994): 273–288. https://doi.org/10.2307/281932.

10. Nigel Brush and Forrest Smith, "The Martins Creek Mastodon: A Paleoindian Butchery Site in Holmes County, Ohio," *Current Research in the Pleistocene* 11 (1994): 14–15.

11. Finney, *Calumet, Canal, and Cuyahoga*, 124.

12. Finney, *Calumet, Canal, and Cuyahoga*, 180.

13. Olaf H. Prufer, Dana A. Long, and Donald J. Metzger, *Krill Cave: A Stratified Rockshelter in Summit County, Ohio, Research Papers in Archaeology*, no. 8. Kent State University Press, 1989.

14. Bradley Thomas Lepper, *Ohio Archaeology: An Illustrated Chronicle of Ohio's Ancient American Indian Cultures* (Wilmington, Ohio: Orange Frazer Press, 2005), https://voyageurmedia.org/wp-content/uploads/2014/06/OA-book_article_06_27_14.pdf.

15. Orrin O. Shane III, H. Prufer, and D. H. McKenzie, "The Leimbach Site: an Early Woodland Village in Lorain County, Ohio," in *Studies in Ohio Archaeology* (1975): 98–120.

16. Brian G. Redmond, "Late Archaic Ritualism in Domestic Contexts: Clay-Floored Shrines at the Burrell Orchard Site, Ohio," *American Antiquity* 82, no. 4 (2017): 683–701, https://doi.org/10.1017/aaq.2017.43.

17. David M. Stothers and Timothy J. Abel, "Archaeological Reflections of the Late Archaic and Early Woodland Time Periods in the Western Lake Erie Region," *Archaeology of Eastern North America* (1993): 29, 64. https://www.jstor.org/stable/40914368.

18. Finney, *Calumet, Canal, and Cuyahoga*, 225–226.

19. Brian G. Redmond, "The OEC 1 Site (33CU462): A Late Prehistoric Period Village Settlement in Northeast Ohio," *Archaeology of Eastern North America* (2009): 1–34. https://www.jstor.org/stable/40914529.

20. Finney, *Calumet, Canal, and Cuyahoga*, 125.

21. Finney, *Calumet, Canal, and Cuyahoga*, 188–189.

22. Mary C. Garvin and Jan Cooper, *Living in the Vermilion River Watershed* (Akron, OH: Western Reserve Land Conservancy, 2008), 96–101.

23. Stephanie J. Belovich, " Defensive or Sacred? An Early Late Woodland Enclosure in Northeast Ohio," *Ancient Earthen Enclosures of the Eastern Woodlands* (1998): 154–179.

24. Brian G. Redmond, "Connecting Heaven and Earth: Interpreting Early Woodland Nonmortuary Ceremonialism in Northern Ohio," *Midcontinental Journal of Archaeology* 41, no. 1 (2016): 41–66. https://doi.org/10.2307/26599928.

25. Brian G. Redmond, "Hopewellians in a Non-Hopewellian World? Interpreting the Hopewellian Domestic-Ritual Landscape at the Heckelman Site in Northcentral Ohio,"

(2020); Brian G. Redmond, Bret J. Ruby, and Jarrod Burks, eds. *Encountering Hopewell in the Twenty-first Century, Ohio and Beyond, Vol. 2*. (University of Akron Press, 2019).

26. Finney, *Calumet, Canal, and Cuyahoga*, 125–127.

27. Charles Whittlesey, *Ancient Earth Forts of the Cuyahoga Valley*, Cleveland: Fairbanks & Benedict (1871).

28. As with all the precontact societies of Ohio, the original tribal names of these groups remains unknown due to the lack of written records prior to the coming of Europeans in the 1700s.

29. David S. Brose, "The Everett Knoll: A Late Hopewellian Site In Northeastern Ohio," (1974), *Ohio Journal of Science* 74, no. 1 (January 1974).

30. Finney, *Calumet, Canal, and Cuyahoga*, 135–136.

31. Olaf H. Prufer, Mark F. Seeman, and Robert P. Mensforth, "The Lukens Cache: A Ceremonial Offering from Ohio," *Pennsylvania Archaeologist* 54, no. 3–4 (1984): 19–31.

32. David R. Bush, David R, "The Valentine Cache Site, Lake County, Ohio," *Ohio Archaeologist* 29, no. 1 (1979): 21–24.

33. Mary L. Simon, Kandace D. Hollenbach, and Brian G. Redmond, "New Dates and Carbon Isotope Assays of Purported Middle Woodland Maize from the Icehouse Bottom and Edwin Harness Sites," *American Antiquity* 86, no. 3 (2021): 613–624, https://doi.org/10.1017/aaq.2020.117.

34. Robert A. Genheimer, ed., *Cultures Before Contact: The Late Prehistory of Ohio and Surrounding Regions* (Columbus: Ohio Archaeological Council, 2000).

35. David M. Stothers and James R. Graves, "The Prairie Peninsula Co-tradition: An hypothesis for Hopewellian to Upper Mississippian continuity," *Archaeology of Eastern North America* (1985): 153–175, https://www.jstor.org/stable/40914257.

36. Emerson F. Greenman, "Two prehistoric villages near Cleveland, Ohio," *Ohio State Archaeological and Historical Quarterly*, vol. *XLVI* (1937), 306–366.

37. David S. Brose, *The South Park Village Site and the Late Prehistoric Whittlesey Tradition of Northeast Ohio* (Madison: Prehistory Press, 1994).

38. Redmond, "The OEC 1 Site (33CU462): A Late Prehistoric Period Village Settlement in Northeast Ohio," 1–34.

39. Finney, *Calumet, Canal, and Cuyahoga*, 188.

40. Olaf H. Prufer and Sara E. Pedde, "The Stow Rockshelter in Summit County, Ohio: The Archaeology and History of Investigations, 1952–2000," in *Caves and Culture: 10,000 Years of Ohio History*, eds. Linda B. Spurlock, Olaf H. Prufer, and Thomas R. Pigott (Kent, Ohio: Kent State University Press, 2006), 27–53.

41. See Knepper and Kern, this volume.

Chapter 4

1. Michael J. Shott, "Estimating the Magnitude of Private Collection of Points and Its Effects upon Professional Survey Results: A Michigan Case Study," *Advances in Archaeological Practice* 5:125–137, 2017. doi: 10.1017/aap.2017.8.

2. Michael J. Shott, Mark F. Seeman and Kevin C. Nolan, "Collaborative Engagement: Working with Private Collections and Responsive Collectors," *Midwest Archaeological Conference Occasional Paper No. 3*. Midwest Archaeological Conference, Urbana, IL, 2018. http://www.midwestarchaeology.org/ sites/default/ files/annual-meeting/documents/ MAC-Occasional-Papers-Vol-3_smaller.pdf.

3. Kevin C. Nolan, Michael J. Shott and Eric Olson, "The Central Ohio Archaeological Digitization Survey: A Demonstration of Amplified Public Good from Collaboration with Private Collectors," *Advances in Archaeological Practice* 10:83–90, 2022. doi:10.1017/ aap.2021.33.

Chapter 5

1. This was one of the final pieces Dr. Knepper wrote in his long and distinguished career as the preeminent historian of Ohio. He did not leave in-text citations for this chapter, so an annotated bibliography of important sources has been appended for further reading on this subject by his friend and colleague Dr. Kevin Kern.

2. The "big falls" was partially covered in 1912 by a power dam that created a lake more than thirty feet deep over a considerable part of the once wild, scenic glens in Gorge Metro Park. As of the date of this publication, plans are underway to remove the dam and return the river to its natural state.

3. These Iroquois (Haudenosaunee) migrants came to be known by contemporaries as *Mingos*, from the Lenape word meaning "treacherous." Here they are called the Ohio Iroquois, while Senecas and Cayugas that remained loyal to the council are called by their tribal names. *Iroquois* is the French term for the Haudenosaunee Confederacy (People of the Longhouse), while the English referred to the confederacy as the Six Nations or Five Nations. Here the name Iroquois is used when referring to the confederacy, as that is the name employed mostly by historic sources in the 1700s–1800s. Today the league of tribes is properly called the Haudenosaunee Confederacy.

4. Local accounts take far too literally the notion that Netawatwees Town was at the big falls. No important chief would place his town within the constricted, rugged confines of the Cuyahoga gorge, an inaccessible place, removed from a navigable river, with no substantial trail penetrating its rock-strewn depths. Nor would he place his village on the flat, infertile, isolated land above the gorge's rim. No Native American town in all of Ohio had such a location. Netawatwees later located his capital town along the Tuscarawas. Lenapes called it Gekelemukpechunk, and whites called it Newcomerstown. In 1772 John Ettwein, Moravian missionary, wrote a description of it. The town center contained forty to fifty lodges (accommodating about 160 to 200 persons) but "some miles upstream and some miles downstream stand more houses and huts which are reckoned as belonging to the town." Earl Olmstead, *David Zeisberger* (Kent State University Press, 1997), 194–95.

5. In 1934, Mrs. J. B. McPherson submitted a report to the Cuyahoga Falls DAR chapter. Her main interest was to document the claim that Mary Campbell was the first white child to live in the Western Reserve. Her research was admirable. She covered the sources, such as they were, but also wrote scores of letters in the hope of finding additional information. One reply put her on the trail of Mary's descendants, the issue of Mary and the man she

married back in Pennsylvania. Relatives confirmed much of Mary's story and added bits of folklore. This report motivated the DAR to advocate naming the rock shelter Mary Campbell Cave, in recognition of the first white child in the Western Reserve. The cave was previously known as Old Maid's Kitchen. In 2019, after further study, including historic research and archaeological investigations that revealed no evidence of Native American occupation of the rock shelter, Summit Metro Parks decided to change the name of the rock shelter back to Old Maid's Kitchen. Information on Mrs. McPherson's research can be found in Taylor Memorial Library, Cuyahoga Falls, Ohio, vertical files.

6. Frequently after a Native American raid, local settlers gathered and set off in pursuit of the warriors, hoping to rescue prisoners and exact revenge. This practice often prompted further retaliation and later became almost a reflex reaction to the frequent raids carried out by both sides in the Kentucky and Ohio borderlands.

7. Local investigators agree that Hopocan had a village or encampment at Nesmith Lake near the southern terminus of the Portage Path. If so, the encampment dates from before Hopocan's chieftainship since, after 1776, his whereabouts are rather well known, with no mention of Nesmith Lake.

8. Consul Butterfield, *History of the Girtys* (Cincinnati, 1890), 48. This is one of many accounts of Hand's campaign. Simon Girty, the frontier's most hated and feared renegade, was apparently with Hand. If so, it was as close as he was known to have come to the Cuyahoga. More recent scholarship has challenged the reports of Girty's unsavory reputation.

Chapter 6

1. "Maps, Mapmaking, and Map Use by Native Americans," in *The History of Cartography, Volume 2*, ed. G. Malcolm Lewis (Chicago: The University of Chicago Press, 1998), 51–182.

2. Louis De Vorsey Jr., "Silent Witnesses: Native American Maps," *The Georgia Review* 46, no. 4 (1992): 709–726. De Vorsey referred to the loss of Native American elders and their oral knowledge through epidemics "was tantamount of the wholesale burning of libraries." To see examples of Native American cosmology, astronomy and cartography, visit these UNESCO World Heritage sites in Ohio, together known as Hopewell Ceremonial Earthworks: Hopewell Culture National Historical Park in Chillicothe including Mound City Group, Hopewell Mound Group, Hopeton Earthworks, Seip Earthworks, and High Banks Earthworks; Fort Ancient Earthworks near Oregonia; Newark Earthworks including Octagon Earthwork and Great Circle Earthworks.

3. Joe Jesensky, "To Kirtland to the Bakers," September 12, 1986, private collection. The Joe Jesensky Papers are not archived in any one place but are held by several individuals and institutions, including the Bedford Historical Society and Akron Summit County Library Special Collections.

4. "The Indian Pathfinders' Association of Cleveland, Ohio," in Jean and Bob Kainsinger, *Cleaveland Hill Farm and Quarry,* http://waltonhillsohio.gov/pdf_waltonhills/en-US/HistoricalDocs/CleavelandHillFarmQuarry.pdf.

5. For further discussion of Native American mapmaking see Louis De Vorsey Jr., "Silent Witnesses: Native American Maps" (1992), especially page 725 where he concludes his

discussion of Native American mapmaking by quoting Colonial American governor Thomas Pownall's commentary on Native American cartographic capabilities: "Indeed all the Indians have this knowledge to a very great Degree of practical Purpose. They are very attentive to the Position of the Sun and Stars, and on the Lakes can steer their course by them…the Habit of traveling mark to him the Distances, and he will express accurately from these distinct Impressions, by drawing on the Sand a Map which would shame many a thing called a Survey. When I have been among them at Albany, and inquiring of them about the Country, I have sat and seen them draw such."

6. Russell K. Pelton to P. P. Cherry, June 19, 1914, in Kainsinger, *Cleaveland Hill Farm and Quarry*.

7. Russell K. Pelton to P. P. Cherry, June 19, 1914.

8. "Clevelanders Mark Old Indian Trails" in Kainsinger, *Cleaveland Hill Farm and Quarry*.

9. Russell K. Pelton to P. P. Cherry, June 19, 1914.

10. Russell K. Pelton to P. P. Cherry, June 19, 1914.

11. *Encyclopedia of Cleveland History,* "Rose, Benjamin," https://case.edu/ech/articles/r/rose-benjamin; "Rose Building," clevelandgatewaydistrict.com.

12. Kainsinger, *Cleaveland Hill Farm and Quarry*.

13. Virgil D. Allen, "Our First Highways and Their Locaters," *Dependable Highways,* October 1915, 11–13. Also found in Kainsinger, *Cleaveland Hill Farm and Quarry*.

14. Virgil D. Allen Papers, private collection.

15. *The Elyria Reporter* (Elyria, OH), September 9, 1893; "Father of Oakland Librarian is Dead," *Oakland Tribune* (Oakland, CA), May 21, 1929.

16. P. H. Kaiser, Esq., *The Moravians on the Cuyahoga* (Cleveland, OH: Mount & Co., Printers, 1894), 2–3.

17. Kaiser, *Moravians,* 2–3.

18. Kaiser, *Moravians,* 12–13.

19. Rev. John Heckewelder, *Map and description of northeastern Ohio 1796* (Cleveland, OH: William W. Williams 1884), http://www.archive.org/details/mapdescriptionofooheck.

20. James Bier, "Modern counterpart of Heckwelder Map of 1796" (Cleveland, OH: Western Reserve Historical Society, 1968), http://web.ulib.csuohio.edu/speccoll/maps/bier.htm. A copy of this map was found in Joe Jesensky's personal papers, private collection. James Bier was born in Cleveland in 1927. After receiving a B.S. degree in geology from Western Reserve University in 1953, he went on to attain a M.S. degree in geography and cartography from University of Illinois at Urbana-Champaign where he taught until his retirement in 1989. He is well known for his books mapping the Hawaiian Islands, http://web.ulib.csuohio.edu/speccoll/maps/bier.html.

21. Russell K. Pelton to P. P. Cherry, June 19, 1914, in Kainsinger, *Cleaveland Hill Farm and Quarry*.

22. Ohio History Central, *Thomas Hutchins,* https://ohiohistorycentral.org/w/Thomas_Hutchins. For more information on Colonel Bouquet, see Knepper and Kern this book. For more information on colonial cartography and the role maps played in imperial ambitions

see Chad Anderson, "Rediscovering Native North America: Settlements, Maps, and Empires in the Eastern Woodlands," *Early American Studies* 14, No 3 (Summer 2016): 478–505.

23. Thomas Hutchins, *A General Map of the Country on the Ohio and Muskingham . . . in 1764* (Philadelphia: W. Bradford, 1765), https://www.loc.gov/item/2001695748/.

24. Walling, H. F. and O. W. Gray, *New Topographic Atlas of the State of Ohio* (Cincinnati, Ohio: Steadman, Brown and Lyon, 1872).

25. William C. Mills, *Archeological Atlas of Ohio Showing the Distribution of the Various Classes of Prehistoric Remains in the State with a Map of the Principal Indian Trails and Towns* (Columbus, Ohio: Fred J. Heer for The Ohio State Archeological and Historical Society, 1914), VIII.

26. William Dancey, "The 1914 Archaeological Atlas of Ohio: Its History and Significance," (Paper presented at the 49th Annual Meeting of the Society for American Archaeology, Portland, OR, April 12, 1984).

27. Dancey, "The 1914 Archaeological Atlas of Ohio."

28. Ephraim George Squier and Edwin Hamilton Davis, *Ancient Monuments of the Mississippi Valley: Comprising the Results of Extensive Original Surveys and Explorations* (Washington and London: Smithsonian Press, 1848). This was the first publication issued by the Smithsonian Institution. Squier, a newspaper editor and Davis, a physician, produced landmark scientific research of the mounds and earthworks built by precontact Indigenous peoples. It is a primary resource for these earthworks that are now mostly obliterated on the surface.

29. Henry Shetrone, "The Indian in Ohio with a Map of the Ohio Country," *The Ohio State Archaeological and Historical Society Quarterly* 27, no. 3 (1918): 272–520.

30. It is likely that most of Virgil Allen's papers were destroyed as the result of a house fire in 1996. Molly Baker Patel, great granddaughter of Virgil Allen, phone conversation with author, February 2, 2020.

31. Joe Jesensky identified Frank Wilcox as a Pathfinder. They knew each other through the Cleveland School of Art. Wilcox likely knew the earlier Pathfinders.

32. Frank N. Wilcox, *Ohio Indian Trails* (Cleveland: The Gates Press, 1933), 19. Wilcox (1887–1964) was a notable Cleveland artist, author, instructor, and historian. He was a modernist American artist and master of watercolor. Wilcox attended and later taught for over forty years at the Cleveland School of Art (now the Cleveland Institute of Art).

33. Frank Wilcox, *Ohio Indian Trails*, ed. William A. McGill (Kent, OH: The Kent State University Press, 1970), endpapers.

34. Lee, James Daniel, *A general map of The Ohio Country and the Northwest Territory of the United States From the Best Information to 1799*, Joe Jesensky's Papers, private collection. Also available at the Cleveland Public Library.

35. Joe Jesensky, no title, 1984, private collection; Jean and Bob Kainsinger, "Indian Trails Passing Through this Area" in *Historic Sites in Our Parks: Sites in Cuyahoga Valley National Park and Bedford Reservation within the Boundaries of the Village of Walton Hills* (Walton Hills: Village of Walton Hills, 2006), 16. Also available online at http://waltonhillsohio.gov/pdf_waltonhills/en-US/HistoricalDocs/HistoricSitesParks2.pdf.

36. Lewis Evans, *A map of the middle British colonies in North America* (1755), loc.gov; George Washington to Thomas Jefferson, January 1, 1788, *Founders Online,* National Archives, https://founders.archives.gov/documents/Washington/04-06-02-0002; Heckewelder, *Map and description of northeastern Ohio 1796.*

37. George W. Knepper, *Ohio and Its People* (Kent, OH: Kent State University Press, 2003); 52–53, 81–83.

38. Clyde R. Quine, *Old Portage and the Portage Path* (Akron, OH: self-published, 1953). See also Wm. I. Barnholth, *The Cuyahoga-Tuscarawas Portage: a documentary history* (Akron, OH: Summit County Historical Society, 1954); Marking the Trail of the Portage Path: Pinpointing the exact location of the trail—Survey Data (Yeck Family Portage Path Memorial Program, 2002).

39. Jim Carney, "River to river: on anniversary of survey, they'll mark route of the Portage Path," *Akron Beacon Journal,* June 18, 1997.

Chapter 7

1. Dr. Lynn Metzger completed a draft of this essay in 2015, shortly before her death. It is based on extensive research she conducted while completing her doctoral dissertation "Cleveland American Indian Center: Urban Survival and Adaptation," Case Western Reserve University, 1989. It has been edited and completed for this volume by her friend and colleague Peg Bobel.

2. Helen Hornbeck Tanner, *Atlas of Great Lakes Indian History* (Norman and London: University of Oklahoma Press, 1987), 162.

3. In 1830 the US Congress passed the Indian Removal Act by a narrow margin. Lawmakers were deeply divided over the measure, but as a result of the law the U.S. government, between 1830 and 1850, forced the removal of about 100,000 Native Americans from eastern regions to lands west of the Mississippi. For more information see the excellent educational resource "Native Knowledge 360°" on the Smithsonian National Museum of the American Indian website: americanindian.si.edu.

4. Reuters, "Wyandot Indians win $5.5 million settlement," Around the Nation, *The New York Times,* February 11, 1985; Marisa Lati, "The U.S. Once Forced This Native American Tribe To Move. Now They're Getting Their Land Back," *The Washington Post,* September 20, 2019. For a deeper look into the Wyandot assimilation, removal, and subsequent settlement in Kansas see Kevin Kern, "'It Is by Industry or Extinction That the Problem of Their Destiny Must be Solved': The Wyandots and Removal to Kansas," *Northwest Ohio History* 75, no. 2:161–168.

5. Marisa Lati, "The U.S. once forced this Native American tribe to move. Now they're getting their land back," *The Washington Post,* September 20, 2019, https://www.washingtonpost.com/religion/2019/09/19/us-once-forced-this-native-american-tribe-move-now-theyre-getting-their-land-back/. Since the Wyandot left in 1843, the United Methodists in Upper Sandusky have cared for the church and cemetery, and have held weekly services in the summers. It is also open to visitors in the summer months.

6. Lynn Rodeman Metzger, "Cleveland American Indian Center: Urban Survival and Adaptation" (doctoral thesis, Case Western Reserve University, 1989), 11.

7. Azusa Ono, "The Relocation and Employment Assistance Programs, 1948–1970: Federal Indian Policy and the Early Development of the Denver Indian Community," *Indigenous Nations Studies Journal* 5, no. 1 (2004): 29–34.

8. See James B. LaGrand, *Indian Metropolis: Native Americans in Chicago, 1945–75* (University of Illinois Press 2005) for a discussion on relocation in Chicago.

9. Metzger, Cleveland American Indian Center, 37–41.

10. Metzger, "Cleveland American Indian Center," 47.

11. Metzger, "Cleveland American Indian Center," 54–56.

12. Metzger, "Cleveland American Indian Center," 56–57.

13. Elaine Neils, *Reservation to City* (Chicago: University of Chicago, 1971), 76, quoted in Metzger, "Cleveland American Indian Center," 54.

14. A *Cleveland Plain Dealer* front-page article announcing the arrival of "Real Indians" was rife with stereotypes. See Wilson Hirschfield, "Real Indians Soon to Call City Home, *Cleveland Plain Dealer*, September 20, 1957.

15. Metzger, "Cleveland American Indian Center," 54–54, 58–59.

16. Metzger, "Cleveland American Indian Center," 75, 172.

17. Metzger, "Cleveland American Indian Center," 118–119.

18. Metzger, "Cleveland American Indian Center," 119, 121–122, 124, 127–29.

19. Metzger, "Cleveland American Indian Center," 129–30; Terry Pluto, "Chief Wahoo compromise makes sense for both sides," *The Plain Dealer*, January 31, 2018; Paul Dolan, "Letter from Paul Dolan: Guardians," MLB.com, July 23, 2021, https://mlb.com/indians/fans/cleteamname/letter-from-paul-dolan.

20. Metzger, "Cleveland American Indian Center," 110, 123–127.

21. Herbert Johnson to Robert L. Steele, July 4, 1972, quoted in Metzger, 126.

22. Metzger, "Cleveland American Indian Center," 99–100.

23. Metzger, "Cleveland American Indian Center," 133–34.

24. Metzger, "Cleveland American Indian Center," 127, 133, 179–80.

25. Metzger, "Cleveland American Indian Center," 130.

26. Metzger, "Cleveland American Indian Center,"158–59, 166.

27. Metzger, "Cleveland American Indian Center," 186–88, 200–205.

28. Metzger, "Cleveland American Indian Center," 193–94.

29. Metzger, "Cleveland American Indian Center," 178–79.

30. Metzger, "Cleveland American Indian Center," 172, 218–227; Glenn Proctor, "Robert Hosick, 60, head of local Indian Center," *Akron Beacon Journal*, January 9, 1985.

31. William Canterbury, "Akron center fights for 'smallest minority'," *Akron Beacon Journal*, November 23, 1978.

32. Jim Carney, "'Unknown' agency sure keeps active," *Akron Beacon Journal*, January 31, 1986.

33. Carney, "Unknown agency," As of 2022, the North American Indian Cultural Center, Inc., continues to provide services out of its office currently located in Tallmadge, Ohio.

The Center is responsible for administration of employment, training, and education assistance for all Native Americans in the State of Ohio via the US Department of Labor's Workforce Investment Act and later the Department of Labor's Division of Indian and Native American Programs Workforce Innovation and Opportunity Act, Section 166, for Native American adults and youth.

34. Interview with Jim LaRue, November 29, 2017.

35. Pat Norman, "Indian cultural center is leaving Canton," *Akron Beacon Journal*, December 18, 1978; Ted Vollmuth, "Indians help their own," *Akron Beacon Journal*, September 18, 1988.

36. Associated Press, "Indians trying to save site they say is sacred ground," *The Newark Advocate* (Newark, Ohio), October 23, 1988, https://www.newspapers.com.

37. William Canterbury, "Petition seeks Ohio site for Indian culture center," February 12, 1976.

38. US Department of Commerce, US Bureau of the Census, "The American Indian and Alaska Native Population: 2010," 2010 Census Briefs (Washington, DC, January 2012).

Chapter 8

1. Improved Order of Red Men, Great Council of the United States. *Record of the Great Council of the United States of the Improved Order of Red Men* Vol. XIV, No. 1 (1908), 697–702.

2. For more detailed analysis of these phenomena, see Philip J. Deloria, *Playing Indian* (New Haven: Yale University Press, 1998) and Robert Berkhofer Jr., *The White Man's Indian: Images of the American Indian from Columbus to the Present* (New York: Vintage Books, 1979).

3. Edmund De Schweinitz, *The Life and Times of David Zeisberger, the Western Pioneer and Apostle of the Indian* (Philadelphia: J. B. Lippincot, 1870), 371–372.

4. Bradley T. Lepper, *Ohio Archaeology: An Illustrated Chronicle of Ohio's Ancient American Indian Cultures* (Wilmington, OH: Orange Frazer Press, 2005), 240–242; E. G. Squier and E. H. Davis, *Ancient Monuments of the Mississippi Valley* (Washington, DC: The Smithsonian Institution, 1848), 301–306.

5. Lucius V. Bierce, *Historical Reminiscences of Summit County* (Akron: T. & H. G. Canfield, Publishers, 1854), 54.

6. Charles Whittlesey, *Ancient Earth Forts of the Cuyahoga Valley* (Cleveland: Fairbanks Benedict, 1871), map in back cover folder; P. P. Cherry, *The Western Reserve and Early Ohio* (Akron: R. L. Fouse Publisher, 1921), map on page 8; Karl Grismer, *Akron and Summit County* (Akron: Summit County Historical Society, 1952), 10.

7. William I. Barnholth, *Fort Island and the Erie Indians* (Akron: Summit County Historical Society, 1958, reprint 1965), 7.

8. David R. Bush and Charles Callender, "Anybody but the Erie," *Ohio Archaeologist* 34, no. 1 (1984): 31–35; Elizabeth Mancz, Jeffrey Hudson, C. L. Huegle, L. M. Hartley, John Marwitt, and Donald Metzger, "A Phase I Literature Search and Phase II Archaeological Survey of the Proposed Fort Island Park Project City of Fairlawn, Summit County, Ohio" (Department of

Sociology, University of Akron, 1988); John L. Marwitt, L. M. Hartley, Eric Olson, and Gavin DeMali, "A Management Summary of the 1989 Field School Excavation at Fort Island, 33 SU 9, Fairlawn, Summit County, Ohio" (Department of Anthropology and Classical Studies, University of Akron, 2016); City of Fairlawn, "Fort Island/Griffiths Park," https://www.cityoffairlawn.com/71/Fort-Island-Griffiths-Park (accessed 15 February 2020).

9. The Mary Campbell Society Children of The American Revolution, Mary Campbell Cave Plaque, 1934.

10. Mark J. Price, "Legends of the Gorge," *Akron Beacon Journal*, May 16, 1999, 15; Emily Mills, "Summit Metro Parks Digging at Mary Campbell Cave," *Akron Beacon Journal*, July 30, 2019; Emily Mills, "Dig Finds No Support for Gorge Metro Park Legend," *Akron Beacon Journal*, February 3, 2020.

11. Belle McKinney Hays Swope, *History of the Families of Mckinney-Brady-Quigley* (Chambersburg, PA: Franklin Repository Printery, 1905), 156–167. The Brady's Leap legend is similar to the McColloch's Leap incident, which is similarly memorialized in West Virginia history: J. H. Newton, G. G. Nichols, and A. G. Sprankle, *History of The Pan-Handle: Being Historical Collections of the Counties of Ohio, Brooke, Marshall and Hancock West Virginia* (Wheeling: J.A. Caldwell, 1879), 134–135.

12. Swope, *History of the Families of Mckinney-Brady-Quigley*, 166; Andrew Bugel, "Brady Lake Voters Dissolve Village," *Record-Courier*, May 3, 2017; Save Brady's Coalition, "Kent, Ohio Community Rallies Around Local Landmark," Press Release, August 22, 2002, http://cleveland.indymedia.org/news/2002/08/2157.php.

13. Josiah Strong, *Our Country: Its Possible Future and its Present Crisis* (New York: Baker and Taylor, 1885), 175–177. Emphasis in the original.

14. Alan Ashworth, "On Arbor Day, Akron's 300-Year-Old Signal Tree Stands Tall," *Akron Beacon Journal*, April 27, 2019; Jennifer Conn, "Davey Tree Expert Co. to 'Adopt' Akron's Signal Tree for 5 Years," Cleveland.com, August 16, 2018, updated January 30, 2019, https://www.cleveland.com/akron/2018/08/davey_tree_expert_co_to_adopt.html.

15. Mark Price, "Portage Path Name Change Leaves Trail of Hard Feelings," *Akron Beacon Journal*, July 8, 2013; Mark Price, "Path to the Past," *Akron Beacon Journal*, September 6, 1998.

16. Kirin Makker, "No. 53 on Main Street," *Winterthur Unreserved Museum & Library Blog*, January 10, 2014, http://museumblog.winterthur.org/2014/01/10/no-53-on-main-street/; Mark Price, "Where is Courtney Park? Finding it is Hard as a Rock," *Akron Beacon Journal*, July 13, 2015.

17. Jeffrey Steele, "Reduced to Images: American Indians in Nineteenth-Century Advertising" in S. Elizabeth Bird, ed., *Dressing in Feathers: The Construction of the Indian in American Popular Culture* (Boulder, CO: Westview Press, 1996), 45–64. It should be noted that image on the one-cent piece was intended to be the idealized Lady Liberty wearing an Indian headdress, but this distinction was almost immediately lost on the public, which continues to call them "Indian Head Pennies" to this day.

18. Mark Trahant, "Our World, But Not Our Worldview," *National Geographic*, December 2018, 126.

19. Rarihokwats, ed., *The Best of Akwesasne Notes: How Democracy Came to St. Regis and the Thunderwater Movement* (New York, Mohawk Nation: Akwesasne Notes, 1974).

20. Rarihokwats, *The Best of Akwesasne Notes*; Case Western Reserve University, "Chief Thunderwater," *Encyclopedia of Cleveland History*, https://case.edu/ech/articles/c/chief-thunderwater (Accessed 15 February 2020).

21. "Chief Thunderwater Dies," *New York Times,* 11 June 1950; Case Western Reserve University, "Chief Thunderwater"; Center for Public History + Digital humanities, Cleveland State University, "Chief Thunderwater," *Cleveland Historical,* accessed 15 February 2020, https://clevelandhistorical.org/items/show/275.

22. Deloria, *Playing Indian*, Chapter 4.

23. Akron YMCA, "A History of YMCA Camping in Akron," https://www.akronymca.org/CampYNoah/About/History (Accessed February 15, 2020); Akron Princesses.org, "About Us," http://www.akronprincesses.org/about-indian-princesses (Accessed February 15, 2020).

24. Hayley Munguia, "The 2,128 Native American Mascots People Aren't Talking About," *FiveThirtyEight*, September 15, 2014, https://fivethirtyeight.com/features/the-2128-native-american-mascots-people-arent-talking-about/; Hannah K. Sparling and Carol Motsinger, "Tribute or Racial Slur: Is it Time for Schools to Give Up Native American Mascots?" *Cincinnati Enquirer,* June 11, 2018, https://www.cincinnati.com/story/news/2018/06/11/native-american-mascots-time-schools-change/676650002/; Ohio House of Representatives, "Miller, Miranda Call on Ohio's Schools to Retire the Use of Native American Mascots," August 11, 2021, https://ohiohouse.gov/members/jessica-e-miranda/news/miller-miranda-call-on-ohios-schools-to-retire-the-use-of-native-american-mascots-107113. As of 2018, Ohio also claimed six of the twenty-seven (22 percent) high schools that still use "Red Men" as their team names.

25. Marc Bona, *Hidden History of Cleveland* (Charleston, SC: The History Press, 2021), 39; Bob Braunwart, Bob Carroll, and Joe Horrigan, "The Oorang Indians," *The Coffin Corner* (Pro Football Researchers Association) 3, no. 1 (1981), 1–17.

26. Ed Rice, *Baseball's First Indian: The Story of Penobscot Legend Louis Sockalexis* (Camden, Maine: Down East Books, Rowman & Littlefield, 2019); Ted Berg, "Neither Chief Wahoo nor the Indians' Nickname Honor the Penobscot Man That Inspired Them," *USA Today,* February 1, 2018, https://ftw.usatoday.com/2018/02/chief-wahoo-cleveland-indians-racist-mascot-nickname-louis-sockalexis-mlb; Anthony Castrovince, "Cleveland Indians to Change Team Name," MLB.com, December 14, 2020, https://www.mlb.com/news/cleveland-indians-team-name-change; Paul Dolan, "Team Name Update: Letter From Paul Dolan," MLB.com, December 14, 2020, https://www.mlb.com/indians/fans/cleteamname; Paul Dolan, "Letter From Paul Dolan: Guardians," MLB.com, July 23, 2021, https://www.mlb.com/indians/fans/cleteamname/letter-from-paul-dolan; Abigail Bottar, "Lake Erie Native American Council Attends First Cleveland Guardians Game," Ideastream Public Media, August 7, 2023, https://www.ideastream.org/race-gender-identity/2023-08-07/lake-erie-native-american-council-attends-first-cleveland-guardians-game.

27. "Wooden Indian to Watch Park," *Akron Beacon Journal,* October 27, 1972; "Toth's Work Honors Indians," *Akron Beacon Journal,* July 7, 1978; Theresa Cottom, "District Plans to Remove Massive Wooden Native American Statue—But Removal Could Get Messy," *Akron Beacon Journal,* August 20, 2018.

28. "Artist's Statues Honor Indians in All 50 U.S. States," *Cape Coral Daily Breeze,* April 5, 2009. https://www.capecoralbreeze.com/news/florida-news-apwire/2009/04/05/ artist-s-statues-honor-indians-in-all-50-states/. In "Toth's Work Honors Indians," Toth has also said of his work, "I am protesting against the plight of the Indians.... Against the theft and trickery through which we took this land ... I want also to honor the Indian as the proud, brave, and dignified people they are."

29. Trahant, "Our World," 121; Berkhofer Jr., *The White Man's Indian,* 111.

30. Doug Livingston, "Indigenous People Retrace Culture on the Portage Path," *Akron Beacon Journal*, October 7, 2019.

31. Livingston, "Indigenous People Retrace Culture"; Theresa Cottom, "Northern Cheyenne Nation joins Akron's First Peoples Day," *Akron Beacon Journal*, October 1, 2018.